THE AGRICULTURAL SOCIAL GOSPEL IN AMERICA:

The Gospel of the Farm
by
Jenkin Lloyd Jones

Edited with an Introduction
by Thomas E. Graham

THE AGRICULTURAL SOCIAL GOSPEL IN AMERICA:

The Gospel of the Farm
by
Jenkin Lloyd Jones

Edited with an Introduction
by Thomas E. Graham

Studies in American Religion
Volume 19

The Edwin Mellen Press
Lewiston/Queenston

The Agricultural Social Gospel: *The Gospel of the Farm* **by Jenkin Lloyd Jones,** Edited with an Introduction by Thomas E. Graham

This is volume 19 in the continuing series
Studies in American Religion
Volume 19 ISBN 0-88946-663-7
SAR Series ISBN 0-88946-992-X

Copyright © 1986 by The Edwin Mellen Press

The Edwin Mellen Press
Box 450
Lewiston, New York
USA 14092

The Edwin Mellen Press
Box 67
Queenston, Ontario
CANADA LOS 1L0

Printed in the United States of America

This book is dedicated by the editor
to the descendants of
Richard and Mallie Lloyd-Jones,
unto the fifth generation
who honour their names –
especially Thomas E. Jones, M. Helen Jones
and Anna Nell Phillip.

PREFACE

During the past eight years I have been working to produce a biography of Jenkin Lloyd Jones. This book has risen from that effort as a way of completing, on his behalf, Jones' final and unfinished task. It has been a small participation in the life I am chronicling.

Because of its place as one piece of a much larger project, many people have made indirect contributions to its production. My research has been supported financially by The Social Sciences and Humanities Research Council of Canada and by the University of Winnipeg. Help and advice came regularly from the staff of the Library, the Dean's office and the Vice-President's office at the University of Winnipeg.

The bulk of the material on Jones' life, including his last draft of "The Gospel of the Farm", is held by Meadville Theological School in Chicago. Faculty and staff there have been generous in their hospitality and cooperation. Special appreciation is due to Neil Gerdes, the librarian.

The other repository of Jones' papers is the Special Collections division of the Joseph Regenstein Library of the University of Chicago. My debt to the librarians there is greater than will appear in this book.

Early encouragement for the preparation of this book came from Paul Hass of the State Historical Society of Wisconsin. Chapters II, VI and XII have already appeared in The Wisconsin Magazine of History, of which he is editor.

I have been heartened by the cooperation and interest of the Lloyd-Jones family. Mrs. Howard Barnett,

Jones' granddaughter, has helped in many ways, including providing specific items of family knowledge. Unity Chapel Inc. - the Lloyd-Jones family as organized to care for the chapel and cemetery that were the family focal points - has given continual support.

Suggestions and criticisms have come from members of Collegium, who have been my community of scholarship in the development of all the Jones' material. John Badertscher and Erin Phillips have also read and discussed my work as the book developed. My family and friends have allowed me to talk out my ideas far beyond their real interest in Jenkin Lloyd Jones.

Final thanks are due to Sandy Cain for the careful preparation of the final manuscript.

TABLE OF CONTENTS

INTRODUCTION   xi

I	HEROES OF THE FARM	1
II	TRANSFORMATIONS OF A COUNTY	22
III	CONCERNING SOIL: PLOWING	40
IV	CONCERNING SEED: SOWING	56
V	CONCERNING WEEDS: CULTIVATING	71
VI	THE HARVEST FIELD: REAPING	82
VII	JOHNNY APPLESEED	103
VIII	TREE PLANTING	121
IX	THE REFORESTATION OF TOWER HILL	139
X	TOWER HILL TWENTY YEARS LATER	154
XI	ROAD MAKING	163
XII	BARN BUILDING	181
XIII	AT THE HORSE FAIR: BREEDING	197
XIV	PIGS AND BABIES	216
XV	THE GOSPEL OF THE MANGER	236
XVI	THE MILK OF HUMAN KINDNESS	256
XVII	THE GRAVE IN THE WOODS	277

INTRODUCTION

Jenkin Lloyd Jones

When Jenkin Lloyd Jones married at age seventy, the event was worth a front-page story with a picture in all the Chicago papers. In papers from Boston to San Francisco it was noted, although in a less prominent way. He was a major public figure, with a lifetime record of efforts for social improvement. Reporting his death, <u>The Citizen</u> of Los Angeles said:

> Just the other day all America paused -- without regard to creed or color -- to drop a tear for the memory of the venerable Jenkin Lloyd Jones, one of the truly great men of past generations.[1]

His greatness lay in his personal influence, but may be suggested by his accomplishments. He was author of several books, editor of a newspaper for forty years, religious leader in Chicago for thirty-four, shaper of mid-Western Unitarianism, organizer of still-active institutions, crusader for social reform and sought-after public speaker in an age of great oratory.

His career almost exactly coincides with the great industrial development of America -- from the Civil War to World War I. He entered the seminary in 1866, after serving as a private in the Civil War, and died a short two months before the Armistice in 1918. When his family emigrated from Wales in 1845, Wisconsin was the wilderness edge of the frontier. When he died, the population of America was more urban than rural.

The first half of his career was closely connected with the revitalization of the Western Unitarian Conference. During these thirty-two years he initiated innovative Sunday School work in the Western Conference, invented the Unity Club, co-founded <u>Unity</u> -- the Conference newspaper, led the Conference in independent missionary initiative from Ohio to Colorado. He pioneered in the ordination of women and fostered a spirit of broad liberalism that disregarded theological limitations.

In 1892 a six-year schism in the Conference was healed by a compromise which Jones understood as a repudiation of his leadership. Coincident with the compromise was his involvement in The World's Parliament of Religions at The Chicago World's Fair of 1893, which reinforced his vision of the wider possibilities of religious unity. The two events together motivated a shift to a more independent religious stance. While he did not cease to be a Unitarian minister, he was little involved in the institutional side of the Unitarian Church thereafter. His church, All Souls in Chicago, paid off its loan to the American Unitarian Association and withdrew from denominational affiliation. After years of planning, he dedicated Abraham Lincoln Center on the south side of Chicago in 1905.

The second half of Jones' career was devoted to bringing his religious insights to bear on the social problems of his time. Abraham Lincoln Center embodied his ideal of how a church should relate to all aspects of city life. Within it were a gymnasium, library, publishing company, manual training shops, kitchens for domestic science classes, social rooms, classrooms and the rudiments of a day-care facility, in addition to a large church auditorium. It also financed and staffed external agencies of civic betterment.

With Abraham Lincoln Center providing support and a corps of dedicated workers, Jones involved himself in all the progressive movements of the early twentieth century. As often as not he was instrumental in founding groups, or at least serving on their boards. All in all he was active in over 150 organizations. A roll call of his involvements would include women's suffrage, prison reform, the humane society, the NAACP, labor relations, reform of city and state government, aid to immigrants and relief of poverty. The two causes that dominated his work were prohibition and world peace. He was a nationally recognized spokesman for both.

In the last four years of his life, he was identified with the peace movement. His previous fame turned to notoriety as he held to his pacifist convictions after the United States entered the War in 1917. By many, including the United States government, he was regarded as seditious.

Although he was a famous man in his lifetime, Jones' name scarcely survived his death in 1918. Friends and associates cherished his memory and the Unitarian Church never quite forgot who he had been, but to the larger world his life left no lasting trace. His significance had been in his living presence more than in his legacy.

He could organize institutions and committees and was able to use many methods of influence and action, but his chief role was that of inspiring and motivating others. His battlefield was the public platform and his weapon was the spoken word. His reputation derived from his ability as a speaker and the intensity, honesty and moral fervor which he conveyed to his audience.

The Gospel of the Farm

Although Jones was often heard in civic and secular contexts, he learned his craft in the church. Fundamentally a preacher, his genre was the sermon. On his lips, though, a sermon and a lecture were not far apart. In content and flavour, his sermons were like lectures. In tone and style, his lectures were always sermonic.

Outside of editorials and one book of World's Parliament extracts, nearly everything he published derived from his preaching. Many of his Sunday sermons were fully reported in the Monday papers and he printed his sermons frequently in Unity. His first book, The Faith That Makes Faithful, was a collection of sermons co-authored by William Channing Gannett in 1883. The World's Parliament inspired two books, one of which was a sermon collection. Between 1899 and 1916 four more books of sermons were published.

By his seventy-fourth birthday, he had accumulated material and ideas for several more books. He wanted to write an autobiography, present his accumulated experience in religious education, give his religious interpretation of evolution, do a study of Mark Twain's writings, publish a series of sermons on Jesus and The Apostles and make a collection of his book reviews. His friends and admirers urged him to realize some of his intentions. The most insistent was one of his part-time secretaries, Mrs. Susan Quackenbush of Portage, Wisconsin. He was persuaded that if he were going to do anything more in the way of publishing, he had little time left to do so.[2]

None of these projects advanced beyond the stage of a sketch or outline. There were three intended books, though, which were near enough complete to submit to publishers: "The Gospel of the Farm", "Abraham Lincoln" and "Peace".

Peace was uppermost on his mind in 1917. Jones' experience in the Civil War had taught him the awfulness and misery of war, and his understanding of evolutionary progress inspired him to believe that war was a dysfunctional remnant of a lower stage of human progress. From the time of the Spanish-American War onward Jones had been outspoken in his denunciation of war and the promotion of peace.

The flag which flew over Abraham Lincoln Center was edged with a white border to symbolize peace. In 1915 Jones was invited to sail with the Ford Peace Ship, and when Ford left the expedition, Jones served for a time as head of the mission. The book he published in 1916, Love for the Battle-Torn Peoples, recounted in successive chapters the virtues and contributions to civilization of each of the belligerent nations as an antidote to the growing spirit of hatred and villain-making.

After the United States entered the war, Jones was among the handful of peace workers to remain consistent. From his pulpit and in the columns of Unity he continued to uphold the ideals of peace and to oppose the war. He was almost the only one of the pacifist ministers able to retain his appointment during the war-fever. For some months during 1918 Unity was prohibited from the mails for its pacifist articles.

Jones gathered a collection of his sermons and speeches for publication as a book on "Peace". Although it was sent to a publisher, he knew quite well that it had little hope of being accepted. The sentiment in the country was for war, not peace, and he was by that time too notorious for his pacifism to expect a sympathetic hearing.

He was far more optimistic about his book on Abraham Lincoln. The interest in Lincoln had been one of the continuous elements in his life. As a youth he had enlisted in the Civil War, mainly to bring an end to slavery. He had understood himself to be fighting with Lincoln in the noble cause. Lincoln was a hero and model for him -- especially as he grew older. Abraham Lincoln Center was designed to be a church that Lincoln would have approved of and felt able to join. In 1904 he and his son Richard were instrumental in stopping the sale of the Lincoln birthplace to a distillery and preserving it as a National Monument. In his suggestion for his own epitaph he wanted to be remembered as a "Lincoln Soldier".

It was no surprise to him that "Peace" was not published, but he was disappointed that he could find no one to accept the Lincoln manuscript, either as a book or series of magazine articles.

The most carefully prepared manuscript of the three, though, was "The Gospel of the Farm". As with the Lincoln book, he was confident that it would see publication.

In 1908 Jones had preached a sermon based on his experience of building a barn on his vacation "encampment" at Tower Hill, Wisconsin, and he printed it in Unity the following week. Former Governor Hoard of Wisconsin saw it and asked permission to reprint it in Hoard's Dairyman, a prominent farm journal out of Fort Atkinson. Hoard also asked Jones to write a series of sermons for the paper to be printed as "The Gospel of the Farm". Jones complied and wrote six sermons which ran roughly every month from January through July 1910.

These six sermons and the barn sermon formed the core of the proposed book. He selected from his other sermons of the past twenty-two years those which related to the general topic of rural life. Although the majority of the sermons were immediately settled on, the final list of contents was not made definite for some months.

The manuscript itself never quite reached its final stage. Preparation continued throughout the search for a publisher, so that none ever saw the copy as envisioned.

There are seventeen sermons in the manuscript. The most recent was preached in 1917; the earliest are from 1895, although one of these is a rewritten version of a sermon first delivered in 1878. All the sermons were first heard by the congregation at All Souls Church, Chicago. Eleven of them were printed in Unity shortly after they were first preached. Five of the six sermons requested by Governor Hoard (chapters 3,4, 5,11,13) appeared only in Hoard's Dairyman. Chapters 6,12 and 15 were printed in both Unity and Hoard's. Chapter 17 has never been published before.

The first two chapters set the tone for the collection; both speak of the hardships and accomplishments of pioneer farmers on the frontier. "Heroes of the Farm" is an appreciation of Hamlin Garland's A Son of the Middle Border. "Transformations of a County" describes the changes in Jefferson County, Wisconsin in the sixty years after 1845.

The four sermons following are from the original Hoard's series. They treat central activities of agriculture: plowing, sowing, cultivating, harvesting. The focus is mainly on the development of machinery and techniques for performing these tasks.

Trees are the subject of the next four. "Johnny Appleseed" and "Tree Planting", both Arbor Day sermons, encourage the planting of trees -- literal and metaphorical. The experiences of reclaiming the waste land of Tower Hill provide a pair of complementary sermons.

Chapters 11, 12 and 13 are a miscellaneous group; their topics are making roads, building barns and breeding horses. The sermon on barn-building is the one that caught Governor Hoard's eye and initiated the series. The others are the remaining two of the original "Gospel of the Farm".

The next group is united by its emphasis on human relationships and family. "Pigs and Babies" is rather similar in theme to "Barn Building", but is more focused on babies than the barnyard. "The Gospel of the Manger" is a Christmas sermon with a strong appeal for peace and unity of the human race. "The Milk of Human Kindness" is a sermon on women and motherhood.

The manuscript concludes with "A Grave in the Woods", returning to the theme of sacrifice and accomplishment by pioneers. It is openly autobiographical and relates to the story of the death of Jones' Uncle Jenkin during the family's first year in Wisconsin.

The surviving correspondence shows that Jones and Mrs. Quackenbush both took a hand in the process of finding a publisher. Their emotions were raised from discouragement to triumph and then dropped to despair. In the opening correspondence, McMillan expressed a cautious interest in the several projects Mrs. Quackenbush proposed to them. Jones had other plans for the farm book and sent it to the Agricultural Department of The University of Wisconsin. When his friend there declined it, he turned to Orange Judd, recommended to him as a publisher of farm books.

After Orange Judd rejected it, he returned to McMillan and had Mrs. Quackenbush send "Peace", "Abraham Lincoln" and "The Gospel of the Farm", to them. The reply led them to believe McMillan would certainly publish the last two at least. They exchanged jubilant letters of congratulations and set about putting the finishing touches on the manuscripts. Jones arranged for a photograph of the grave in the woods to accompany the farm book and involved himself in straightening out a knotty problem in Lincoln's ancestry.

In May they "were bereaved" when McMillan rejected both books with a vaguely-worded letter. The farm manuscript was sent off to Doubleday, who promptly rejected it, and then to Lippincott. Lippincott did not publish it, but their rejection letter was not preserved. Jones wrote Mrs. Quackenbush to keep trying "if it takes all summer".[3]

The summer of 1918 had too many troubles of its own. The Post Office banned <u>Unity</u> from the mails, and most of Jones' energy went into dealing with that problem. In September he was operated on for hernia, after which he had a severe attack of angina, which had been chronic for two years. He died on 12 September without being able to do anything more toward publishing the manuscript. During the next two years Mrs. Quackenbush made a few efforts to find a publisher for "The Gospel of the Farm", but to no avail. The manuscript now reposes with most of the rest of Jones' papers in the Jenkin Lloyd Jones Collection at Meadville Theological School in Chicago.

"The Gospel of the Farm" is very much like the books of sermons that Jones had been publishing during the previous twenty years. Like them it is a collection of some of his best sermons, joined by a common theme. In style and message it was not inferior, but in this case he seemed to have lost his audience.

Certainly a part of the reason lay with the impact of the war on the publishing business. Both Orange Judd and McMillan mention it in their rejection letters.[4] Jones' reputation as a pacifist and as one suspected of "sedition" clearly played a part as well. The curt note from <u>Atlantic Monthly</u>[5] seems to be rejecting Jones personally as much as it rejected the opportunity to serialize the Lincoln manuscript.

I would not discount those reasons, but would also propose that something more fundamental was taking place. "The Gospel of the Farm" is a fairly typical example of Jones' thinking and style; it contains in matured form those elements which made his reputation. The failure of the manuscript to see print is an indication that what was popular and influential in the decades before the War was no longer able to command attention or admiration.

The abrupt fading of his reputation supports this interpretation. After the printing of his obituaries, he drops suddenly into obscurity. It is rare to find any mention of him in articles or books on the history of the period, even those which deal with movements or events in which he was prominently involved.[6] This volume of sermons demonstrates the reasons for both his fame and his later obscurity.

Jones' Preaching

A great many of Jones' sermons appeared in print, and he expected people to read them, but in structure and style they are clearly meant to be heard, oriented to the ear rather than to the eye. The sentences are long and oratorical. Flourishes of word and image crowd into the sentences; long lists of items set up a momentum that rolls the sentences forward. Many sentences link clause after clause in an extended chain of ideas. Sentences will change direction, sometimes more than once, in their rhetorical course. Jones also inserted digressions into the middle of a sentence. It was difficult to arrive at a consistent and clear system of punctuation for the text because the real punctuation was done by pauses and vocal inflections, independent of conventional eye-oriented punctuation.

The larger shape of the sermon is as much ear-centered as the individual sentences are. In most cases the progression of the sermon is by means of intuitive connections more than by a logical order. It is a structure designed to carry a hearer through a series of emotional experiences, culminating in moral resolution. Often one is hard-pressed to say what a particular sermon is "about" -- and yet most sermons have an undeniable unity.

"The Milk of Human Kindness", Chapter 16, was originally a sermon on the Genesis story of the creation of woman, although in this context it is hard to see. It begins with the importance of mammals in evolution, and moves to the contributions of human motherhood to civilization, digressing on the significance of monogamy. Abruptly it shifts to the value of the cow and discusses the economics of milk production, ending with the importance of sanitation and quality control. Since pure wholesome milk was the concern of women with babies, this leads Jones back to mothers again, but not before a digression on temperance -- milk as a substitute for beer. The concern for pure milk is one example of the great influence that women have exerted on behalf of all the children of the world. A story about his own experience with a mother wolf allows him to stress the strength of mother-love and the superiority of altruistic love over "wolf-love". Approving the contemporary movement for women's rights, he dwells on the role women can play in society -- especially on behalf of world peace. The sermon closes with a plea for "the fusion of male and female" in the enterprise of civilizing humanity.

As disorganized as that sounds in outline, the sermon itself works rather well. It is moving and persuasive as long as the words are allowed to exert their own power. One must let the rhetoric have its own way and be content to ride the stream.

The form the sermons take is characteristic of the way Jones had been preaching since the mid-1870's. After a few years of experimentation, he found or invented the form that more and more became his stock in trade. His sermons would occasionally have a Biblical text, as half of these do, but the sermon was rarely governed by it. The text served only as a motto or at most a place to begin or end. Many times the stated text does not figure in the sermon in any way.

In the place of Biblical matter the anchor of the sermon was some piece of factual information. It might be an advance in science or technology; it might be a fact of natural history. In these sermons, most strikingly, he uses the history of some aspect of agricultural technology -- the development of the reaper in Chapter 6, for example. The material for these histories is drawn from standard works on the subject -- Bailey's <u>Cyclopedia of American Agriculture</u> or Brisbin's <u>Trees and Tree Planting</u>, among others.

Often Jones would find his theme in a particular book. He favored novels, but in "The Gospel of the

Farm" the two book-sermons are based on biographies: Hamlin Garland's autobiography and a biographical narrative about John Chapman by a county historical society.

The most effective bases for his sermons, though, are his own experiences. The collection contains sermons grounded on several incidents connected with his summer holidays at Tower Hill, on a visit to his childhood farmstead, a trip to Murfreesboro, Tennessee and the story of the death of his Uncle Jenkin.

The main part of the sermon will usually be a lengthy re-telling of the history, event or story, with frequent side comments and digressions. The narrative is done with the intent to underline some point or quality that he sees in the story.

Typically, the last part of the sermon will be an attempt to draw out the "lessons" to be derived from the narrative. This may involve a metaphorical shift from the "lower fields" of nature to the "upper fields" of the spirit. In the sermon on sowing, for instance, after having discussed how man has improved on nature's seeds and methods of sowing, the lesson has to do with improved ways of "sowing" ideas and achieving higher moral yields.

In the better sermons the lessons are less mechanical. "Pigs and Babies" begins with the building of a pig-pen and rather rapidly turns to a contrast between the way farmers care for pigs and the life of babies in Chicago slums. It moves beyond that to discuss the need for more significant care than that given to pig-babies -- care for the moral, intellectual and spiritual development of children. Frequently the lesson never appears at all. The narrative itself takes over and the sermon hardly gets beyond it. Near the end of "Johnny Appleseed" Jones confesses:

> I have made several unsuccessful attempts to leave the apple trees of Ohio and the apple-planter of the frontier and go in search of spiritual applications, of ethical lessons, but every attempt fails. ...These trees teach their own lesson, deliver their own messages.[7]

The lessons are secondary in most of the sermons. The points Jones really wants to make are built into the narratives themselves. In the sermon on reaping, while he includes a few brief lessons, the real point is made in the story: the rapid advance of society to reduce drudgery and nourish the world better, as it was achieved by the ingenuity, determination and cooperation of some outstanding men.

Poetry was one of Jones' special interests. He frequently preached on great poems and was a founding member of the American Browning Society. It is not surprising, then, that poetry appears often in the sermons. Each one was supposed to have a poetic preface; over half have extensive poetic quotations. Browning, Tennyson, Longfellow, Kipling and several minor poets find a place in the sermons. Some of the quotations are apt and some are not. The long quotation of "M'Andrew's Hymn", a poem about steamships, in the sermon on reaping is quite irrelevant except for its general stress on the beauty of machinery. Like the sentence structure and organization, the poetry is there for the ear. Declaimed, as it would have been, it became another way of evoking an experience in the audience; it is used at least as much for its music as for its meaning.

In their form and style, the sermons were first-class entertainment. They created a range of emotional experiences; they told stories of interesting things; they conveyed a sense of a "personality". As much as a novel, a play or a concert -- and there would be a bit of all three in the platform presentation of these sermons -- they gave pleasure and enjoyment. During much of his career, Jones was asked to give lectures in small churches in order to revive the interest of the congregation, give it status in its town or attract outsiders to its doors. Part of his fame rested on his ability to do these things consistently.

Reading the sermons in print does not, of course, produce the same effect as a "live performance". In the absence of the living voice, though, his words are sufficiently well-crafted that it takes little imagination to create a vicarious sense of the speaker's presence. The sound of the voice still resonates on the printed page.

While the entertainment value of the sermons is real, that was not for Jones -- or his audience -- adequate justification. Their primary importance was their high moral purpose.

The common theme of these sermons is the rural life. Jones chose his subjects from the activities of farms and farm folk: settling, planting, growing, reaping, animal husbandry. These were experiences with which he and many of his generation grew up. The topics were part of the memories, if not the life, of a large number of people.

Jones makes very effective use of these memories. He draws much on the life he lived as a child on a pioneer farmstead both to make vivid his subject matter and to provide a contrast with contemporary farming.

These personal reminiscences unintentionally provide for the modern reader an album of pictures of the way life was on the frontier a century and a quarter ago and give a bonus for the reading of them.

In the rural life he saw a whole host of fundamental moral values. Farming was the first major move of humanity toward civilization; it produced settled communities, co-operation, family stability. Tilling the soil and planting trees were the acts of progressive men and women in times past which created the advanced life of the present. Tilling and planting in the present were sacraments of rededication to progress and a useful preparation for further advances. The farm was the primary school of life.

Farm life called for vision and faith in the power of God in nature. "...humanity must needs make direct connection with Divinity in the wheat field at least....he enters into partnership with the eternal powers in the orchard, if nowhere else."[8] The power and adaptability of nature fascinated Jones. When he looked at seeds, the nature of soil, the capacity of barren ground to renew itself, the sensitivity of animals, the work of rivers and glaciers, he led his hearers to marvel at the Force that governs the world. One value of farm life was its close touch with this Force and the resulting sense of its immediate presence.

In the midst of the war he took comfort in the civilizing ability of nature and farm life.

> Let the sword-bearers do their devilish work to the utmost. Yet the peasant life of Germany, France, England, Russia, Austria, Belgium will remain. It will

continue to be sweet, tender, loyal so long as there are little lambs to be nurtured, little calves to be fed, little colts to be trained; so long as there are little chickens to be loved by little boys and girls; aye so long as there is a flower to be watered by care-burdened housekeepers. While man continues to plant trees, set out parks, preserve places of beauty, so long will the procession of life, not of man alone, but of all of life, move toward the heights of gentleness, tenderness and forgiveness.[9]

Nature by itself, though, was only the beginning place. The farm is nature with human effort added. For all her power, nature is inefficient, inadequate and clumsy. The story of the farm is the story of human attempts to improve on nature. The plow does a better job than the wind; hybrid seed-corn is better than Indian corn; fenced land is more productive than open. Intelligently planted, cultivated and harvested wheat fields will feed more people better. Carefully bred and cared-for cows produce more milk to nourish more healthy babies.

But not for Jones was the "conquest" of nature. He looked instead to a thoughtful, planned co-operation with nature. Tower Hill was reforested not because he defeated the natural, but because he protected the land and allowed the natural forces to work unimpeded.

Farming was hard work -- soul-deadening, body-killing work. Jones knew that from his own childhood.

"Indeed life on the farm seems an endless, almost hopeless, battle with weeds out-of-doors and flies indoors."[10] He escaped to the seminary to get free of it. Several of the sermons retell in some detail the hardness of that life.

Many of them also chronicle the endeavors by which this drudgery has been alleviated. He sang thankful hymns to the steel plow, the self-binding harvester and macadamized roads as much for the ease they brought to the everyday life of the farmer as for their economic and social impact.

While farm life -- especially that on the pioneer farm -- was hard, and while all efforts to make it more pleasant were worthy of celebrating, it was the people who lived that hard life and fought its battles who were the heroes of civilization. Their efforts, foresight, determination and sacrifice transformed the wilderness America into a prosperous nation. Jefferson County was a microcosm of America, and its story in Chapter Two is the story of the whole country.

Unknown heroes like Hamlin Garland's father and his own uncle, along with wealthy and famous men like Cyrus McCormick, had dedicated themselves to their tasks with determination, courage and vision. Out of their lives came the fulfillment of twentieth-century America. The lesson, of course, was that similar dedication and vision were demanded of his hearers. The farmers and the farm-improvers were to be models and inspirations for the present day.

What started on the farm culminated in the city. The farm was the arena of the human accomplishments of previous generations, but in the twentieth century it was the city that needed this firm application of human will and intelligence. The living conditions of many in the city were deplorable, vices of intemperance and greed despoiled individuals and society as a whole; those who lived in comfort too often misused their prosperity to their own detriment. These elements of city life are to the modern world what the forests, marshes and rocky fields, weeds and flies were to the pioneers and farmers. They are to be fought against and overcome with the same effort and sacrifice.

This is the real message of the "Gospel of the Farm" -- a challenge to city-dwellers. They are to use the same intelligence that developed the reaper, surfaced roads, devised modern barns and improved horse breeds to raise the quality of life in the city.

> When shall we bring the chivalry of the home up to the standard of this chivalry of the stable? When shall we bring human husbandry to the heights reached in horse husbandry? ...When will human tenements, wherein men and women bring forth and rear babies, be brought to the standard of the stable in the point of good air, good water, good feeding and gentle treatment? When shall we have as good laws, as wisely executed, for the prevention and suppression of disease in human society as now are found on our statute books concerning the denizens of the barnyard?[11]

The problems of the city, though, are not of the same order as those on the farm. Rural problems were primarily physical ones. The farm called for effort to create a material prosperity, to reduce physical drudgery. These things are needed in the city too, but they are only the beginning. The city provides opportunity for development on a different level. Jones speaks often of the need for accomplishments in "the realm of the spirit".

On the lips of a more conventional preacher one would expect that phrase to have to do with things like God, salvation, piety and faith. For Jones it carried a more humanistic meaning. "Spiritual" for him was a word for the intangible elements of human life and society. It denoted those features of life that related to more than the basic needs of survival and comfort. It named a constellation combining intellectual growth, social structures, human relationships, ethical activity, aesthetic appreciation and personal improvement. In one instance he explains the phrase "realm of the spirit" as encompassing "morals, politics, civic weal and religious liberty".[12]

The importance of the city lay not merely in the fact that it was the place where contemporary pioneers were called to work, but also in the fact that it provided scope for this higher and more significant kind of pioneering -- pioneering in spiritual things. If the farm was the primary school of character development, the city was to be the university.[13]

The clear aim of all these sermons was the working out of this relationship between farm and city. Farm life and agricultural improvements are good in themselves and formed an indispensable foundation for civilization. They were also the scale model to be enlarged in the city, so that greater goods might be accomplished and a higher civilization achieved.

Jones was confident that the task could be done because the heart of his faith was the reality and inevitability of the evolutionary process. The story of the universe was the story of the slow, but inexorable, development from inanimate matter, through primordial life, plants, animals and barbarian man up to the civilized state of present human society. All the stories from history, biography and personal experience that he recounted in his sermons were episodes in this larger story of progress. They were the specifics by which one can come to see evolution as a cosmic fact, and the nature of its action. Furthermore, the process had not come to an end. Jones' studies taught him that "there is a groping toward beauty, a leaning toward duty, a climbing toward the light, everywhere discoverable in the mighty progressions of life, growing more and more mighty in its upward reach".[14]

He expected the continuation of growth in the future as much as he saw it in the past. What had taken place on the farm would in some way take place in the city as well. Evolution was as applicable to the spiritual realm as it was to the physical. In fact the spiritual was its real realm. The push of evolution was toward more and more advancement in human society and relationships. It tended toward "international comity", "the elimination of the brute", toward the conquest of the world by love and gentleness.

It was in this confidence that Jones' religious faith was founded. Evolution was not a blind mechanism. It was the working of the Divine in concrete forms. If one looks with perception, one sees that the material world and the Divine are one and the same. As Jones comments in Chapter 3, "We never know which is premise and which is conclusion, which fact and which symbol... One of the great strengths of the farm is the clarity with which this truth can be seen there."[15]

The spirit of human beings is equally a manifestation of the Divine. It is the means by which evolution continues. The stories that Jones tells are examples of the Divine force in human minds. The burden of the sermons is the appeal to release and apply that force, allowing the evolutionary process to continue through his hearers, so that like the pioneers and inventors he spoke of they might also be a blessing to posterity. He lays this out partly as a challenge and partly as opportunity.

> It is hard to analyze, but it is easy to recognize, this urge of the spirit towards new adventures, the irresistible hunger to add a plus to life. O to feel the joy of creating, the challenge to the mind as well as to the hand, and the inspiration of trying to transform the ideals into the wealth of the world.[16]

The message of Jones in these sermons is founded on the farm experience -- a subject that would reach the lives and memories of most people of his generation. His recognition of its difficulties, praise for its accomplishments and appreciation of its fundamental values were validations of their -- and their nation's -- past. The transference of attention to the cities addressed the present realities and defined the moral tasks of the day. Relating these to the farm made them comprehensible and possible. Faith in the evolutionary process provided a divine sanction for the tasks and goals as well as lively hope to motivate the audience to take up the challenges.

The combination is irresistible. The common

heritage -- especially of the Midwest -- is sanctified by the sermons. The present moment is given crucial importance. Noble aspirations are summoned to attach themselves to difficult, but realizable, goals. And the whole is given meaning by placing it into a cosmic context. Delivered in a format that entertained while it exhorted, it is easy to see why the dispenser of it attained to popularity and influence. Jones' reputation as lecturer and preacher was made by sermons like these.

The Rejection of Jones

In 1918 his popularity was rapidly diminishing and in a very few years would be only a memory to his close associates. There is no doubt that the war is a prominent cause in this process. Jones' involvement in The Ford Peace Ship brought him ridicule and hostility. He retained the personal loyalty of his congregation, but even they disagreed with his unbending pacifist stance. The Post Office ban on his newspaper hinted at treasonous activity to the nation at large. For the moment, at least, he was more notorious than famous.

The war had also given birth to a strong sense of "the enemy". Germans, including Austrians were spoken of in harsh terms as barbarian, bestial or even demonic. But Jones' message was founded on a vision of the universal community of humanity in which the "enemies" were ignorance, greed, intolerance and self-indulgence and the "allies" were all concerned men and women, undivided by nationality, race or theology. This central theme of his preaching would be met in the wartime consciousness not just with indifference, but with active hostility.

Much is also made of the shattering effect of the

war on the optimism of liberals and the liberal message. The hope in inevitable progress and growth toward goodness was severely damaged by the fact of the war and the misery created in its continuance. While there is some truth to these assertions, it seems an oversimplification -- at least in relation to the United States. Certainly the decade after the war was just as optimistic, in the popular mind at least, as the two decades before. The optimism, though, was of a different kind. And while it may be a dramatic convenience to use the war as a benchmark in describing the change, the change itself was not the result of the war. There were longer-term forces at work and it was those which spelled the end of Jones' power to command audiences -- and the decline of the liberal movement of which he was a leading figure.

In these sermons Jones heralded the advances in technology and science as events in the evolutionary movement. They had transformed nature into farms, were transforming farms into cities and could transform cities into paradise. The ingenuity of the human mind working with ever-unfolding revelations of nature and energized by the spirit of the pioneer would create a material and spiritual greatness. And he saw this as a self-generating process. The more the advances, the greater the resources for further advance.

But his faith betrayed him. The technological changes in the late nineteenth and early twentieth centuries slowly led to the urbanization of America. With it came a generation which neither knew nor remembered the farm. The hardships, the inescapable sense of nature and the kind of character these produced were vanishing all the while Jones was writing and preaching. The link by which he attempted to connect with the basic identities of his audience gradually failed to find anything to attach to.

There is some indication that, at least in a vague way, he recognized this. In the latest of these sermons, "Heroes of the Farm", written in 1917, he pities the child who has "never known the high discipline of unsatisfied longing", whose life is "poisoned with luxuries". In the same sermon he says:

> There is reason to fear that the pioneer has over-reached himself. The reaper and the automobile, yes the telephone and aeroplane have so occupied the energies of the pioneer that the intelligence, the conscience, aye, the self-directing forces are in danger of falling out of his life.[17]

Jones was not afraid of the city, nor did he long for a return to a rural Eden -- as some of his contemporaries did. The city was a large step forward for humanity, but it was as yet imperfect and needed much intelligent effort to lift it out of the "alarming degeneracy", "greed and passion...ambition and speculation" that characterized it. It needed the farm in the same way that the university needs the primary school. The cities were now populated by those who skipped primary school, and his message could not reach them.

He rarely lost his hopefulness, but on this matter, he occasionally had to look to the appearance of some new infusion of the pioneer spirit from outside. The new immigrants represented such a possibility. It might be that they would be the reinforcements that could stem the decay and inner weakness of America.[18]

Technology had struck at the entertainment value of Jones' sermons as well. The telephone, automobile, moving pictures and the phonograph, all of which Jones endorsed and took advantage of, were much more exciting ways of spending leisure time than hearing lectures and reading sermons. It is hard for us to believe that at one time people really did look forward to lectures and voluntarily spent afternoons reading sermons. It is not hard to see, though, that given new and more varied opportunities, people would take them up instead.

The liberal message was closely mingled with its medium -- the lecture-sermon. When that failed to attract, the message declined as well.

The success of Jones' message depended on tapping the sense of moral purpose in his hearers. He presented them with a duty and an opportunity for ethical endeavor on behalf of the improvement of society -- national and international. Co-operation with divine evolution was the centre of his religion. Unless there was a corresponding religious sentiment in his hearers, the message would not be received.

Robert Bellah points out that throughout the period covered by Jones' lifetime a purely private pietism was growing up that emphasized only individual rewards. "Religion itself finally became for many a means for the maximization of self-interest with no effective link to virtue, charity or community."[19] Bellah also points out that by the early decades of the twentieth century the meaning of human life was summed up in the word "success".

To the extent that religion had become private and its goal success, then no appeal to the broader well-being of humanity or to growth in the "spiritual" side of life would be likely to find a ready response.

The religious underpinning of the liberal message was deteriorating. In another late sermon, "Tower Hill Twenty Years Later" (1916), Jones tries to address the issue.

> I resent the implication that the church is chiefly an "institution" for human benefactions....Unless through all our bread-doling and hand-directing activities there stream great floods of thought and life, science and poetry, we have misdirected high energies in ineffectual activities. The golden key of conservation is discrimination between things more important and less important. There is a spiritual economy as well as a physical economy. "Seek ye first the kingdom of Heaven, and all these things shall be added unto you."[20]

The world in which Jones grew up and carried on his ministry had changed while he spoke to it. The fundamental verities of the farm receded out of memory; the moral earnestness and social conscience shrank to private piety and personal ambition. The grand vision of spiritual progress thinned out to one of material prosperity. The war brought hatred and suspicion in place of the ideal of a universal community. And the entertainer no longer entertained.

"The Gospel of the Farm" appeared too late to reach its audience. Jones -- and liberals like him -- spoke and wrote out of the aspirations of the nineteenth century and they required of their audience the sharing of those aspirations. He endorsed the hopes of his age, seeking to enlarge and ennoble them as well as striving to fulfill them. He saw technology as the means both to that enlargement and fulfillment, and he became its evangelist. But technology produced something different from his vision. The means to achieve progress was realized, while the aspirations were discarded. The evangelist was made obsolete by his own gospel.

THE TEXT

Jones had gone a long way toward preparing his manuscript for publication. It exists as a typed draft of an extensively rewritten version of the sermons. It has a great many editorial corrections in Jones' hand. A separate sheet contains a hasty list of some of the poems selected to accompany each of the sermons.

Because Jones wrote for the ear instead of the eye, his sentences often appear sprawling and ungainly on the page. The main task of editing has been to re-punctuate these sentences to make them easier to read and to conform to modern conventions. I have tried to avoid changing the structure, however, so that the original oral flavour could be retained.

Very rarely have I changed the words themselves. A few spellings have been modernized and once in a while a sentence has had to be altered to make it comprehensible or grammatical.

Jones sometimes inserted sentences or paragraphs into the sermon which badly interrupted the sense of what he was saying. In some cases I have omitted those intrusions, always indicating the omission in a note. Wherever the omitted material has seemed to me to have intrinsic interest, it has been reproduced in the notes.

The text contains an abundance of quotations from the authors he had been reading or his favorite poets. As befits the sermon style, Jones often does not identify the sources. To the extent that it is practical, I have attempted to provide identification for his quotations. Sometimes this has not been possible, either because the sources are too obscure or else there were too few clues to their origin. Jones read widely and much of what he read has passed out of currency. He also made much use of anthologies and secondary sources for his material. For a full identification of all his sources, one would need access to Jones' own library.

There are many references in the sermons to persons and events that were part of the common consciousness of the early twentieth century, but are no longer recognized seventy years later. Where I thought it helpful, I have supplied information in the notes to aid in understanding Jones' allusions. When the sermon itself clarified the reference, I have added no comment.

The notes have also been used to pass on minor items of information about Jones himself and the times in which he lived.

Each of the sermons is preceded by a short introduction. In addition to providing information about the dates of composition and previous publication of the sermon, I have tried to set each in the context of Jones' life and thought. The introduction also indicates, so far as Jones had selected them, the poem that would have appeared with the sermon in the book as he planned it.

The Gospel of the Farm is not fully what Jones intended to publish. I have not felt free to guess the poems that were not specifically named, nor did it seem useful to print the text of the poems. The addition of notes would have been unnecessary had the book appeared in 1918. Apart from these differences, however, this is, as much as I could make it, the last book of Jenkin Lloyd Jones.

NOTES

1. The Citizen (a Los Angeles labour newspaper), 3 January 1919. A clipping found in The Jenkin Lloyd Jones Papers, Joseph Regenstein Library, University of Chicago, Box VI, Folder 9.
2. Jenkin Lloyd Jones to Herbert Myrick, 16 January 1918. Jenkin Lloyd Jones Collection, Meadville Theological School, Chicago, (hereafter MTS) Letterfile "Jenkin Lloyd Jones 1918 A-Z".
3. Jones to Susan Quackenbush, 24 May 1918. MTS Letterfile "Jenkin Lloyd Jones 1918 A-Z".
4. Orange Judd Company to Jones, 2 March 1918. MTS Letterfile "1918 M-Z" and Jones to Susan Quackenbush, 24 May 1918. MTS Letterfile "Jenkin Lloyd Jones 1918 A-Z".
5. Editor, Atlantic Monthly to Susan Quackenbush, 4 April 1918. MTS Letterfile "1918 A-L".
6. The only exception is the Ford Peace Ship. Jones' role in this has been adequately noted.
7. "The Gospel of the Farm" manuscript. MTS Drawer XVI, Chapter Seven, "Johnny Appleseed" (1905), p. 13.
8. "The Gospel of the Farm" manuscript. Chapter Three, "Concerning Soil -- Plowing" (1908), p. 1.
9. "The Gospel of the Farm" manuscript. Chapter Fifteen, "The Gospel of the Manger" (1911), p. 14.
10. "The Gospel of the Farm" manuscript. Chapter Five, "Concerning Weeds -- Cultivating" (1909), p. 3.
11. "The Gospel of the Farm" manuscript. Chapter Thirteen, "At The Horse-Fair -- Breeding" (1909), p. 15.
12. "The Gospel of the Farm" manuscript. Chapter Two, "Transformations of a County" (1905), p. 14.

13. Jones used this image in a sermon, "The Spiritual Value of Country and City: A Comparative Study" 15 September 1895, MTS Sermon File, No. 796.
14. "The Gospel of the Farm" manuscript. Chapter Fifteen, "The Gospel of the Manger" (1911), p. 13.
15. "The Gospel of the Farm" manuscript. Chapter Three, "Concerning Soil -- Plowing" (1908), p. 13.
16. "The Gospel of the Farm" manuscript. Chapter One, "Heroes of the Farm" (1917), p. 11.
17. Ibid., p. 16.
18. "The Gospel of the Farm" manuscript. Chapter Fourteen, "Pigs and Babies" (1914), p. 11.
19. Robert Bellah, "New Religious Consciousness and the Crisis in Modernity" in Varieties of Civil Religion ed. Robert Bellah and Phillip Hammond (San Francisco: Harper and Row, 1980), p. 170.
20. "The Gospel of the Farm" manuscript. Chapter Ten, "Tower Hill Twenty Years Later" (1916), p. 7.

I

"Heroes of the Farm" is the most recent sermon in the collection. Jones preached it to his congregation, All Souls Church in Chicago, on 16 December 1917. By that time the possibility of "The Gospel of the Farm" as a book had been raised, and initial enquiries sent out. The sermon appears to have been written with the book in mind.

It serves as a good introduction, by raising the two main themes of the collection: the value of rural life in developing both individuals and the nation and the effort that social improvement calls for.

In form it is a review of Hamlin Garland's autobiography, Son of the Middle Border, which had just been published the previous summer. He knew Garland and the tone of the review is intimate and chatty rather than literary. He praises the book, as most did, for its honesty and realism.

One of the attractive elements of this sermon is that Jones, now in his mid-seventies, allows himself to reminisce about his own childhood on the frontier, often matching stories with Garland.

The sermon was published in Unity the week after it was preached.

Jones had partially selected a list of prefatory poems for each of the sermons in the book. The chosen poem for "Heroes of the Farm" was the first five stanzas of Rudyard Kipling's "The Explorer" -- an apt choice. In his notes, though, he mis-names it "Pioneer".

HEROES OF THE FARM

> Now Jehovah said unto Abram: Get thee out of thy country, and from thy kindred, and from thy father's house, unto the land that I will show thee. And I will make of thee a great nation, and I will bless thee, and make thy name great; and be thou a blessing.
>
> Genesis 12:1,2

I can hardly trust myself to write of Hamlin Garland's recent book, A Son of the Middle Border, for it seems so personal.[1] It is like talking about myself. I got there before my friend Hamlin; I anticipated his story by twenty or more years. I know whereof he speaks and more. His book will stay as a remarkable contribution to literature because it portrays life in its pioneer achievements in the Mississippi Valley.

Hamlin Garland undertook a dangerous task, and woe to him who shall try it after him. In mid-life, while still in the strain and struggle of the battle, with a career not yet at its high-water mark in the literary world, he stopped to tell his own story; and

— — — — —

[1] The opening paragraph has been omitted, as a kind of false start.

he has succeeded to a remarkable degree.[2] The author has succeeded so well that in the order of things it would seem that he now ought to die, for it will be hard to open up his story again. There scarcely seems room for any new triumphs or fresh achievements.

Mr. Garland has told in a plain, simple, frank fashion the hard experiences of un-named and un-honored thousands. He has spoken for, and of, the brave army of pioneers who carried the banners of American independence, education and intelligence over the Blue Ridge, through the forests of Pennsylvania, Ohio and Indiana, across the prairies of Illinois, Iowa and Nebraska, on over the Rocky Mountains to the beyond. It is a plain, simple story of the pioneer, for the first time so far as I can recall, told with great frankness on its dark as well as its bright and beautiful side.

Oh, we have plenty of "Songs of the Pioneer", plenty of the "Romances of the Prairies", plenty of the poetry which men in slippers and easy chairs have attributed to cowboys or plowboys! But Hamlin Garland has put into the story the dust and the mud, the sweat and heat of the harvest field, the chills and the chilblains of winter, the nerve-testing and soul-wearying "chores". He has shown us the pinched life of the women, the meager lives of children. He has reported the tyrannical preoccupations of pioneer fathers. All this and more he has told in such a way that it takes on the grace and charm which art can throw over the grimmest facts, the severest realities.

The story opens in Wisconsin. A little boy ran away when the weary soldier returning from the war laid

- - - - -

[2] The next sentence is omitted.

aside his musket and said, "My little man, won't you come to Daddy?" The mother, who had kept the hoe bright while the father followed Grant and Sherman through the three years' struggle at the front, brought the pillow on which to ease his head. Soldier fashion, he preferred to lie on the floor to rest himself. But the father came back from the war with the discipline of Sherman and Grant in his blood. The soldier-farmer was a direct product of New England. His mother had taught him to love Emerson, Whittier and Holmes. Thus the boy found himself the child of a restless pioneer.

They called the narrower valleys "coulees" along the upper Mississippi where the French have left their trails in the vocabulary of common life, but farther south along the Wisconsin where I belong, they called them "pockets" and "hollows". Now, alas, the boys and girls have come home from college and the "hollows" have become "vales" and the "pockets" are "ravines". This soldier-farmer grew restless on the valley farm that was crumpled up on either edge. He at first visited and then explored the vast and waiting spaces of Iowa and Minnesota. He was enamored of the "smooth ground" so easily cultivated. So he picked up wife and little children and left the Wisconsin valley farm behind him, in search of a better chance, although his successor converted it into a model dairy farm and perhaps made more money than the wandering pioneer ever did before or after his three, four or more moves. This restless settler had no sooner fairly established himself on a three-hundred acre farm in Iowa and stocked it with the necessary equipment of reapers, mowers, plows, cattle, pigs, sheep and chickens, than he read of the still cheaper and wider fields of Dakota. Then he longed for a thousand-acre wheat field. And so the story continues to the end. It is the story of a restless, relentless, industrious emigrant -- the story of thousands upon thousands who helped make the Middle West.

This man's religion was a simple, but to him an adequate, one. His son says, "Dad would stop in the middle of a swath any day to tell about the end of the world." He was a Second Adventist and had it figured out to perfect clearness. His favorite hymn was "On the Other Side of Jordan".[3]

But although he got to where there were three hundred acres of wheat to harvest, herds of cattle to manage, plenty of pigs to sell, he never got to where "sister Hattie" could have the organ she coveted or the mother the ingrain carpet on the floor for which she longed. To the end she hungered for the most common elegancies and conveniences that would seem to be the birthright of a New England-derived family.

Hamlin Garland grew up neighbor to one whom, after he returned from his eastern experience, he found still living in the little stone hut he built as a pioneer. This thrifty man said, "I always meant to build a good house and make a granary of this stone building, but I have never got around to it." No, he never got around to it, though he probably had a bank account and a mortgage or two on his neighbors' farms, but these to him meant only a more strenuous life, and to his family more self-suppression.

William Dean Howells says of this book, "It is the first time that an actual farmer, not an 'agriculturalist' but a real farmer, has ever broken into the realm of literature." I want to testify that he has

- - - - -

[3] Jones misread; it was Garland's Grandfather McClintock who was the Adventist.

done it successfully. I speak confidently not as a literary critic, but as one who has been there. Most of what he has described I have seen, much of it I have been.

The meagerness of a boy's life on a western farm, the premature responsibilities, the confining burdens are overlooked and neglected by the spic-and-span new social worker of today. The reader of current literature knows all about the hard lot of the mill-hand and the boys and the girls in factories -- not too much, nor is it any too soon to take note of them, but the hard lot of the boy and the girl on the frontier, nay, the boy and girl still on the farm -- even in the prosperous Middle West -- has escaped the philanthropists and is still much omitted in the studies of the social reformer.

All these hardships, the heart and head starvation, come out in the story of this boy who had "responsibilities" at seven years of age. It was his task to bring in the kitchen firewood, to break nubbins for the calves and to shell corn for the chickens. At ten years of age he must reach up to the handles of the plow as he directed the team on a quarter-mile furrow. It was a proud day when father told him he might take the team and do the plowing, but long before noon the young legs were weary and the pride had all gone out of it. As the most tender episode of that hard experience, he thinks of little Frank slipping out, through the never-failing thoughtfulness of the mother, with a precious cookie and perhaps a cup of milk.

How distinctly he recollects the farm work that encroached upon the winter term of school and pulled him out of it before the term was over. Here again the story is so autobiographical that I do not know whether

HEROES OF THE FARM

I am talking for Hamlin Garland or for myself. I never see the boys and girls bounding out of school with their books and throwing up their caps in great glee because school is out and vacation is on without thinking of the doleful pathos of the "last days of school" in _my_ life. I was more grown and more developed than I care to confess before I could ever leave school without bitter tears. Oh, the agony of those autumn days in which I knew that we could not get round to husking the corn in time for me to begin school when the term began! I was always three, four or five weeks late. And I was always scrimped on the other end because plowing, harrowing and planting must begin before the end of the spring term. I remember how I used to envy the girls, and thought it was no wonder they could get ahead because they could begin with the school term and continue to the end -- an achievement which the farmer's boy scarcely remembers ever to have realized.

In the fullness of time came the Grange Movement. It found in the elder Garland a responsible agent. Great hopes were awakened by this new industrial tool that was to bring justice to the farmer and equalize profits and help him to get ahead.

The hopes of the farmer and his wife have been recorded and to a degree appreciated, but the dreams of the farmer's boys and the shy yearnings of the farmer's daughters which were awakened by this Grange movement have never been thought worthy of record, and they are but vaguely hinted at even by Mr. Garland, the poet laureate of the prairie farm.

When the county organization wanted an agent to buy the grain and to take charge of the elevator in the Iowa town, Mr. Garland was the man. For one happy winter there was a break in the routine and drudgery of the farm. The family moved into town, where the mother did not have to see to the calves and tend to the butter and milk. A few luxuries did creep into that village home. They could go to the meat market and have an occasional bit of fresh meat, which on the farm they never expected except perhaps at hog-killing time -- when there was a revelry in head-cheese, souse and liver.

In this village was established the "fresh-water college" in which Hamlin Garland received his training. It was where he made the acquaintance of the masters of literature, became enamored of Shakespeare, resolved that he was going to make an orator of himself; there he became a leader of debate, an organizer of agricultural movements -- and that is more than many big colleges do for the boys of today.

Mr. Garland dates the awakening of his life not to a revival meeting led by some evangelist preaching a lurid gospel of hell fire, as so many farm boys do, but to a sermon he heard in this Iowa village from a wandering Methodist missionary -- a young man who had not yet completed his college course and who had the rare hardihood to preach on art and the message of beauty.

> With most eloquent gestures, with a face glowing with enthusiasm, the young orator enumerated the beautiful phases of nature. He painted the starry sky, the sunset clouds, and the purple hills in words of prismatic hue and his rapturous eloquence held us rigid.
> We have been taught, he said in effect, that beauty is a snare of the evil one; that it is a lure to

destroy, but I assert that God desires loveliness and hates ugliness. He loves the shimmering of the dawn, the silver light on the lake and the purple and snow of every summer cloud. He honors bright colors, for has he not set the rainbow in the heavens and made water to reflect the moon? He prefers joy and pleasure to hate and despair. He is not a God of pain, of darkness and ugliness, he is a God of beauty, of delight, of consolation.

In some such strain he continued, and as his voice rose in fervent chant and his words throbbed with poetry, the sunlight falling through the windowpane gave out a more intense radiance, and over the faces of the girls, a more entrancing color fell. He opened my eyes to a new world, the world of art.[4]

It was a very plain little "Commencement" that marked a sad going out into life of this young farmer lad, but he had at least achieved one or two things that softened the burdens of an awkward boy. He had at last reached a respectable hair-cut; he had been to a barber and no longer felt conspicuous on account of the unkempt condition of his back hair. He had also

- - - - -

[4] From Chapter XVII of <u>Son of the Middle Border</u> (p 164f in the 1962 reprint by MacMillan).

achieved a pair of shoes which enabled him to shed the cowhide boots that were clumsy and so uncomfortable. (He had always longed for a pair of trousers that would not climb up forever to the top of his boots.) Last but not least, he had a suit of "store clothes" in which to graduate.

His father, like the good honest Yankee he was, said, "My boy, your time is your own. I cannot give you anything, but you have a right to your time." So this boy, burdened and prematurely old, who had never been allowed to come in contact with girls except as he had conversed with them at a dance, started out to hunt his career. School teaching was the first step, of course, but lecturing, oratory, public life, politics perchance, lay farther on. But if not any of these, always teaching was his opportunity.

It was a pilgrim's progress eastward, back to the old friends in Wisconsin. There was a long hunt for a job. Disappointed by schoolboards, penniless, caught in a storm with no place to spend the night, he ventures to knock at the door of a farm house. The good wife was out getting him something to eat when, in an ungracious way, overwhelmed with his disgraceful plight, he seized his hat and stole away into the storm again rather than confess his impecuniosity.

We next find him walking the "purline plate" of a barn in his stocking feet with a good-natured Swede, thereby developing ingenuity and perfecting his education as a carpenter. He became an expert shingler, which held him in good stead when he found himself penniless in New England.

At last the farmer boy won his way to Boston. He had saved enough to pay for his board for a while. He found a position as teacher in the Boston School of

Oratory. He led an underfed and precarious life, but the prairie boy was pushing forward. Always with literary ambition he at last had a manuscript accepted by Harper's, for which he was paid twenty-five dollars. Forthwith Hamlin, the loyal son, bought silk for a dress for his mother and the autobiography of General Grant for his father. The mother sent back a grateful and tearful acknowledgement, confessing that all her life she had longed for a silk dress; and the boy expresses his regret that he could not have been there to receive in person her gratitude.

The story brings our farmer boy back west again. He finds the Garland homestead now on a Dakota prairie. His father is still trying to get the better of the encroaching chinch bug. The same awful bug invaded my Wisconsin home so that we would have to stop the reaper and sweep off the accumulated pests before the machinery would run. We gathered them up from the reaper platform by the bushel. But that is my story, not Garland's.

His father was forever following the lure of new lands. Next he reads of the citrus-fields of California and of the benignant climate that avoided blizzards. But it remained for Hamlin and his younger brother Frank, who won his honors on the stage before Hamlin did in literature, finally to carry back the tired father and mother to the Wisconsin bluff country, stopping on the way to visit the World's Fair.[5] But the machinery of the mind as well as of the body was worn out, and after two days of the World's Fair the mother said, "I am tired," and the father said, "Take me

— — — — —

[5] The "World's Fair" is the World's Columbian Exposition held in Chicago in 1893.

away." And thus in middle-life this loving son at last was able to install the worn-out father and mother in an improvised "Garland homestead" up in New Salem, Wisconsin.

Thus ends this story of pioneer anxieties and hardships. There comes into this life of a son of the Middle Border scarcely a touch of romance such as books deal in. It is true that he stopped off a train to see "Alice" on his first journey in search of a career. She walked up and down the street of the little town with him for one twilight hour; she told him she was sure he would succeed. Later there is an incidental allusion to the fact that Alice is dead, but that is all.[6]

We see the pathos of this farmer's wife out West, the meager life and the uninspired drudgery mingling with the inspirations of the field and of nature. Woman's life on the farm is wanting in the changes that bring the farmer within reach of the contagion of a growing world. The monotony of the life of the farmer's wife is well described in a poem by the same author:

> I've seen that woman once a week
> Ever since that very day in church,
> When Ben turned round 'n kissed her cheek
> And the preacher knelt to pray.
> I've watched her growing old so fast --
> Her breath just flickered toward the last.
>
> Wasn't old, nuther, forty six - No,
> Jest got humpt, an' thin an' gray,

- - - - -

[6] I have omitted the next sentence.

> Washin' an' churnin' an' sweepin', by Joe,
> F'r fourteen hours or more a day.
> Brats o' sickly children every year
> To drag the life plum out o' her.
>
> Worked to death. Starved to death,
> Died f'r lack of air an' sun --
> Dyin' f'r rest, and f'r jest a breath
> O' simple praise fer what she'd done.
>
> An' many's the woman this very day
> Elder, dyin' slow in that same way.[7]

The life of the farmer's wife on the frontier would be a tragedy were it not enhaloed with the large results written in the pride of countries, the triumphs of states and the boast of nations. The exhaustion has been forgotten but the glowing experiences still abide.

Into this story of the long furrow, the limited schooldays, the heavy boots, the awkward clothes, come the ameliorations of Beadle's dime novels and the New York Tribune ("the try-bune" as we used to call it). I do not know how to educate a child today without the old-fashioned school reader of the little old country school house. Hamlin grew up on McGuffey's as I found in Sander's, not only a school book, but a rich treasury of permanent literature. It was too early for Tennyson and Browning, but there were Wordsworth and Scott and their associates, and there was as much of Shakespeare as we could digest. There were Daniel Webster's speeches and much beside. Hamlin grew up on Ray's Arithmetic and Mitchell's Geography. I could

- - - - -

[7] Hamlin Garland's poem "A Farmer's Wife" (last four of six stanzas), published in Prairie Songs, 1893.

revise the list by substituting Davies' <u>Arithmetic</u> and adding Clark's <u>Grammar</u>.

But all this story -- long in the living, short in the telling -- is punctuated by such episodes as this: "Hamlin, get up! get up! Your father is very ill. You must go for the doctor." And the boy plunges into the dark for a horseback ride through a tempest for five miles on what was scarcely a road -- only a trail, and he brings back the doctor.

Notwithstanding the grimness of it, this was a favored home. There was music always. For the mother could fiddle; she could play the old hymns. The father used to say that his wife could go to the store in the morning to buy calico and wear the dress for supper. "She knit all our socks, made our shirts and suits, carded and spun wool, did all the housework, and still had time to help the boys with their kites and bows and arrows."

This frail woman adjusted herself to six different homes when she was not half-way through, and Hamlin does not tell us how many more homes there were. She followed the restless father who always believed that he ought to have a "bigger farm and cheaper land". This westward urge made him the restless pioneer, and he died, I fear, a dissatisfied and disappointed man. He was one of the "Pioneers" of whom Hamlin Garland sings:

> They rise to mastery of wind and snow;
> They go like soldiers grimly into strife
> To colonize the plain. They plow and sow,
> And fertilize the sod with their own life,
> As did the Indian and the buffalo.[8]

- - - - -

[8] The whole of Garland's short poem, "Pioneers", also from <u>Prairie Songs</u>.

Much of this story doubtless sounds like foreign speech to those who are not old enough to reach back into the early life of the Middle West. A few who read these pages may know what it is to husk corn with chapped and bleeding fingers. Some may know what it is to have chilblains that make it an agony to get one's boots off and more agony to get them on again. It was a poor winter that did not give me half a dozen frozen noses or ears on the way to and from school.

I am in search of the "gospel of the farm". What about the pioneer life of the soul? Where is the "Out West" of the spirit? What are the conditions of life that make all this not only tolerable but enjoyable, not only endurable but inspiring? It is hard to analyze, but it is easy to recognize this urge of the spirit towards new adventures, the irresistible hunger to add a plus to life. Oh, to feel the joy of creating, the challenge to mind as well as to hand, the inspirations of trying to transform ideals into the wealth of the world!

Where is the "Out West" of the spirit? Where does it begin? A cowboy poet, Arthur Chapman, has answered the question in a poem which at one time was said to be the most popular poem in the West, conceived out there under the shadow of the Rocky Mountains:

> Out where the hand clasp's a little stronger,
> Out where the smile dwells a little longer,
> That's where the West begins;
> Out where the sun is a little brighter,
> Where the snows that fall are a trifle whiter,
> Where the bonds of home are a wee bit tighter,
> That's where the West begins.

> Out where the skies are a trifle bluer,
> Out where friendship's a little truer,
> That's where the West begins;
> Out where a fresher breeze is blowing,
> Where there's laughter in every streamlet
>   flowing,
> Where there's more of reaping and less of
>   sowing,
> That's where the West begins.
>
> Out where the world is in the making,
> Where fewer hearts in despair are aching,
> That's where the West begins;
> Where there's more of singing and less of
>   sighing,
> Where there's more of giving and less of
>   buying,
> And a man makes friends without half-trying--
> That's where the West begins.[9]

Religion begins out there also. The joys and inspirations of the prophet are interpreted by the life of the pioneer. The leader in the realms of the spirit parallels the experience of the men who converted the wild prairie into gardens, who made Wisconsin the great dairy state, Iowa the great corn state and Minnesota the great wheat state. The Pioneer and the Prophet are intruders in the domain of nature. They represent a human plus -- a something added to the utmost reach of nature.

It is a lonely business for the prophet! It is living away out west on frontier lines. But out there

─────

[9] Arthur Chapman (1873-1935), "Out Where The West Begins". Jones must have been dozing when he selected this poem. It exemplifies the "Romances" to which he objected earlier.

lie the consolations of religion, out there are found the inspirations of life.

The World's Fair wearied the worn-out farmer; it was too much for the exhausted mother. But their blood and sinew, their brains and lives had entered into the glory of that World's Fair. Its triumphs were first won by them way out there on the prairie; its achievements were first chopped out of the forests, coined out of the mines.

So must the inspirations of religion ever come through the pioneer. What is the matter with the churches that they are not full? I do not know. But I do know that the prophets of God are never found in crowds -- the advancing columns of human nature are never popular. Pioneering is solitary work, so solitary that if I were to express the pain and burden of Hamlin Garland's story in one word it would be "lonesomeness". The solitary quality of the log house in the clearing, the cold pioneer frame house on the unbroken horizon of Iowa or Minnesota, spells loneliness. I have seen them; I have been there. I know them, and without doubt "loneliness" is the word. But at the same time they are inspiring on account of the social forces working in and through them. Comfort came from the unrealized crop that was <u>going</u> to pay the mortgage -- if not this year then next or the year after that. Although it was ten-cent corn with ten percent interest in Kansas, Kansas was still inspiring even in the old days of chinch bugs and grasshoppers.

Is it not easy now to find the inspirations of the pioneers in the realm of the spirit? The lure of the ideal in the social realm, oh, how invaluable it is!

For all the frankness and literary skill displayed by Mr. Garland in this book, I fear that his most valuable revealments will either be wholly missed or misunderstood. Only those who have been there can read between the lines the story of the intellectual foundation and spiritual accumulations of the Middle West. Those horny-handed, hard-headed, grim pioneers were unconsciously state-builders. What "up-to-date" young man on the farm or elsewhere can understand, much less appreciate, the picture of the wheat-buyers and neighboring farmers in the little prairie village eagerly waiting for the arrival of the Chicago train on Monday, and then on winter days gathering round the hot stove in the elevator to listen to someone read aloud Ingersoll's last lecture. In this day of distrust of the daily paper -- its confessed opportunism, its censored religious news, its vivisected sermons -- who can understand the significance of the amount of sanity that went with the Chicago paper which every Monday morning distributed through all the villages along all the trunk lines throughout the Mississippi Valley the richest word spoken in Chicago pulpits on the Sunday previous. The old <u>Inter-Ocean</u> built for itself a large Monday clientele because for several years it published in full the sermons of David Swing.[10] A Boston paper secured for itself a similar ascendancy over its rivals by virtue of its printing weekly the wise words of James Freeman Clarke.[11]

- - - - -

[10] David Swing (1830-1894), former Presbyterian minister. After a celebrated trial for heresy, he founded the Independent Central Church in Chicago.

[11] James Freeman Clarke (1810-1888), missionary, educator, scholar, leader in the Unitarian Church.

It was over this road that Hamlin Garland travelled into his intellectual activity and spiritual earnestness. Those prairie discussions led him into the fellowship of Henry George and to an acquaintance with Walt Whitman. Edward Everett Hale secured for him library privileges in Boston, and he became the interpreter of Darwin, Haeckel, Herbert Spencer, and John Fiske, men that to the end of this story were his inspirations and guides.

The prairie farmers in the Middle West were the pioneers of thought; many of them rough-hewed their way to the advance lines of religious and political thinking. Their homes ceased to be lonely because they were companioned by great leaders and comforted with great thoughts. The ideals they dreamed of ameliorated and finally obliterated the gruesome exposures and overwork.

Father Garland was consoled and comforted by the thought of the speedy coming of the Lord from heaven to wipe away the sins of the world and establish his kingdom here on earth. The son found similar comfort and inspiration in the dream of a social reconstruction, an economic escape from industrial injustice, a new balancing of society -- perhaps through Single Tax or Socialism, or through a more general diffusion of education. No matter what, it added a spiritual plus to the heroism of the farm, it touched barnyard drudgery with the leaven of thought. The experiences of the harvest fields and the corn-husking were illumined with political enthusiasms and cultural ambitions.

I wish Mr. Garland had told us whether Uncle David's threshing machine was a "J.I. Case" or a "Buffalo Pitts". But that is unimportant. The great thing to know is that this expert with the axe, this champion rail-splitter and successful runner of threshing machines clung to his violin to the end. The old man disappears with the fiddle in his stiffening hands.

The great compensating factor that stands out through his book is that the pioneer took his orders from within; his inspirations came from above and beyond. Never-realized was the farm that made the farmer's life not only endurable but desirable. Colonel Higginson[12] read the Thanksgiving Proclamation of the pioneer in his poem that gives thanks for "The Things I Miss":

> Sometimes there comes an hour of calm;
> Grief turns to blessing, pain to balm;
> A Power that works above my will
> Still leads me onward, upward still,
> And then my heart attains to this --
> To thank Thee for the things I miss.

The piano that never arrived, the spring wagon that was never realized enriched that home. The hardest things for the dear mother to turn her back upon as she returned to the shelter of the Wisconsin hills were the windswept graves of two darling daughters.

The comforts, the inspirations, the triumphs the settler missed ultimately came into the community. They enriched the countries and ennobled the states. Pity the children who have never known the high discipline of unsatisfied longings, ungratified expectations; pity the child who has but to cry and the candy comes, needs only to tease "Daddy" and the automobile arrives, whose life is poisoned with the luxuries that come whenever he makes sufficient fuss.

Perhaps my friend Hamlin worried a little too

- - - - -

[12] Thomas Wentworth Higginson (1823-1911).

much about his dress, but better be uneasy in homespun and a home-made suit of clothes than to play the silly dude, like the over-dressed student of styles such as are sometimes seen parading the streets and boulevards of today. Garland speaks of the girls at the "exhibition" who were more distressed over ill-fitting sleeves than they were over their dramatic shortcomings, but they are less to be pitied than their sisters who are still more conscious of their sleeveless arms.

Do not miss the import of this story. In this revealment of the story of one family is found the rise and origin of the democratic state, the hope of humanity.

There is reason to fear that the pioneer has over-reached himself. The reaper and the automobile, yes, the telephone and the aeroplane, have so occupied the energies of the pioneer that the intelligence, the conscience -- aye, the self-directing forces -- are in danger of falling out of his life.

There is an intangible frontier which calls for a new race of pioneers.

II

During the last thirty years or so of his life, Jones spent his summers at Tower Hill in Wisconsin, a mile or so from the family's farms. It was both his place of rest and the location of his Summer School of Religion. Every autumn on his return to Chicago he preached an "after-vacation sermon" based on some experience or observation of his summer. Several sermons in this collection are that type. This is his after-vacation sermon for 1905, preached on 8 October and printed in Unity on 26 October.

At the conclusion of the Summer School, on 22 August, Jones and the teaching staff rewarded themselves with a week-long excursion by horse and wagon-- "gypsying" they called it -- through southeastern Wisconsin. It became a kind of pilgrimage for Jones as he led the group to the first family homestead near Ixonia.

Through most of the sermon Jones looks back to the Jefferson county of his childhood, in order to show how far the area has progressed. It gave him a chance to share his memories, and modern readers a chance to glimpse the way life was in the 1850's.

Jones' notes indicate that the prefatory poem was

to be "The East and The West". Most likely he meant Matthew Arnold's sonnet, "East and West" -- a poem that fits at least part of his theme.

TRANSFORMATIONS OF A COUNTY

My earliest recollections of life are in a log house surrounded by heavy forests, the clearing scarcely reaching at any point the boundaries of the little farm, the title to which came direct from the government at a dollar and a quarter per acre. The presence of neighbors was testified to by our ears more often than by our eyes; the ring of the woodman's ax and the tinkle of the cow-bells revealed more than we could see.

My father avoided the broad prairies or even the more accessible "openings" that were available to the adventurous pioneer who dared make a claim, because to the eyes of the Welsh immigrant the absence of trees suggested a desert. Land that "could not grow a horse switch" was no place for a man to provide for a large and growing family. So out of pathetic ignorance, he accepted the challenge to battle. He made his claim to one hundred and twenty acres of the heaviest forest in the Rock River Valley in the county of Jefferson in what was then (1845) the territory of Wisconsin. Hither the wife and seven children were brought, myself the babe in arms. It was necessary to chop a tree in order to catch a glimpse of the sky; the logs for the house were near at hand.

In this log house the first twelve years of my life were spent. I cannot remember the earlier privations nor yet the more numerous pleasures that gathered around this home in the woods -- the second house in what came to be a thrifty Welsh settlement, rejoicing in Welsh lore and worshiping the God of their fathers in the love of their fellows. But my recollections do reach back to the Indian, the deer, the trapper, the peddler, the weekly mail, the itinerant preacher and the gruesome battle with mosquitos and malaria. The heavy timber land that followed the valley of the Rock River was interlaid with marshes like jelly in a layer-cake. The marshes could be crossed only on log-ways -- the logs laid side by side for wagon roads and end to end for pedestrians. These marshes were the despair of the traveller and the fertile hatching place of mosquitos and malaria. We now know the connection between the two, then unsuspected. It was a fortunate year that did not bring with it three or more months of ague in the spring and fall seasons.

Next to saleratus and salt, quinine was the most staple necessity. The shelves of the country store carried large supplies of "India cologogue", "Wahoo bitters", "Bile Beans" and other sure cures for chills and fevers. She was a thriftless housewife who did not lay in a goodly store of smart-weed, boneset, pennyroyal, prickly ash-berries, and other "yarbs" that would come handy in the ague season. When all other topics for conversation failed -- when even the weather was exhausted, the fireside talk was sustained with new cures or old recipes for "breaking" the "chills and fever". He was uninitiated indeed who did not have a personal experience, with its special cure, to offer. The curative merits of jallop, mandrake, ipecac, blue mass, castor oil, seidlitz powders and wet-sheet packs were discussed by experts. Never was empiricism in medicine more honestly based on actual experiments.

The industrial problems of my childhood were the

removal of the forests, getting rid of the logs, building roads through the marshes and clearing the land of boulders, for the glaciers had done a rollicking business in the transportation of "hard heads" and boulders into Jefferson county.

The first problem of the farmer was to get rid of the trees. How the great blazing log-heaps lit up with lurid light the springtime nights! I remember how my father used to get up at midnight to rebuild the burning piles of oak, elm and basswood, the ashes of which offered the only article of commerce in the process. These were carefully heaped up and protected from the rain until the big wagon would come along and buy the ashes at a cent or a cent-and-a-half a bushel, to be carried off to the ashery and there converted into crude potash for shipment further east where it would be made into saleratus. In the back end of the big wagon was a case of goods - blue jeans, needles, threads, calico and tinware - from which store the ashes were paid for.

When the trees were chopped off and the stumps had slowly rotted away, the little field was still peppered with "nigger heads" - boulders big and small. These must be gathered in piles and worked into stone fences, or piled up so that in the fullness of time they made ready-to-hand material for basements of barns, walls, bridges, wells, quaint store-houses and the foundations of roads across the marshes.

After twelve years of what seemed to be an almost hopeless battle with stumps, stones and ague, my parents once more ventured on a change, and gathering their children -- now ten in number -- moved into the more open country. Eighty miles away they found more elbow room on the prairie - land less infected with malaria germs.

Fifty years after this escape from the woods, I led a touring party on a vacation ride back to, and around, the old homestead. We breakfasted sumptuously in the brick house reared on the spot where once the old log house offered its unbounded hospitality to the emigrants. We travelled the length and breadth of Jefferson county, found everywhere improved roads, beautiful homes, well-trimmed lawns and, so far as Wisconsin permits, attractive orchards and gardens still continuing the thought and skill of the "old country". Cows stood belly-deep in clover where fifty years ago they sank in the mire. Many a time as a bare-footed boy, I was sent flying through the woods to summon the neighbors to come and help pull a cow out of the marsh. Now happy Jerseys walk daintily with unsoiled feet over the same ground. The forests are gone; only here and there along the roadside a veteran oak or a maternal elm remain as honored witnesses to the marvellous transformation - survivals of a lost glory.

In my boyhood recollection, oxen were the only beasts of burden and the ox-sled was the vehicle for summer and winter. When the new wagon, all green and red, came to our house and when some years later the three-year-old filly was bought from the drove of horses that came all the way from Ohio -- tied head to tail in single file -- the children on the way home from school came out of their way to see the interesting curiosities.[1] Since then prancing coach horses and cushioned surreys have become the commonplaces of that countryside, while the automobile everywhere menaces

- - - - -

[1] One sentence was omitted here because it disrupted the progression of his idea. "Now and then parents stretched their piety enough to come round by way of our house as they went home from church."

the safety and disturbs the serenity of the turnpiked road. In short the backwoods settlement of fifty years ago is now on the main street of summer tourists. It is the center of one of the most favored agricultural regions of the Northwest. The county has a world-wide reputation for its cheese, its butter and its eggs, for it is the home of W.D. Hoard[2] and his <u>Dairyman</u> -- he who has made classic the phrase "Treat your cow as if she were a lady".

Here and there, black on the hillside or down by a springside, is still to be seen the crumbling relic of some old log house that for a time did service as a barn or as a chicken house on its way to oblivion. But the farm houses now are solid brick or stone mansions, oftentimes with stained glass transoms over the front windows and doors, and hard-wood floors on the inside. They are furnished with refrigerators for summer and steam heaters for winter. Of course the log school house has long since given way to the more commodious frame or brick one and even that is now menaced by the town grammar and high school. The grandchildren of those who were happy if they could win attendance for a short winter term while they worked in the fields in summer time are now full of university ambitions, steeped in the college lore of fraternities and football.

What has brought about this marvellous physical transformation? What has made of the formidable forests in the county of chills and fever, a park of beauty - a county not only of home comforts but of home

─ ─ ─ ─ ─

[2] William Dempster Hoard was governor of Wisconsin from 1889-91. Jones had known him since the 1870's. He was the original instigator of "The Gospel of the Farm" and is referred to several times in these sermons.

luxuries, a country-side famous for its prosperity? And this within the memory of one who, without boasting, can say, "All of which I have seen and a part of which I have been?"

My friend, ex-governor Hoard, whose weekly paper, The Dairyman is read wherever progressive farmers live and is an authority in Denmark, Scotland and Australia as it is in Pennsylvania and Oregon, would say that the cow has been an important factor in this transformation, and his claim is well substantiated by facts. Mr. Hoard has served his state well as governor; he was the defender of the public schools at a time when they were seriously menaced by organized political forces. But he has served his day and generation best by preaching what he calls "The gospel of the cow". In the interest of this gospel he has brought the farm nearer to the university; he has courted science, converted the secrets of the laboratory into their economic equivalents in the creamery. Once he wrote to me:

> The literature of the cow is a broad sea, hard to determine without much patient research as to just what would be of interest to you.
>
> Going back into the old Hindoo literature, we find an abundance of allusions to their ideas of the great question of the motherhood of the cow. Max Mueller tells us that in the old Sanscrit they compare the clouds of heaven to the cows, calling them "the cows of heaven", and when they dispense genial rain they speak of it as

"the milk of the clouds". When Cadmus set out in search of his lost sister, Europa, and consulted the oracle of Delphi, the oracle told him to follow a cow and wherever she went he should go, and when she stopped finally and filled herself and lay down to rest, there he should build a city, and thus we are told arose the city of Thebes. So you see, way back in the early dawn of history, the cow was a home-builder, city-builder, and a nation-builder. Mr. White of Kenosha County many years ago said, "I always speak to a cow as I would a lady." In this he recognized instinctively the femininity and motherhood of the cow. In this instance as in many others, the refinements of a perfect humanity is the summum bonum of commercial wisdom. Those dairymen and breeders who carry out these doctrines to the fullest extent, who treat their cows with the utmost kindness, are almost universally successful financially with them.

You speak of Jefferson County and its high cultivation and comfortable homesteads. This has been the field of my most strenuous labor, of course, being in close contact with the people. My two papers have been teaching the doctrine of dairy improvement, soil improvement, home improvement and particularly stable improvement for a good many years, and while a large proportion of the farmers seem on the surface to pay but little attention to what is said, yet, on the whole, I can see there is a constant upward climb in the conduct of the herds and farms and the results obtained therefrom.

All credit, then, to this benignant connecting link between the grass of the field and the stomach of the man; the cow is a milk-making machine, designed by nature but perfected by human nature. All honor to him who has caused alfalfa fields to flourish in Wisconsin -- hundreds of acres of which we see in early September yielding their third crop of the season. It was worth a pilgrimage of a hundred miles to see the serene faces and to look into the gentle eyes of Hoard's herd of forty pure-blooded Guernseys that looked up half in love and half in wonder as the admiring tourists drove into their velvet pasture. It did not detract from the amenities, the poetry, the civilities, the inspiration of the scene to know that each member of the herd was estimated by hundreds - and not by tens - of dollars and that there were those whose commercial value would be told in four figures. It is an added argument for the civilizing power of progressive farming to know that this prophet of the creamery, this champion of the Guernsey and friend of the Jersey is financially successful in his venture - that Hoard's farm probably yields a profit comparable to any of the profitable farms of Jefferson County.

TRANSFORMATIONS OF A COUNTY 31

But with all due respect to the cow, I must urge that she is but a secondary cause for the prosperity of the county. The cow herself is the effect of a more primal cause. This county abounds in Jerseys, Guernseys and Holsteins; it has great butter and cheese industries. We found there hundreds, aye, thousands, of workmen busy in manufacturing dairy supplies and barn equipment. But back of the cow are the Hoards, the Fargos, the Goodriches, the Favilles and the Jameses, who are products of Jefferson County. To study the story of the pioneers in any county of the upper Mississippi Valley is to take a course of instruction in the development of spiritual power. It is to come upon a first-hand revelation of the potency of mind. To apprehend the story of this county's transformation is to discover the foundations of morals and the secrets of religion.

The first pioneers in the valley of the Rock were young men from the hills and valleys of New England and eastern New York. They represented the stalwart stock of the Green mountains, the Adirondacks and the Genesee valley. Born in the woods and forest-trained, they were drawn hither by the timber and the water power; they set themselves early to the work of harnessing the Rock River and its tributaries. This county was staked out by these direct descendants of Puritan power. These immigrants of the 30's represent the American forerunners. Then in the 40's the waves of European immigration broke upon the forests of the Rock River Valley; on the crest of this wave I was carried thither. German, Irish, Norwegian, English, Scotch and Welsh home-seekers poured in. In 1838 there were but four hundred and sixty-eight people in the county, but those four hundred and sixty-eight included a band of men who could construct dams, build saw mills and grist mills with their own hands and manage them. Those four hundred and sixty-eight bear names that have long since become household words, not only in the county but in the state and nation. The men who laid the foundations of that county's prosperity were men who believed not only in the resources of the wilderness but in the resources hid in the more mystic depths of their own souls. They believed in human nature; they stood with open arms to welcome the creative tide of foreign lives that surged toward them; they received them as a banker receives fresh deposits over his counter.

When my father had bought his one hundred and twenty acres of land for one dollar and a quarter an acre -- land which is now worth more dollars than it was then worth cents, and had bought a yoke of oxen and two cows, he had one round gold sovereign left in the palm of his hand. There he found himself in that forest in the month of May -- too late for any plowing or planting for that year -- with a family of nine to feed. A son of New York had already harnessed the Rock River to a sawmill six miles away from the cabin. He looked into the eyes of this Welshman and with prophetic insight, saw something to trust, something to invest in. Through an interpreter he said to the man who knew no English, "Go back to the woods; go to chopping and chop, chop, chop all summer and next fall. Next winter when the snow is on the ground, haul the logs to the bank of the river two miles distant, roll them onto the ice and when the spring freshets come, float your logs down to my mill. Meanwhile I will open an account with you and keep your family in flour and salt until the logs arrive for pay."

This or something like it was the story of

thousands of the pioneers who helped bring about the marvellous transformation of Jefferson County. Wit, aptitude, energy made common cause with industry, with honesty, with tireless patience and unconquerable ideals. The statistics of this county's cows pale in interest and significance when compared with the story of this county's brains. The county has raised men whose names are familiar in the nation's annals - men who have made themselves felt in the pulpit, at the bar, by the bedside of the sick and in the legislative halls of state and nation. When the union was imperiled and when freedom was threatened in the house of her friends, Jefferson County wrote its story with the blood of these patriots and their successors bred in these log houses.

But Jefferson County has sent out a larger army still who have fought and are still fighting the forces of ignorance - who have made the country schoolhouses glow-points in the history of our advancement, by the light of which this marvellous transformation has been wrought well within the limits of a century and the memory of thousands still living. To study the transformation of this county is to study the power of the human mind, the possibilities of human growth, the resources of common humanity -- triumphant whenever humanity is crowded to its best, compelled to its mightiest, lured to its noblest, either by inward or outward necessity.

The material statistics of our county challenge the admiration -- aye, the wonder -- of the intelligent student, but the social history, the spiritual story of Jefferson County is still more interesting. Watertown, Jefferson, Fort Atkinson and Lake Mills are pearls strung on this patient river and its obedient tributaries. These towns and others have their shaded streets, parks, public libraries and high schools, wherein the best methods of education are brought to bear upon hopeful, industrious boys and girls. All this in fifty years makes the epic of Jefferson County, short as it is, a classic in spiritual transformation.

When we pass from a study of the economic aspects – may I say the physiology of the county – into a study of its sociology, we awaken another class of emotions, perhaps find sources of grave anxiety as well as high encouragement. These early pioneers had other trials than mosquitos and malaria; stumps, marshes and stones were not the only enemies to be overcome or obstacles to be removed before the wilderness could be transformed into a garden, and rose and apple trees be made to grow in the place of bramble and poison ivy.

The immigrants of the 40's were a home-sick lot. Well might they read with choking voices the plaint of the Hebrews when they hung their harps on the willow tree and could not sing the songs of Zion in the land of the stranger. I can well remember the terror that seized me and the cry that followed me when, in the new log schoolhouse (which turned out to be literally in the middle of the road, for it was built before the road was surveyed), the new "school ma'am" spoke to me in a language I could not understand – the English of the statute. Fortunately my first school ma'am was a bi-linguist and she could dispel the forlorn feeling which her English inspired by some soothing sentences in my mother tongue.

My father's log house was one with a loft reached by a ladder for the older children and trundle beds for the younger ones, and still it promptly became the objective point for hundreds and thousands of immigrants, the distributing point for a continuous stream of Welsh settlers. During twelve years of strenuous test the limits of the hospitalities of that house were never reached. When the inside was full, there was the stoop on the outside and then the hay mow in the barn and the shade of the garden trees. Always there was ample room for all who came.

I have spoken of the neighborly rally when a cow had sunk in the mire, but only those who have lived in that network of pioneer sympathies - who have inherited the blessed memories of neighborly exchanges which belong to the frontier - can understand how the poverty of things helped swell the riches of spirit, how the inspirations and consolations of the intangible nerved the arm to fight with forest trees, poisonous fens, pestilential breezes, arctic cold in winter and torrid heats and forest fires in summer.

The sociology of the pioneer was simple but it was intense. The social fabric of the settlement had few decorations, but it was vital; cut it anywhere and it would bleed. The communion of the backwoods was more sacramental than anything the creeds could define or understand. The logging bee, the house-raising, the quilting bees, the butchering and harvesting days, the rally to help the widow, the co-operative harvesting of the sick man's crop and the husking of the orphan's corn were eucharistic seasons in which the communicants partook of the very body and blood of the Master in ways they little realized and to an extent they could never understand.

"Here it is! Right here is the spot, Jenkin! Here is where the old schoolhouse stood. Here is where the door was where you used to go in, Jenkin, Bach!"[3]

- - - - -

[3] "Bach" is a Welsh term of endearment.

The old man was bent and twisted under the burdens of eighty-three years as he located for the tourists the long-vanished log schoolhouse. Meager was the curriculum, crude was the instruction, far, far away from the boasted "new education". That schoolhouse knew nothing of "nature studies" or "character-building" or "manual training" in a pedagogical sense, and still there was more than academic tuition in those old log schoolhouses which laid the foundation of a democracy magnificent, because it was democracy actual. Within those old log schoolhouses Scandinavian and Celtic, Germanic and English, French, Canadian and Indian blood were mixed as in a witch's cauldron and out of the mixture came a new something, unlike any of them, but still partaking of the virtues of all of them - the true American citizen. The citizen's pride of birth was lost in the joy of living. The clannishness of the home was transformed in the school room. Webster's Elementary Spelling Book disintegrated the creeds, ameliorated the prejudices of the sects, eliminated the dogma from practical ethics and from the working religion of the settlement. It was the hand-book that introduced the sons and daughters of foreigners into the universalities of literature and formed the Esperanto in which the various dialects of Europe were merged.

    I dare not attempt to compare the sociology of the Jefferson County of today with the sociology of the Jefferson County of the 40's and 50's as I remember it and as it is written in the earlier annals of which the rising generation is far too careless. We may well wonder if the larger house with its carpet on the floor, its piano and picture embellishments contains a contentment and sincerity, a simplicity of the spiritual life as much richer and larger than that of the old log house as is the brick mansion than the house in the clearing.

Webster's Spelling Book and the New York "Try-bune", perhaps one religious paper and the weekly mail formed the connection between the home and the great world. On these lines did the mind of the child travel towards its culture. In mastering these it received its training.

How meager were the privileges! What parent now-a-days would trust a child to such inadequate tutoring? And still it is a perfectly proper problem in pedagogy to ask whether your manual training, your special courses, your examinations and reviews, even your high school preparations and college accomplishments are giving the children of today the relish for knowledge, the appetite for information, the vital acquaintance with the heroes of history, the working intimacy with the forces that make for good citizenship and high government, which the boys and girls received in the old schoolhouses with their spelling schools and speaking days, and the love that clung to the apron strings of the sweet though unsophisticated little "school ma'am" whose gingham apron and blue ribbon daintily arranged at the throat lifted her into the realms of fairyland – made her seem, to the bare-footed boys and girls who blushed when she spoke to them and trembled when she kissed them, a sylph-like being dwelling apart in a land of sweetness. I speak from tender and well-defined memory.

If culture is to be interpreted in terms of character, and character is to be tested by the potency of will, the joy of the heart, it is a question which educators may well face – whether the physical transformation of Jefferson County is paralleled with an equivalent cultural advance.

One study more is due this story of a county's transformation. The old-fashioned circuit-rider is largely a thing of the past; the primitive exhorter, the camp meeting, the crude theology, the grievous chasm between things sacred and things secular are largely gone. Let them go -- if only the devoutness, the consecration, the delight in heavenly things, the peace of spirit, the serenity of soul, the sense of God in the heart and of providence in the life remain! Do they?

I will not venture an answer. I am content if this study of the transformation of Jefferson County leaves us in the presence of great spiritual facts, real spiritual questions.[4]

I would fain convert this story of Jefferson County into a parable of the heavenly life - the life of today. The United States still has its spiritual forests with their miasmatic swamps and pestiferous mosquitos. There are sociological hard-heads, social boulders, political stumps to be removed in our country before garden beauty and meadow wealth will become possible.

What man has accomplished in the realms of nature, man can and must and will accomplish in the realms of the spirit. We could not, if we would, return to the simplicities of the wilderness, the perplexities of the settlement. But we are still confronted with pioneer tasks in the realm of morals, politics, civic weal and religious liberty. What the fathers accomplished on the lower fields, the sons must achieve on the upper fields. Blessed be the pioneers

- - - - -

[4] I have omitted the next paragraph. Its connection with the rest of the sermon is tenuous and its presence created a confusion.

who are busy ditching the marshes of political corruption, converting the wilderness in the realms of morals into corn fields and orchards. The analogies are so palpable, so pressing, so convincing that I need not attempt to state, much less enforce, them. Let the men and women of this second decade of the twentieth century apply themselves to their tasks with the courage, fortitude, consecration and single-mindedness which the pioneers of Jefferson County applied to their tasks in the fourth and fifth decade of the nineteenth century. Then when their bodies are dust in grass-grown graves, others will bless them for their pioneering as we now bless the pioneers who prepared for us a way in the wilderness.

This chapter originally appeared in the **Wisconsin Magazine of History** 67:2, and is reprinted here with permission.

III

This sermon began the "Gospel of the Farm" series for <u>Hoard's Dairyman</u>. It was published 21 January 1910. The other sermons in the series - in the order they appeared - are Chapters IV, V, XIII, XI and VI.

Jones tried out all the <u>Hoard's</u> sermons on his own congregation first, and then rewrote them, pretty much as a group, for the newspaper. "Concerning Soil: Plowing" was first preached 9 May 1909 at All Souls Church, Chicago.

The structure of this sermon illustrates well Jones' characteristic form and the weaknesses that he was sometimes liable to. The first half is given to telling the history of the development of the modern plow and to describing the nature of soil. This serves him in the same way as a Biblical text serves a more orthodox preacher. He then attempts to apply by analogy the data of his story and description to the ethical and social situation of his hearers.

The application here is pretty general and sketchy. It turns on the use of metaphors, none of which is developed very far. In the end the point of the sermon is simply that of a correspondence between the matter of plowing the soil and improving human life. The aim of the sermon is to generate motivation for progress in personal and social life.

"Welsh - 12th Century" is Jones' note for the poem to accompany the sermon. It is hardly possible to discover what he had in mind.

CONCERNING SOIL: PLOWING

The gospel of the farm is the gospel of exact bookkeeping, of discipline, of intelligence, of profound piety. On the farm there is no place for infidelity; humanity must needs make direct connections with divinity in the wheat-field at least. There mortal man is in constant communion with the unseen forces; he enters into partnership with the eternal powers in the orchard -- if nowhere else.

Bible texts may be obscure, the proper rendering of Hebrew and Greek roots may be uncertain, but there is no uncertainty as to the connection between the cherries on the bough and the roots in the ground. A mystic transformation does take place when dirt, water and air are converted into turnips, clover, wheat, corn and apples. The miracle of the harvest field is beyond distrust; here is no place for skepticism. Nowhere do the laws above more clearly establish their kinship with the laws below than upon the farm. Here one vocabulary serves, so closely does the life of the field tally with that of the spirit. "Cultivation", "training", "fertilizing", "plowing", "subsoiling", "planting", "weeding", "watering" are terms that lend themselves with equal clearness to the preacher and the farmer; character and corn are the results of analogous processes.

Some twenty-eight hundred years ago Micah saw his

people as a field to be plowed. More than nineteen hundred years ago the greatest of preachers delivered the most pertinent sermon ever spoken from the pregnant texts of the field, the seed, the garden, the roadside, the mountain and the beach. Since his time the inventions and discoveries of the laboratory and the revealments of science have multiplied the analogies and intensified the lessons.

But he alone can fully understand the call of the furrow who has walked between the horns of the plow, followed by the buoyant robin and the demure farm hen. He who has watched the roll of the sod and the breaking of the clods, felt the thrill of the plowshare cutting through the web of roots -- bringing to light hidden life, filling the air with the wholesome aroma of the earth -- begins to realize a near-by God. Under such circumstances the song of the bird finds an echo in the hoping heart of the plowman.

Every plowman feels, though it took a Daniel Webster to state, the exultation of plowing:

> When I have hold of the handles of my big plow, with four yoke of oxen to pull it through, and hear the roots crack and see the stumps all gathered under the furrow out of sight, observe the clean surface of the plowed land, I feel more enthusiasm over my achievement than comes from my encounters in public life in Washington.[1]

- - - - -

[1] Most of the material on plowing, including the quotations, is taken from J.B. Davidson's article, "Tillage Machinery" in Volume I, Chapter 11 of Bailey's <u>Cyclopedia</u> cited below.

CONCERNING SOIL: PLOWING   43

At other times the farmer may see ominous signs in the sky and be depressed with the thought of the drought or the freshet which seldom arrives. But at plowing time there is no place for depressing notes; if there is any remnant of the boy's whistle left in the heart of the man, it works at this time.

The frontispiece of L.H. Bailey's great four-volume <u>Cyclopedia of American Agriculture</u>[2] is the picture of a plow deep-set in the ground. Underneath are the words: "The Greatest of Implements".

The story of the plow is the story of civilization. When this story is told in its proper perspective, the plow-makers will stand higher and their names will be more often upon the lips of school boys than will those of the great field marshals of history. The plowman, not the soldier, represents the nation's real safeguard -- the ultimate defense of the community. He who causes bread to spring out of the ground, not he who takes it out of the mouths of women and children, is the true hero.

Society took an immense step forward with the perfection of the plow. The older civilizations were largely confined to the alluvial lands in river valleys because the ancient plow, a crooked stick or some clumsy amplification of the same, could make no impression except on such soil; their feeble scarifying of any harder soil was ineffectual. When at last men fitted an iron point to the crooked stick and hitched an ox or an ass to it, mankind took a great stride forward.

- - - - -

[2] Bailey's <u>Cyclopedia of American Agriculture</u> (New York: The Macmillan Company) was first published in 1907 and had gone through five editions by 1917. Jones draws heavily on this set of books for information in several of these sermons.

In the tribal days of the Hebrews we read that they "went down to the Philistines to sharpen, every man, his share and his coulter". In 1730 we read of Englishmen importing Dutch plows "chiefly made of iron". According to Bailey it was not until 1840 that a plow factory was established in England.

Thomas Jefferson, great on so many lines, brooded over the plow problem. He noticed when in France that oxen plowed with collars and harnesses. He drew elaborate mathematical designs for an ideal plow. Webster was prouder of his achievements in designing a breaking-plow than he was of persuading a jury.

Charles Newbold, a man of New Jersey, in 1797 devised a method of casting in iron the mold-boards for a plow. The farmers rejected the product because, they said, iron poisoned the soil and interfered with the growth of plants.

Then came Jethro Wood, the hero of the modern plow. He perfected the mold-board and paid the price of the pioneer. The agricultural as well as the religious prophet must ever travel the thorny road. Said William H. Seward:

> No citizen of the United States has ever conferred greater benefit on his country than has Jethro Wood; none of her benefactors have been so inadequately rewarded.

Wood died in want, but he left the plow behind him -- a great destroyer of hunger.

A good plow must be self-scouring. The rough cast-iron with its porous surface was of little use in the rich prairie soil of the West, because it was not self-scouring. When the man had to stop every few rods to clean the plow with his paddle, plowing was very tedious as well as inefficient. But when in 1868 James Oliver developed the process of hardening cast-iron so that it would take a more polished surface, plowmen took a new hold; the "Oliver Chilled Plow" is still widely advertised and extensively used throughout the South, where a single mule plows the cotton field.

Grand Detour, on the banks of the Rock River in Illinois, is now less than a deserted village. The railroad gave it the cold shoulder and the prosperous city of Dixon sprang up nearby; it was first overshadowed and then absorbed. But Grand Detour should still be a farmers' shrine, for there in 1837, over eighty years ago, John Deere made a plow out of an old cross-cut saw blade, and that steel plow made the cultivation of the vast areas of the Mississippi valley possible. In 1838 he made three plows; in 1839 ten were built; next year there were forty turned out; five years later his factory was removed to Moline and it had a capacity of turning out ten thousand plows a year. In 1886, in the ripeness of eighty-two years, this Vermont blacksmith died a multi-millionaire. He had been mayor of the thriving city of Moline, president of its leading bank, a builder of its public library, a contributor to many charities. His biographer speaks of him as "a man of great power and decision of character, sympathetic and generous".

But all these titles and honours are incidental; his great contribution to humanity was the steel plow. There are other claimants to this honour. William Parlin of Canton has recently been placed in the Illinois Hall of Fame as a pioneer plow-maker, and his claim is enforced by the existence of one more "greatest plow works in the world", which places the little city of Canton on the map as beloved of farmers. When the true story of the subjugation of the Mississippi valley is written, the list of the trappers, explorers, colonels, generals -- even the great railroad builders and the more recent captains of industry -- will pale in the presence of the story of Oliver, Deere and Parlin, the plow-makers; of Studebaker, the wagon-maker; of McCormick, the maker of reapers.

But the hammer implies a nail, the plan a board, the ax a tree, and the plow the soil. I must not let the plow-makers crowd out the plowing. The tool implies a task.

Who will teach us the Gospel of the Soil? Whence came it? What is it? What are its possibilities, this meager covering of the earth out of which comes all life -- plant and animal -- food, clothing, shelter -- everything material with which man has to deal? It is such a thin film on the surface of the globe that it is impossible to indicate a cross section of it by any scale -- just a few inches on the flinty hillside, not more than eight or a dozen feet in the richest farm lands of Illinois. Yet out of this little blanket of dirt year after year and century after century comes the measureless growth of grass and corn, hay, oats, clover and shrubbery, grape-vines, apple and plum trees, pines and oaks. And this little peeling of earth is but rotten stone, crushed rock, disintegrated strata, with a curious, almost intangible, plus of some thing or things gotten out of water and air. Clay is powdered granite, sand disintegrated quartz, loam a mixture of clay and sand, reinforced by the debris of the life it has produced.

> The mills of God grind slowly
> But they grind exceeding small.[3]

- - - - -

[3] Longfellow's translation of one of the "Poetical Aphorisms" of von Logau.

CONCERNING SOIL: PLOWING

says Longfellow. He had in mind the mills of justice, the spiritual edicts of the Almighty, but it is just as applicable to the physical world. The millstones used in grinding the granite and crushing the quartz are chiefly wind, water, cold, heat, sunshine and frost.

> No rock so hard but that a little wave
> May beat admission in a thousand years.

The grim face of the mountain is scarred by dew, hollowed and undermined by frosts, carved by the wind.

It takes a strong team and a good plow to turn up eight inches of soil. That is indeed deeper plowing than the farmer thinks of, for his plowshare strikes back of the millenia of human life, the aeons of vegetable and animal life -- oftentimes back of all stratified rock into the primeval lavas, the fire mists that slowly cooled into the wrinkled mass of unstratified fire-rock that forms the backbone of our globe. This in the measureless aeons was disintegrated, the debris carried by water, laid down upon the floors of the ocean, lifted again by the troubled planet distressed with the boiling, bubbling lava within.

But there is more than this, much more. The rock elements are comparatively few -- whether it be ground granite, dissolved limestone, or crumbled quartz. These alone will yield but meager lichens, mosses, sage-grass and stunted shrubs. The nobler wrappings of grasses, flowers, grains, fruits and forests come not until that something else is added, of which the farm books are so full nowadays, the preservation and increase of which is the constant quest of the skilled farmer -- "humus".

What is humus? Who can tell? It is all that I have mentioned, plus a something drawn from the air - some old, strange combinations to which science gives mysterious names, but of which it can offer little explanation -- something elaborated in the marvellous plant laboratories that have gone before. It is what remains of past life, the decayed bodies of dead organisms, the cemetery that holds what is left of the life that once rejoiced in the sunlight and slaked its thirst with dewdrops and showers. It is this new and finer plus, the something that makes the barren rock soil fertile, that changes prairies into meadows, thickets into orchards, grazing places into gardens.

Now we come in sight of the prime mission of the plow, the great missionary work of the plowman. Here is the next word -- "tillage". It is that manipulation of the soil which will make it more retentive of moisture, which will hold more effectually the wealth of past life and in due time and process make this wealth again available to new growth, sucklings of a new crop, babes of a higher order.

Now we have our "Message of the Plow". The three great words of the tilled field are:

Soil: the grindings of the cold, dead structure, arranged in the bed in which organic life has been cradled; the enriching of that bed with slow accumulations of passing life, enabling tasseled corn, rose bushes and hickory trees to raise on stepping stones of this dead past beauty, strength, fruitfulness.

Humus: the accumulations of life -- past failures making for future successes; lichen, sand burr, mullen and thistle, yielding up their lives that beans, pumpkins, clover, corn and wheat may become possible.

The Plow: a successful extension of man's cooperative hand, accomplishing in an hour what would take nature, unaided, centuries of farming; that which hastens the decay of the sod and sweetens the acid with sunlight; the hoe raised to horse-power; the spade acting continuously as fast as the horses can walk around the field.

How painfully and at what cost have the elaborations of the thought-fields and heart-fields of humanity been developed! What great blocks of **granite** stolidity, what flinty surfaces have been ground by the small but tireless chisels of time, in order to make social the soil that grows the luscious fruits and nourishing grains of human character. What tillage of mind and heart has it taken to clothe barbaric ruggedness with beauty, gentleness and tenderness! These soul-fields, like the earth-fields, have been enriched by the humus of human experience -- the life deposits of those gone before, by the failures and painful disasters of the men and women who have gone down in defeat and disappointment, but not to utter rack, not to final ruin and everlasting loss. Our soul-fields have been enriched by their lives; out of their disappointments have come triumphs, their tears have grown smiles.

Samson's riddle is the secret of civilization. Bees have built their nests in the grinning skeletons of death, and honey is found in the lion's jaw. Whittier gave expression to the same secret when he wrote:

> The grain grew green on battle plains,
> O'er swarded war-mounds grazed the cow;
> The slave stood forging from his chains
> The spade and plough.
>
> Where frowned the fort, pavilions gay
> And cottage windows, flower-entwined,
> Looked out upon the peaceful bay
> And hills behind.

> Through vine-wreathed cups with wine once
>   red,
> The lights on brimming crystal fell,
> Drawn, sparkling, from the rivulet head
> And mossy well.
>
> Through prison walls, like Heaven-sent hope,
> Fresh breezes blew, and sunbeams strayed,
> And with the idle gallows-rope
> The young child played.
>
> Where the doomed victim in his cell
> Had counted o'er the weary hours,
> Glad school-girls, answering to the bell,
> Came crowned with flowers.[4]

"Tillage" is quite as much the word of the school room and the church as it is of the meadow and the garden; something can be done in enriching the fields of thought by artificial methods. Here as there, "boughten" fertilizers are more or less available, but the wisest agricultural scientists tell the farmer to be wary of them. At best they are but exceptional and not permanent and essential elements in profitable farming. The great problem of the farmer is the proper manipulation of the soil that he has, a wise conservation of the field's own resources. Barnyard manure is better and more available than machine-made or laboratory-prepared fertilizers. The skillful farmer is trusting more and more to "green manures", allowing the field to enrich itself. Cow-peas, soy beans, clover and alfalfa lay hold of the elements of the air as well as of water and of solids and convert them into life-producing

- - - - -

[4] Stanzas 11-15 of Whittier's poem, "The Reformer".

stuff. They under-drain the fields, make mellow the loam, blanket the earth -- saving the delicate and fugitive substances from the depredations of burning sun, scalding winds and drenching rains.

All these have their equivalents in the spiritual fields. Ideas, emotions, amusements, the sweet recreations that we call "leisure" or, perhaps, "indolence", all help to enrich the field so that it will grow more ideas, better deeds, finer feelings.

I cannot go into the story of the bacteria in plant life, those curious, persistent, unpaid aids of the farmer. The question of "hired help" is an oppressive one, the constant plaint of the farm-home, but the farmer should not ungraciously overlook the splendid corps of helpers furnished him by nature. The providence of the field is lavish in farm hands, reaching from the invisible microbe without which germination would be impossible, up through the angle-worm that does what the plow cannot do in aerating the soil, through countless bugs and beetles -- more of them friends than enemies of the farmer, up to the birds, who plant without charge and pick off the bugs without pay, and on till we find the stock which roams the pasture to its enrichment and transforms the roughage of the field into delicious milk, toothsome butter, juicy beefsteak and appetizing mutton chops.

So it is in the fields of the spirit. The moralist owes more than he can ever tell to the microbes of doubt and distrust, the angle-worm of curiosity, the dashing flight of reckless birds that on outstretched pinions dare to sail the upper air.

All the large problems in agriculture today are the large problems in sociology as well. The reclamation of swamp lands, the conservation of soils from erosion, the draining of marshes and the irrigation of desert tracts are the mighty things to be accomplished in the soul-fields as in the earth-fields. Great things are being done in this direction by the husbandman in both fields; more things are to be done. Our agricultural colleges are more successful than our theological schools in teaching better social husbandry. The spiritual farmer is not content with his agricultural reports. He must help drain the soggy fields of stupidity, the stagnant marshes of ignorance, irrigate the arid plains of individualism and selfish greed; he must conserve the wastages in the human field, be patient with the slow forces, believe in the essential fertility of nature -- whether material or human -- in the sublime vitality and fecundity of the universe.

Then, too, the parent as well as the farmer must not forget the plow in the plowing. There are too many moralists who still seek to prepare the social field with the old Egyptian crooked stick for a plow, or at best the cast-iron plow of medieval days -- now grown very rusty -- to which the soil clings, and instead of a furrow we have an irritating scratch that leaves only a scar. In this tilth of the spiritual fields we need the modern plow of advanced thought and fearless science, a thought plow perfected by experience and brought down to date.

Thomas Jefferson, who improved the plow, was also the writer of the Declaration of Independence. Abraham Lincoln, who could sink the ax deeper into the wood than any other woodsman in the settlement, was the very man who laid the ax to the root of slavery and brought the poisoned tree low.[5]

- - - - -

[5] The next sentence has been omitted as a confusing digression.

CONCERNING SOIL: PLOWING   53

The books tell us that in eight inches of soil, the possible reach of a plow, covering one acre of land, there are twenty-four thousand pounds of the fundamental elements necessary to plant life. This is the basis upon which the farmer is to work. It is the province of the skillful husbandman not only to get, year after year, the crop of this soil, but to do it without exhausting the supply -- nay, actually to increase the fertility. Skillful dairy farming and green manuring greatly enhance the fertility of the field year by year.

So lavish is the God of the soul that truth, love and justice increase by production. Light is not lessened by lighting your neighbor's lamp. It is increased. There should be no cowardly, niggardly faithlessness in regard to the higher resources of human nature. The dirt that distresses the house-keeper and offends the dainty, is, as Emerson said, "but misplaced earth, soil wrongly placed". The garbage that is a menace to life in the city may be made the source of new life on the farm. The sewage that brings disaster when neglected and uncared for will, when put into the right place, make tomatoes, watermelons, roasting ears, strawberries and Belleflower apples of most flavour.

Note how futile has been my attempt to keep the fields apart. I rejoice in the splendid confusion. I meant to reason from the plowing in the field to the plowing in the church, from the plowing of the farm to the plowing of the ministry, from the husbandry of the farm to the problems of the school lot, but I have utterly failed. We cannot keep them apart; we never know which is premise and which is conclusion, which fact and which symbol, so identical, confusing, interchangeable are the facts and tasks involved.

Of only one thing we are sure: that there is good stuff worth tilling in both fields. The patience, science, skill, faith which make orchards grow on flinty fields, pastures out of boggy swamps, alfalfa and watermelons out of sandy soil, which can so manipulate compacted clay that it will grow great corn and luscious grapes will, when applied to the problems of human husbandry, make -- within limits -- kind and gentle men out of the dissolute, co-workers out of enemies.

The student of history can no longer doubt that the bog land of humanity can and must be drained, that the arid lands of the human heart can and must be irrigated and that this is to be done by conserving the waste, utilizing the roughage, applying tile or dike as case may need and, above all, by accumulating the spiritual humus, by carrying into this higher husbandry the patience, persistence, the sagacity, the determination to keep at it -- to work with and not against the God of things as they are, which brings such splendid triumphs on the farm.

If sorrow and defeat is to come to us, if the American Zion like the ancient one is to be made as a plowed field and our Jerusalem to become a heap of ruins, then, still, if not with us, in spite of us, "The law and word of the Lord will go forth and he will judge between many people, and they shall beat their swords into plowshares and their spears into pruning hooks".

We must not be mean and rebellious. Rather, let us take hold of this plow-making business, rejoice in the plow-men of the soul, become co-workers with the great agriculturalists in the realm of the spirit with the Jethro Woods, the James Olivers, the John Deeres, the William Parlins. It is not hard for us to name them: in modern times, the Beechers, the Philips Brookses, the Theodore Parkers and the Channings; further back the Martin Luthers, the St. Francises and the Augustines; and -- most of all -- the great Plow-man of Nazareth who nineteen centuries ago tilled the Judean field in so skillful a manner that he became the great farmer in the fields of the spirit for all time.

IV

Far more than most of Jones' later sermons, this one makes explicit use of a Biblical Text. Jesus' parable of the sower, in Matthew's version (Matthew 13: 4-18), gives him both beginning and end, and it is used as part of the application section.

His "liberal" standpoint leads him to treat the Bible rather differently. For him it is mainly a record of the sayings and doings of sensitive religious people of the past - of whom Jesus is the pre-eminent one. The major difference between Matthew's Gospel, for instance, and Bailey's Cyclopedia of American Agriculture is that the Gospel is explicitly religious, while Bailey only implicitly so. God's nature and activity are revealed in both -- but not identified as such by Bailey.

It is one of Jones' cardinal principles that everything is a unity; one law governs material and spiritual realities. Since sowing wheat and educating children are two versions of the same thing, then observing nature, reading a Department of Agriculture Bulletin and studying the Bible, all three, lead the receptive mind to Truth.

This second sermon in the Hoard's series was

first preached at All Souls on 16 May 1909, revised and published in <u>Hoard's Dairyman</u> 18 February 1910.

As with the previous sermon, the poetic preface is only indicated as "Welsh - 12th Century".

CONCERNING SEED: SOWING

The parable of the sower is one of the most characteristic and suggestive in the New Testament. The gospel of the seed has been preserved in three different versions in the record which contains the teachings of the Galilean carpenter, the great out-of-doors preacher. In the seed nature reaches not only her maximum energy but her transcendent ingenuity, delicacy and beauty. All the wild and fierce forces of nature seem to tend toward the seed. While studying rocks, waves, stones, air and water, we may venture to talk of "blind forces", "purposeless energies"; if we are very reckless, we may even speak of "chance" and the "wanton play of atoms". The swinging of the planets may be but the yielding of inert masses to a "mathematical necessity" -- whatever that may mean. Astronomy is an exact science because it deals with a few simple, but far-reaching, facts and forces. Weight, bulk, distance determine the rhythmic motions of the stars and the apparently wayward journeyings of the comets.

But once we come within the realm of organic life, then quality counts, not bulk - texture, not size. It is not anything that can be weighed, measured or analyzed, but an elusive potency, an intangible mystery, the nature of which may not be discovered, but whose existence cannot be denied, which represents what we call "life". For the perpetuation of this "life" all the forces of time and space, the realities that appeal to sense, feeling or thought focalize. "Creation groans", as Paul puts it, to bring forth life. The creative will revels in the task of perpetuating itself. For this purpose torrents are subdued and distilled; the last and highest achievement of water is wrought in the dew-drop; tornadoes, hurricanes, mighty trade winds are tamed and tempered that they may achieve their highest results in the summer breezes that wave the wheat fields into fructifying billows and sway the nodding plumes of corn until they yield a fertilizing breath.

The revelations of the telescope are awe-inspiring, but those of the microscope woo the spirit into confidence and trust -- finer, more consoling, more God-revealing. An undevout astronomer may be mad, but it was an astronomer who said, "I have swept the heavens with my telescope and have found no God." Yet the investigator with the microscope, the student of the germ, breaking into the realms of littleness exclaims:

> There is no unbelief.
> Whoever plants a seed beneath the sod
> And waits to see it push away the clod,
> Trusts he in God.[1]

But it is not my purpose to dwell upon the marvels of the laboratory, the delicacy and exquisite balance of forces and substances, the fine compoundings of chemicals, the motherly anxiety with which nature surrounds the mystic germ, protecting it from the vandal forces of nature, providing it with the nourishment fitting to its infancy, tucking away in the chambers of its commissariat just the food to its liking and to its

- - - - -

[1] "There is No Unbelief" by Lizzie York Case. Stanza 1.

CONCERNING SEED: SOWING   59

needs until, so to speak, it is old enough and strong enough to go alone and feed itself. But all this and much more belong to the story of the seed.

It is worth our while to stop on our way to the sowing to note the charming variety, the wonderful diversity, of seed. We do not need books - not even a short course in an agricultural college - to make impressive the lesson of the seed. We need only to stand in front of any country store in springtime and note how charming the coloring, how inspiring the variety, how curious the forms of the seed exhibited there. What a store of curious knowledge the farm wife must possess before she can intelligently buy her two dollars' worth of garden seeds! Can you at a glance tell the difference between parsnip and turnip seed, carrot and lettuce seed, early or late peas, sweet or popcorn, sunflower, radish, squash, melon and pumpkin seeds? Can you tell which is cucumber and which is musk-melon?

But all this is easy compared with the finer art of selecting flower seeds - convolvulus, portulaca, nasturtium, candytuft, petunia, zinnia, poppy, snapdragon, balsam. No, no! This is expecting too much of a plain farm wife; she must trust to the labels and rest in the integrity of the grower.

But back of this marvellous display of color and form lie row upon row of open sacks with the later brands, the most approved varieties, of wheat, oats, rye, corn - eight-row, twelve-row, sixteen-row, yellow and white sacks of timothy and clover seed, alfalfa, millet and rape.

All these are but a few samples out of the millions of distinct individualities which Nature grows on her farm. The hard-shelled nut, the toothsome cherry, the luscious strawberry, the winged maple key, the pine seed - a diminutive aeroplane designed to travel by wind or by water, all are seeds. The nourishing element in banana, apple, grape, melon, wheat, oats, corn, hickory-nut, cocoanut and all other nuts are by-products of nature - incidents, not accidents, on the great highway of life - the trend of which is always to make life perpetual, to keep this old world of ours planted and growing.

So intent is Nature on this end of reproduction, so determined is she not to be balked, that she has overloaded her dice. In order to be sure of doing it, she has tremendously overdone it.

Here my study breaks down for want of adequate knowledge. Who can state in a paragraph the splendid fecundity of Nature as shown in the awful fertility of a fern frond? John Muir estimates that one of the great trees of Mariposa, the <u>sequoia gigantea</u>, will ripen annually millions of seeds, and that the seed products of one of the main groves of the Sequoia in a fruitful year would suffice to plant all the mountain ranges of the world.

To one trained to the close thrift of a New England farmer, nature displays an appalling wastefulness in these directions. The wastefulness becomes aggravating, distressing, when we note how determined she is to fill the corn field with fox tail, how hard one must work to keep "pusley" out of the garden, "jimson weed" out of the barnyard and burdock off the roadside.

But even here Nature knows what she is about. Her dirt is most profitable when worked up. The new material of the back yard is more available for the next transformation in the posy bed of the front

CONCERNING SEED: SOWING

yard. What she may not have garden-room for comes handy to feed her stock, which includes worm, bird, squirrel, fox, deer, moose and man.

But Nature's passion to breed, her determination to grow things would be baffled and defeated were it not for her wonderful ingenuity in seed-sowing. Here we come upon the most unexpected surprises, the unspeakable ingeniousness of the great farmer. The amazing skill, energy and patience she displays. How ingenious, marvellous, diligent her methods of sowing and planting! The winds and floods, birds and creeping things are all drafted into the service. To some of the seeds wings have been given; to others keels; to others arms; to still others thorns and briers - anything to get themselves scattered. Sometimes the plant shoots its children away and sometimes it drags them down.

Henry M. Simmons[2] entitled his wonderful sermon on the seed, "An Old Parable Extended". He tells us: "Sowing is the work, not only of half the human race but of the whole plant world and a large part of creation." He shows how the dandelion lifts its head when the seed is ready to spread its parachute that the wind may carry it into the next county, how the thistle head guards itself until ripe, then unfolds its silken sails that the wind may sow one of its seeds in Michigan and its brother in Maine. Says Henry Thoreau:

> I feel highly complimented when
> Nature condescends to make use of
> me without knowledge, as when I
> help scatter her seeds in my walk,

- - - - -

[2] Henry Martyn Simmons (1841-1905). Minister of First Unitarian Church, Minneapolis and Jones' frequent vacation companion.

or carry burrs and cockles on my clothes from field to field. I feel as though I had done something for the common weal, and were entitled to board and lodging. I take such airs upon me as the boy who holds a horse for the circus company, whom all the spectators envy.[3]

Thoreau noticed that in December the winged seeds of the birch were blown over the thin-crusted snow, spreading for many thousand miles a table for the birds. He noticed further that the pine groves of Massachusetts grow crescent-shaped, indicating the circle of the wind-sowing, while the oak and the hickory, which must trust to the squirrel and other animals for their planting, spread irregularly. He distrusted the old theory of the long-surviving germ that lay dormant in the earth, waiting for the proper conditions to sprout, and was inclined to think that the oaks that follow the pine were planted by Nature's seed-bearers after the cutting; or rather, they are ever being planted and they are ever growing, but the dominant pines doom them to short life until they are removed. He tells us that if we look through a thick pine wood we will detect many little oaks, birches, and other seedlings springing from seeds probably carried into the thicket by squirrels or blown thither by the winds, but these are soon over-shadowed and choked by the pines. This planting, he thinks, may be carried on annually, and the plants annually die. But when the

— — — — —

[3] A passage similar to this is found in A Week on the Concord and Merrimack Rivers, Chapter 8, "Friday". (The exact quotation is probably from the Journals.)

pines are cleared, the little plants survive and grow to be an oak forever. This close observer further reminds us that we have not made sufficient allowance for the work of the squirrels and the birds in dispersing seeds.[4]

Down in Tennessee, in the heart of the cedar country, I bemoaned the day when all the cedars would be gone, but the old liveryman called my attention to the fact that along all the old fences there were hedges of young cedars growing up, planted there by the robins which fed on the cedar seeds and dropped the germs along the fences upon which they alighted.

My forestry friend in Wisconsin insists that the persistence of the black oak and the scarcity of the white oak in many sections is due largely to the fact that the squirrel, finding the black oak acorn bitter, plants it in the hope that it may sweeten in time for winter use, but the white oak acorn, being very toothsome, is eaten on the spot by the little gourmand. Like the thriftless farmer the frolicsome little prig makes no provision for seeding time.

Thoreau further calls our attention to the fact that the cherry is so hung on the tree that the bird planter cannot pick it on the bough; he must gather it on the wing and consequently fly away with it, enjoy his delicacy and drop the pit where it will have a chance to grow. Thus, says Thoreau:

> A bird's wing was added to the cherry stone, which was wingless. It does not wait for wind to transport it. I know of some handsome

- - - - -

[4] The material for this paragraph is taken from Thoreau's essay, "The Succession of Forest Trees".

young English cherries growing in our woods which I think of transplanting back to my garden.[5]

Every cherry tree has its bird, every nut tree its squirrel - many of them, and our sage of the woods is not sure but the birds have the best right to the cherries and squirrels first claim to the nuts.

In my last study I noted that Nature is a poor plowman. She prepares the soil inadequately and with difficulty. Her drainage is clumsy and her irrigation a total failure over vast areas. When the human farmer comes along to drain the marshes, water the desert, clear the forest, turn up the sod, he not only "makes two blades of grass grow where one grew before", but by virtue of his superior skill in sowing, supplants grass with apples, weeds with wheat and corn.

Man has come to realize that Nature is a clumsy sower, as well as a poor plowman; for all her ingenuity, her planting is very inadequate. The human farmer not only prepares the ground but puts the seed just where it will best thrive. He covers it at the proper depth, protects it through infancy and garners it in its maturity. The winds, birds and floods do pretty well, but man beats them far and away. He carries the alfalfa seed from Chile to California, from California to Wisconsin; he finds barley in Western Asia, puts it into his pocket, plants it on the banks of the Rhine and ultimately along the Columbia.

According to Bailey's _Cyclopedia_, one Stephen Coe carried from Eastern New York in 1836 a single pint of beans, planted them in Orleans county in Western New

- - - - -

[5] "The Succession of Forest Trees" contains a passage similar to this, but this exact quotation is probably from his _Journals_.

CONCERNING SEED: SOWING 65

York, and three years later his son sold a load of thirty-three bushels. From this beginning, the bean crop of Orleans county in thirty years reached over a million bushels.

Not only has man improved on Nature in the distribution of plants, but he has improved on her methods in planting them. Nature broadcasts, man drills. Where she sows, he plants, thus conserving the resources of the soil and permitting no waste places.

But more interesting than all this, man triumphs over Nature in his skill in improving the seed itself; he increases the crop by developing the quality. He eliminates the sickly, the dwarfed, the non-fertile and uses the strong, the splendid, the fertile. "Agronomy" is a recent word in the farmer's vocabulary; it represents the very poetry of farming; it is the science of seed, or something like it, and its triumphs are most startling. We now read of "Corn Breeding Associations", "Seed-Corn Specials". Year after year Iowa has traversed her splendid prairies with railroad trains which stop at the stations where the farmers, previously summoned, are gathered to note the exhibit of, and to listen to lectures on, improved breeds of corn as well as improved methods of planting and cultivating. One of the Year Books of the United States Department of Agriculture reports ninety-six Iowa counties thus traversed in two years, and several thousand lectures given to over two hundred thousand farmers. The corn-growing states of the Union have their seed-corn experimental stations, and another report from the Department of Agriculture tells the farmer that the immense corn crop of the United States could be increased to the value of one hundred million dollars simply by a wiser selection of seed; another hundred million could be added by the better drying and storing of the seed selected, still another hundred million by better care of the growing plant, and still another hundred million by better care of the soil. Even then this vast increase would represent but one-fifth of the present farm value of the corn crop. The Year Book then proceeds to show how one hundred bushels of sound, mature corn per acre has been produced in Wisconsin, where the average yield from careless or unenlightened farming was perhaps thirty-five bushels or less.

All that the stock breeder has learned in regard to the value of cross-breeding of animals, thus developing milk-yielding cows, trotting horses, varieties of dogs and pigeons -- curious or profitable, is now being applied to the improving of seed by cross-fertilization, artificial pollenization and similar subtle processes. The boys in the University of Minnesota have been selecting and planting wheat kernel by kernel, and by the skill of the hand fertilizing the pistil of one stalk with the pollen obtained from another, thus arriving at startling results which have produced unlimited expansion of the productivity of the earth.

In 1899 the Wisconsin Experiment Station secured six pounds of a Swedish variety of oats, improved the same by selection, and five years later no less than five million bushels of Swedish oats were grown by Wisconsin farmers from this seed, which has since been tested and distributed by the Montana and Idaho Stations. Two new pure lines of Kerson oats have been developed by the United States Department of Agriculture and the Iowa Agricultural Experiment Station. A large number of tests by farmers show ten percent increase in yield. The Department estimates that

CONCERNING SEED: SOWING 67

if used on the present oat acreage of Iowa, the annual increase in that state alone would be from twelve to fifteen million bushels.

Jesus in his parable fixed the highest limit of productivity at one hundred fold - and that was the result of good ground. But the modern farmer who wisely selects and skillfully develops his seed knows that this is a wholly inadequate yield. One bushel of seed corn will plant six acres of ground. The one hundred bushels to the acre which have been harvested by experts yields six hundred fold.

When the Europeans arrived, they found the Indians cultivating corn in America, but their corn had but eight rows on the cob, and the kernels were small and flinty. Now we have our eighteen-row corn and fifty or more kernels in a row, giving nine hundred kernels to an ear; and the Illinois farmer does not boast of a stalk unless it carries two full ears and an additional small one. This makes a possibility of twenty-three to twenty-five hundred kernels of corn grown from one kernel.

All this about farm work - the seed and the sowing of the field. I have said nothing of the human work. Need I say anything? The approved methods of the lower fields apply to the upper fields. Sowing has ever been suggestive of faith; the sower has always been an attractive subject to poet, artist, orator and preacher. To cast seed into the ground in the face of storm and blight, of freshet and drought has always been an act of faith. But the modern man with his selected seed, his drill, his modern appliances has injected an element of knowledge and scientific accuracy into the sowing, and we now have the old trust in God with a human plus - an added element of confidence in man, which throws new light upon his task and awakens new inspiration in him who would deal with seeds of thought and plant fields of the spirit.[6]

This sermon is as pertinent to city as to country folk. Alas! how much bad sowing is there in our municipalities! How much poor planting in our cities! The old religion, like the old farmer, made sowing a simple duty; conscience was easily satisfied; seeds were promptly divided into good or bad, and the crop was either grain or weeds. But now it is not good or bad seed; it is better or worse seed. Will we plant twenty-bushel or eighty-bushel corn, seed gathered from nubbins or from the full ear?

Let us think of the brains of our boys and girls, the hearts of men and women, as fields to be sown. Given schools, churches, clubs, libraries, museums, galleries, theatres - all the machinery of soul-cultivation - the product may be stunted, stultified, dwarfed, unless the seed be wisely selected and properly perfected.

It is not enough to read, but it is a question of "What are you reading?" It is not enough to go to school; the question is, "What are you being taught when you go there?" It is not enough to go to church; the question is, "What of the seed sown?" What of the fructifying power of the grain there planted?

The parable of the sower, as Jesus rendered it in my text and context, concerned itself with soils, surroundings - environment we call it. As we read the parable today, we find a new element injected, viz.,

- - - - -

[6] The next paragraph, on modern methods of communication, is such an abrupt and intrusive shift of topic that it has been omitted. The remainder of the manuscript is missing. What follows has been taken from the printed version in Hoard's Dairyman.

CONCERNING SEED: SOWING

the quality of the seed. Well did my friend Simmons say: "Thus, life is not only to be preserved, but improved; only the fittest can grow to ripeness and reproduction."

All the old incentives remain, but now there is an added incentive to scrutinize the grain, to improve the quality of the seed. Says Thoreau:

> He who eats the fruit should at least plant the seed; aye if possible, a better fruit than that which he has enjoyed. O thou spendthrift! Defray thy debt to the world. Eat not the seed of institutions as the luxurious do, but plant it rather, while thou devourest the pulp and tuber for thy subsistence, that so perchance one variety at least may be found worthy of preservation.[7]

The sowing resources of Nature have been greatly increased by the ingenuity of man. As the output of the Illinois corn field exceeds that of the New England Indian, so should the mentality, morality, spirituality of today exceed that of our fore-elders. If we would only give as much attention to the multiplying of ideas in the brains of our children as we give to the multiplying of kernels of corn on the cob, if we would only apply ourselves as diligently to the growing of motives in the hearts of our boys and girls, of graces in our homes and devoutness in our churches as we do to the perfection of wheat and the development of the potato and the tomato!

- - - - - -

[7] From A Week on the Concord and Merrimack Rivers, Chapter 4, "Monday", (p 125 in the Princeton edition of 1980).

Let us open our New Testaments again and read this old parable in the light of the new thought and the larger experience: Yea, verily, unto us it is given to know the mysteries of the kingdom of heaven. For whomsoever hath, to him it shall be given and he shall have abundance; but whosoever hath not, from him shall be taken away even that which he hath. Let not our ears be dull any more or our eyes blind any longer:

> For verily I say unto you, that many prophets and righteous men desired to see the things ye see, and saw them not; and to hear the things which ye hear, and heard them not: Hear, then, ye, the parable of the sower.

V

The six sermons of the original "Gospel of the Farm" series are of uneven quality. One wonders if, as the series progressed, Governor Hoard regretted asking Jones for them. From a passable beginning with "Plowing", the second - "Sowing" - was weaker, and this one on "Weeds" is very thin and unstructured. If it were not for the sake of the unity of the series, Jones would have done well to leave it out entirely.

The series picks up again after this low point. Jones leaves Bailey's <u>Cyclopedia</u> behind and bases his material on narratives or his own experience. His style really demands a story of some sort for him to tell and comment on. As much as he tries to generate a story out of Jethro Tull, it never gets off the ground - and neither does the sermon. Compare the vitality and coherence of the next sermon - based on the life of Cyrus McCormick - with this one.

Perhaps an indication of Jones' own uneasiness with this sermon is the fact that he did not choose a prefatory poem for it.

After being preached to his All Souls' congregation on 23 May 1909, it appeared in <u>Hoard's</u> 18 March 1910.

CONCERNING WEEDS: CULTIVATING

The kingdom of God is likened unto a man that sowed good seed in his field; but while men slept, his enemy came and sowed tares also among the wheat, and went away. But when the blade sprang up and brought forth fruit, then appeared the tares also.
                    Matthew 13:24-26

<u>The New Horse-Houghing Husbandry; or, an essay on the Principles of Tillage and Vegetation. Wherein is shown, a method of introducing a sort of vineyard culture into the cornfields, in order to increase their products, and diminish the common expense, by the use of instruments lately invented. London, Printed for the author, in the year 1731.</u>

The book with the above title and its author, Jethro Tull, have a large place in the history of modern agriculture. This Englishman, travelling in southern Europe, noticed that the vineyards were being cultivated between the rows, and on his return wrote this book advocating that wheat, oats and all crops should be drilled in order that they might be tilled with horses between the rows.

The wonder of one hundred and eighty and more years ago still remains. Bailey in his <u>Cyclopedia of</u>

CONCERNING WEEDS: CULTIVATING   73

<u>Agriculture</u> quotes from this quaint treatise as follows:

> Tis strange that no Author should have written fully of the Fabric of Ploughs! Men of the greatest Learning have spent their Time in contriving Instruments to measure the immense Distance of the Stars, and in finding out the Dimensions, and even Weight of the Planets. They think it more eligible to study The Art of plowing the Sea with Ships, than of tilling the Land with Ploughs; they bestow the utmost of their Skill learnedly, to promote the natural Use of all the Elements for destruction of their own Species, by the bloody Art of War. Some waste their whole Lives in studying how to arm Death with new Engines of Horror, and inventing an infinite Variety of Slaughter; but think it beneath Men of learning (who only are capable of doing it) to employ their learned Labors in the invention of new (or even improving the old) Instruments for increasing of Bread.[1]

Mr. Tull in his curious and rare book thus reasoned:

> Too much Nitre corrodes a Plant;

─ ─ ─ ─

[1] All the material on Jethro Tull, including the quotations, is taken from Bailey's introductory essay to Chapter 11 of Volume I of the <u>Cyclopedia</u>.

> too much Water drowns it; too much
> Air dries the Roots of it; too much
> Heat burns it; too much Earth a
> Plant never can have; that is the
> Food of all Plants. The Soil is
> the Pasture of Plants.

He recognized that this system of tillage would render the ground moist, and make more available the resources of the earth. Says Bailey:

> Tull's theories were incorrect, but
> his practice was good. Tillage is
> surely of first importance, and
> every commonwealth might well raise
> a monument to the memory of Jethro
> Tull.

Mr. Tull in his preface disposes of much of what he called the "ornaments of learning" bestowed upon agriculture by ancient and modern writers. He refers to some "late great man" as

> The Cicero of the Age, who having
> perused all their Books of Husband-
> ry, ordered them, notwithstanding
> their Eloquence, to be carried upon
> a Hand-Barrow out of his Study, and
> thrown into the Fire, lest others
> should lose their Time in Reading
> them, as he had done. He declared
> he could not, for his Life, guess
> what those Authors would be at; for
> they treated of an Art wherein they
> had formed no manner of Principles.

In distinction, from those works, Tull declares that his book was "founded upon principles, which if they be true (for I can only say I think them so) they must be, as all Truth is, Eternal; and yet are not extant in any Author that I can find or hear of".

This book passed through many editions, the latest of which seems to have been issued under the editorship of William Cobbett in 1829, bringing the subject down to that date.

Tull's work called new attention to the plow and its varied uses. The work he started has been carried on to this day in library and machine-shop with ever-deepening intensity. Our universities now employ learned men to teach ever-increasing classes of boys and girls the theory and practice of soil-cultivation; machine-shops are putting out increasing varieties of cultivators, all of which are more or less ingenious modifications of the plow - new and improved applications of Jethro Tull's "Horse-Houghing".

Complex, fascinating to the mind and, I might add, demoralizing to the farmer's pocket-book are the various instruments devised for cultivating fields. How attractive these devices may become can be appreciated only by a farmer boy whose legs and arms have grown weary and stiff in handling the old-time cultivator. How he longs for a new machine, some better contrivance that will lessen the toil of cultivating the corn and potatoes, something that will more certainly kill the weeds. Harrows, shovel-plows - single and double, one-horse, two-horse cultivators, cultivators with tongues and tongueless cultivators - with seats to ride on and with no seats - these and many other devices are now in the market. The chief end of them all seems to be to down the weeds.

Indeed life on the farm seems one endless, almost hopeless, battle with weeds out-of-doors and flies indoors. Professors in our agricultural colleges and settlement workers in our cities may offer learned and elaborate protests against the lamentable tendency of country boys and girls to rush to the city, but the plain truth of the matter is simply this: they are tired of fighting weeds and flies in the country. From the time the seed is put into the ground until the last onion is gathered and the last squash is in the cellar, it is weeding, weeding, weeding - with hand, with hoe, with cultivator and whatever instrument you use - the thumb and finger of the hand or the polished hoes of the mechanical cultivator. It is back-breaking, knee-stiffening work in the garden, horse-weary, leg-weary, soul-annoying work in the field. Surely the "tares" are such persistent foes, such enemies to good crops, such irritants to good nature, that it does seem as though some evil one, as the text implies, had previously sown the troublesome seed for pure mischief, if not for something more malign.

However the parable of the tares may be interpreted, one thing is sure: modern science does not bear out the literal interpretation of the text. There is something to be said in the interest of the tares, and he who would profitably use the parable for spiritual purposes must bear in mind the words of an old teacher of mine: "The thought of this passage is richer than its language."

The interpretations of science, enforced by the practical experience of the farmer, establish one or two very plain conclusions concerning cultivation, whether the fields in question are to yield grain or ideas. Whether the crop is for the nourishment of bodies or brains we shall find that the same gospel applies to farm and school-room, garden and home. Good corn and good boys are raised by the same process;

CONCERNING WEEDS: CULTIVATING   77

sweet girls and sweet melons demand very much the same tilling. Somehow the field and the fireside call for treatment strangely similar.

Among the plain conclusions of science and experience, as regards cultivation, are:
1. Weeds come not from Devil-sowing; they have their uses.
2. True tilling should look not to the destruction of the weed but to the promotion of the grain; hence cultivation means encouragement of the good rather than destruction of the bad.[2]

Carlyle and Ruskin have written much of the social fields. Mark the inevitable analogy in the term. Society is a "field" to cultivate, or better yet, a "farm" with many fields. We have at last reached agricultural sense enough to recognize the law of community. No farmer can grow what he pleases or allow his roadside trees to go untrimmed or his fence corners untilled without trespassing on his neighbors' rights. Willingly he accepts the strict legislation against noxious weeds, knowing that in proportion as they are enforced are his interests advanced. The time has gone by when a farmer can stand on his rights to grow what he pleases, to breed what he likes and as he likes.

We are not so far advanced in recognizing the law of community in our social farming. It is impossible to have a sanitary city on the old theory of liberty that allows the individual to do as he pleases, the parent to direct or neglect his children as he chooses. We are just beginning to see that the individual's

- - - - -

[2] The paragraph which follows this is a rather pointless attempt at defining "a weed". It has been omitted in the interests of the coherence of the sermon.

right ends where the interest of the community begins. Herein lies the philosophy as well as the justification of the so-called "Dry" movement. The anti-liquor legislation represents the most encouraging, most progressive triumph in social farming since the abolition of slavery.

The laws on many of our state statute books prohibiting the manufacture and sale of cigarettes to immature youths are no infringements upon the rights of the individual; they are simply applications of the law of good tillage; they are fighting noxious weeds in the interest of better crops.

Man is a social being. In proportion as he is human, in that proportion is he capable of nurture, of cultivation, of being farmed. A growing indifference to social claims, a decline of respect for churches and Sunday sobrieties prove thriftless farming and indolent farmers in the social realm; they indicate a criminal toleration of noxious weeds or else a dependence upon inferior plants and seed. Grasses and weeds come where grain and fruit might be cultivated. The question of a better city as well as the question of fuller granaries is largely a question of better farming.

Thoreau records that in the early history of his town, hay-makers from Sudbury would come down in large numbers and unite with Concord in clearing the weeds out of the river in the shallow places and the larger streams emptying therein, in order to improve their meadow lands. Something like this must be done in the streams of social life that flow through our cities. We must clear our meadows of the less desirable plants that the more desirable ones may have a chance to grow.

The social farmer is learning that plants cannot be divided into two classes -- good and bad. Weeds represent the desperate attempts of nature to occupy the waste places, to utilize neglected ground. The better the ground, the more ample the weeds and the more scandalous the shiftlessness that permits them to grow. An old barn-yard, the place where the pigs were once penned, the chip-yard where the wood-pile used to be offer at once the best opportunity for burdock and jimson weed or for an onion bed. Which will it be?

Our Concord philosopher again noted that he found the ranker vegetation where the shanties once stood along the railroad, but he did not go there for delicate wild flowers. Similar phenomena are observed in the social field in the city flora, where luxury fattens the ground for weed growths. Says our Concord farmer:

> What an army of non-producers society produces, -- ladies generally (old and young) and gentlemen of leisure so-called! Many think themselves well employed as charitable dispensers of wealth which somebody else earned, and those who produce nothing, being of the most luxurious habits, are precisely they who want the most, and complain the loudest when they do not get what they want. They who are literally paupers, maintained at the public expense, are the most importunate and insatiable beggars. They cling like the glutton to a living man and suck his vitals up. To every locomotive man there are three or four deadheads clinging, as if they

> conferred a great favor on society by living upon it. Meanwhile they fill the churches, and die and revive from time to time. They have nothing to do but sin and repent their sins. How can you expect such blood-suckers to be happy?[3]

Finally, then let us realize that weeds are the results of civilization because it is the civilized man that has learned to discriminate between the less profitable and the more profitable plants. The ethnologist must notice that the savage cannot disperse seed equal in quality or quantity with that of the civilized man. Beggar-ticks and burrs do not adhere to the bare skin, but they do stick to the woollen raiment of the modern man.

So we come back to the truth which the great Preacher of Nazareth caught sight of. He recognized that tares, once sown, require great skill in the removing if the wheat is not to be injured. Perhaps it is better to let them grow for a while than to menace the life of the more valuable but less hardy plant. Rudeness in the social field is as unwise as it is in the garden. The cultivator must be careful lest his cultivation destroy the good in the passion to remove the bad. "Horse-Houghing" must ever be in the interest of the corn, and the kindly Providence that sows all plants will encourage and co-operate with the hand that discriminates in the interest of the best.

"I criticize by creation", was the saying of the greatest of artists, Michaelangelo.[4]

- - - - -

[3] This quotation is probably from Thoreau's _Journals_.

[4] Jones always wrote "Michael Angelo" - as though it were a given name and a surname.

Let not the weeds scare us in either field; they will disappear in the well-tilled ground by virtue of the corn and of the wheat that will overshadow them. The sand burrs that infested Tower Hill when we first took possession of it for a summer encampment twenty years ago are well nigh gone; their place has been supplanted by white clover, bluegrass, ferns and growing pines. They were but brave pioneers in Nature's army, holding the dismal territory, waiting for better husbandry. The true farmer in any field, like Michaelangelo, must criticize by creation. He who would improve garden or man, meadow or woman, must cultivate the better crop in such a way that the inferior will never come to maturity and in due time will disappear for want of seed - the well-meaning but inefficient seed of lower kind.

In some such way as this is the kingdom of God to come - on the farm and in the city, in the field and in the home, where cows and horses flock and breed and where poets and philosophers thrive and multiply.

VI

Thanksgiving Day was a festival that Jones never failed to celebrate. It was for him the major American holy day and called forth some of his best sermons. "The Harvest Field: Reaping" was his Thanksgiving Day sermon for 1909, preached on 21 November.

The beginning, with its disparagement of official proclamations for their hypocrisy, is typical of many Thanksgiving Day sermons. The matter of harvesting gives him his connection with Thanksgiving, but the sermon itself is rather distantly tied to the usual themes of the day.

Although this was All Souls' Thanksgiving sermon, it was also the sixth and last of the series prepared for Hoard's Dairyman. This one appeared in two parts, 8 and 15 July 1910. Recognizing Hoard's first claim, Jones did not print it in Unity until 6 October 1910.

Jones chose to preface this sermon with the poem, "The Singing Man" by Josephine Preston Peabody -- a seven-page poem, too long to serve as a preface. It seems likely that what he intended was just the first stanza - an appreciation of the sense of satisfaction in the labor of reaping grain. The rest of the poem is an indictment by contrast of factory labor conditions, rather out of harmony with Jones' point in this sermon.

THE HARVEST FIELD: REAPING

Thanksgiving proclamations are loaded with phrases about "the divine forethought and care", "the bounty of the year", "abundance of the fields", "teeming acres", "golden grain", "the good health and good cheer" of each particular year.

This is well. But there is danger that these phrases may grow conventional and stilted and carry with them a degree of cant and hypocrisy. The sweat-hardened farmer sings his Thanksgiving hymn to the "bountiful God" with a mental reservation, and responds with a chuckle to the more honest, qualified prayer of the devout come-outer whose grace before a meager meal was, "Lord, we thank thee for the salt; the potatoes we raised ourselves!"

I would not abate one whit the reverential gratitude for the primal forces of nature -- light, heat, water and soil, for the beauty as well as the fertility of hillside and valley, the glory of mountain and river, the sublimity of the stars, the inspiration of the sunrise, the peace of the sunset, the benignancy of the darkness that brings sleep to tired eyes and restoration to weary mind and body. I still would urge that all this stops short of the finer, higher and -- consequently -- later marvels of the harvest field. Old Bible texts and the swing of the old hymn tunes dear to our grandparents are precious to us, but from them we miss something of the glory that belongs to humanity. Why cannot we bring our piety down to date? Why in church on Sunday must we still sing, pray and preach about "sickles", "flails", "threshing floors", "winnowing fans" and "mill stones", instead of talking about "reapers", "threshing machines" and "roller-mills"?

I share with Mr. McAndrew in Kipling's hymn an impatience bordering on indignation with the "Viscount-loon -- wi' Russian leather tennis-shoon an' spar-decked yachtin' cap", who, after having been shown round and through the great ocean liner, said:

    "Mister McAndrew, don't you think steam
        spoils romance at sea?"
    Damned ijit! I'd been doon that morn to see
        what ailed the throws,
    Manholin', on my back---the cranks three
        inches off my nose.
    Romance! Those first-class passengers they
        like it very well,
    Printed an' bound in little books; but why
        don't poets tell?
    I'm sick of all their quirks and turns---the
        loves and doves they dream--
    Lord, send a man like Robbie Burns to sing
        the Song o' Steam!
    To match wi' Scotia's noblest speech yon
        orchestra sublime
    Whaurto---uplifted like the Just---the tail-
        rods mark the time.
    The crank-throws give the double-bass, the
        feed-pump sobs an' heaves,
    An' now the main eccentrics start their
        quarrel on the sheaves;
    Her time, her own appointed time, the rocking
        link-head bides,
    Till---hear that note?---the rod's return
        whings glimmerin' through the guides.
    They're all awa! True beat, full power, the
        clangin'-chorus goes
    Clear to the tunnel where they sit, my
        purrin' dynamoes.

THE HARVEST FIELD: REAPING 85

> Interdependence absolute, foreseen, ordained, decreed,
> To work, ye'll note, at any tilt an' every rate o' speed,
> Fra' skylight-lift to furnace-bars, backed, bolted, braced and stayed,
> An' singin' like the Mornin' stars for joy that they are made;
> While, out o' touch o' vanity, the sweatin' thrust-block says:
> "Not unto us the praise, or man---not unto us the praise!"
> Now, a'together, hear them lift their lesson --theirs and mine:
> "Law, Order, Duty an' Restraint, Obedience, Discipline!"
> Mill, forge and try-pit taught them that when roarin' they arose,
> An' whiles I wonder if a soul was gi'en them wi' the blows.
> Oh, for a man to weld it then, in one trip-hammer strain,
> Till even first-class passengers could tell the meanin' plain![1]

Rudyard Kipling has come very near to singing the Song of the Steam Engine. He is as yet the Poet Laureate of the ocean liner, that greyhound of the deep. For this, spite of the imperfections and, in many directions, lamentable reactions of his songs, he deserves an honored place upon our book shelves. Let us try to think devoutly and with religious humility of the human investment that should enter into our harvest song of gratitude.

- - - - -

[1] Taken from "McAndrew's Hymn" by Rudyard Kipling.

Who will sing for us the Song of the Reaper -- not the man but the machine? Who will write for us the Epic of the Wheat Field, the Drama of the Modern Harvest? The Lord of Heaven and Earth was made manifest in the flesh and brains of Jethro Wood, James Oliver, John Deere and William Parlin -- the great plowmakers, who made the big crops of the West possible. Let us note how Cyrus McCormick, the Mannys, William Deering and their brilliant associates made the saving of that crop possible. Paraphrasing George Eliot, we may well say: God gives us wheat, but not without the help of man in the harvesting of the same. God himself cannot fill our elevators with the best of wheat without the best of men to help him.

Wheat itself, which has been called the food of civilization, the staff of life, representing as it does thirty-four per cent of the bread-producing products of the world, is largely man-made. Grant Allen, the scientist, says, "Wheat, to the botanist, is a grass, a degraded lily." Primitive man, far back, began to tame and train that lily. Herbert N. Casson, author of The Romance of the Reaper[2] and the Life of Cyrus Hall McCormick[3], to whom I am indebted for much material in this study, says:

> We do not know when or where the prehistoric Burbank lived who undertook this education of the wheat-lily. But we do know that wheat has been a food for at least five thousand years. We find it in

- - - - -

[2] Published in New York by Doubleday Page and Company in 1908.

[3] Published in Chicago by A.C. McClurg and Company in 1909.

the oldest tombs of Egypt and pictures on the stones of the Pyramids. We know that Solomon sent wheat as a present to his friend, the King of Tyre; and we have reason to believe that its first appearance was in the valleys of the Tigris and the Euphrates, near where the ancient city of Babylon rose to greatness.[4]

Wheat, like so many of our domestic animals, is a plant that cannot live without men's help. It is a tamed weed, dependent upon the co-operative hand of man. Mr. Casson estimated that if the human race were to perish from the earth, wheat could not survive more than three years. A German economist argues that wheat was the original cause of civilization, not primarily because it is the most available of foods, but because it persuaded primitive man to quit his killing industries and take up instead his tilling activities. When man began to turn up the sod and to plant seed, he ceased wandering in search of more game and better grazing; the nomad became a settler. Then the marvellous drama of civilization began, and man entered upon the sublime career during which he has become the homemaker, the conqueror of continents, the builder of cathedrals, the founder of colleges.

My father brought with him from over the sea his "hook" -- a smooth-edged sickle hammered out by hand on the anvil. My earliest harvest-field recollections are of a little golden field in the clearing with half a

- - - - -

[4] Jones is in error here. This passage is not in the Casson books.

dozen or more men and women, diligent with their sickles, cutting the precious grain -- literally by the handfuls, after the manner practised on the rugged hillsides of Wales. This soon gave way to the more rapid swing of that marvellous Yankee device, the American "cradle". One of the last things I did before giving up my boyhood life on the farm for the service of the Union, and exchanging my blue jeans for the blue uniform of the north, was to "cradle" with an older brother a ten-acre field of oats.

But some six years before this, the reaper had entered our harvest field. The first one I remember required a man to follow after it on foot, pulling off the sheaves as they were laid low on the platform. The next reaper made provision for the man to ride as he "raked off". In some machines he was hung behind the driver and was dragged backwards while, with a curiously constructed tool, he pulled off the grain as it accumulated. An advance was made when the man was permitted to stand face forward, watching the grain as it fell and throwing it off with a pitch-fork. How well I remember the anxious harvest weeks with the old John P. Manny reaper, with its sickle-bar forever breaking -- every break calling for the cessation of activities and idle hours for seven or eight high-priced binders. Meanwhile I, the boy, dispatched on old "Jane" -- the one-eyed, white mare -- would gallop as for life across three miles of prairie to the shop of the hunchback blacksmith who would weld the broken weapon with which the battle against hunger and debts was being desperately waged!

Next there swept into our wheat field with great pomp and procession the first "self-raking" reaper of the neighborhood, the "Palmer & Williams". The

THE HARVEST FIELD: REAPING

neighbors had gathered to watch with incredulous eyes the marvellous deeds of a machine that would rake off its own sheaves. A high functionary of the company came out to set it a-going, but alas! it was a short-lived triumph. The reel and the rake, like the legs of an epileptic, were poorly co-ordinated; they were constantly getting entangled with one another. The reel, if high enough to give the rake a chance to steal in and catch the short grain that grew on sandy soil, would be too high for efficiency; when lowered so as to secure good cutting, the rake would be interfered with in its work of scratching the grain off the platform. The verdict of that season, in that neighborhood, was that self-raking reapers were plausible for long, straight grain on ideal fields, but unavailable for short and tangled grain on rough fields. Consequently, they were impractical; "they would never work".

So the non-raking Manny led the strenuous harvest with five to eight binders following hard after, binding the sheaves dropped in the trail of the machine. The circuit was divided into stations; round on round the men went, travelling one-fifth or one-eighth of the circuit while the machine completed the round. Happy and efficient was the man who could reach the end of his "station" in time to straighten his back, catch a moment's breath or take a swig at the jug sheltered in the shock with its refreshing mixture of vinegar, molasses, ginger and water (known by a familiar name which I have forgotten) before the machine was on him for the next race.

In due time came the exhilarating news that a couple of boys in Illinois had perfected a machine by which the grain was elevated to a platform on which two men stood erect while they bound the wheat and threw off bundles while they rode, as it were, in their carriage. This "Marsh Harvester" was the wonder of the time and seemed to be perfection in the way of reaping machines. But its triumph was short-lived. Its success bargained for a noble defeat. Then to the incredulous farmer came the news of a machine that itself could bind the sheaves (first with wire, later with twine) and carry them along until they could be dropped in piles ready for the shockers.

This story of the reaper was at one time overwhelming to the enlightened imagination, and yet it has all been achieved within my memory. And thousands are still living who can trace in their own experience the revealing inspirations.

My story begins with the <u>annus mirabilis</u>, the wonderful year of 1809. It was the year of Lincoln, the great emancipator of the slave; of Darwin, the great emancipator of the human mind; of Gladstone, the great commoner; of Tennyson, the Poet Laureate; of Mendelssohn, the sweet singer; of Bonar, the great hymn-writer; of Holmes, the Autocrat of the Breakfast Table. But an emancipator second to none of them, a prophet whose message is as far-reaching as any, was born the same year, to whom too little homage has as yet been paid by the purblind readers of books, the sophisticated dwellers in cities, and alas! sadder yet, the graceless and complacent rustics who regret their descent and their surroundings.

Away off among the beautiful hills of Virginia, on the margin of the Shenandoah Valley (through which, fifty-four years later, Sheridan's horsemen raided the fields), Cyrus Hall McCormick was born. Robert McCormick, his father, was a Scotch-Irish immigrant after the order of John Knox -- a thrifty Presbyterian who owned

THE HARVEST FIELD: REAPING

four farms, two grist mills, two saw mills, a melting furnace, a distillery and a blacksmith shop. His dexterous hands could make a walnut cabinet or an iron crane. His humble blacksmith shop built of logs is, I believe, still standing. The Muse of Invention haunted the place, and this shop was the cradle of the Romance of the Reaper. Robert, the father, had invented a hemp brake, a clover-huller, a bellows, a threshing machine, and had tried his hand at a reaping machine, but had given it up; he could not make it go. Cyrus, the son, grew up in a home where the wool, flax and cotton were spun and made into clothing. His mittens, caps, coats, trousers, shirts, stockings and shoes were all home-made. Candles were molded, carpets woven, hams cured, soap boiled, apples dried and sugar made all in and around the home where the McCormick children -- eight of them -- grew up, and whatever of character, power, courage and vision can be studied was also home-made.

Cyrus inherited the dreams of his father and his father's failures as well. He began where the fifteen-year failure of his father ended, and in 1831, less than a century ago, with one horse in the shafts and a boy on the back of the horse, Cyrus McCormick, at twenty-two years of age, started his reaping machine -- and it worked!

The next year he ventured to advertise, but nobody wanted to buy. It was nine years before he sold a single machine. In 1840 he sold three; in 1841 there were no sales; in 1842, seven; in 1843, twenty-nine; in 1844, fifty; in 1845, one hundred and ninety-six. Some time in 1847 the young inventor had a vision, a wild dream, that perhaps he could make a million dollars out of that machine. With three hundred dollars in his belt he started westward, travelling mainly on horseback. He studied the pioneer villages, saw cattle and pigs eating grain on the prairies of Illinois, to garner which was beyond the ability of the human hands available. He determined to plant himself in the muddy, swamp-soaked, ragged village on the banks of Lake Michigan, and the next year, 1848, five hundred machines were made in Chicago. In 1884, thirty-six years later, fifty thousand machines were made in his own shop, and there were five hundred thousand reaping machines in use throughout the world, doing the work of five million men in the harvest field. The little town of ten thousand in 1847 was by then a city of six hundred thousand. It had become the great wheat city of the West, the granary of the world, because it was and has continued to be the reaper city of the world.

But large, inspiring, thrilling as is the story of Cyrus Hall McCormick, it is not so large as the story of the reaper. There are pre-McCormick, extra-McCormick and post-McCormick elements in the reaper romance. McCormick's was the forty-seventh patent issued. Twenty-three men in Europe and twenty-seven men in the United States besides himself had bent themselves to the task. The pages of the patent office reports are gory with reaper fights. Some of the most famous legal battles in the history of the United States courts were fought over reaper patents. Some of the brightest achievements of American lawyers are recorded here. It was in a reaper fight - McCormick vs. Manny - that Edwin H. Stanton made his ten thousand dollar speech in Cincinnati. In the same trial Abraham Lincoln figured and was snubbed by the pompous but brilliant Stanton. Later as President he heaped coals

THE HARVEST FIELD: REAPING 93

of fire upon the head of the cocky Cincinnati attorney by giving Stanton's great power an unexpected and adequate field for action. Lincoln made the man that derided him his inimitable Secretary of War.

Mr. McCormick was beaten at Cincinnati, as he was in most of the courts, says his biographer. But the greatest battles of the reaper were not fought in courts of law. It was a merry war of manufacturers and agents fifty years long. The trials of strength and skill, the contests of the harvest fields, rendered the struggles of the race-course and the fierce strain of football teams tame and vulgar in comparison. The perennial theme for discussion among the farm boys of my day was the rival merits of the various reapers represented in the neighborhood. Bearded grangers forgot to talk politics and ignored sectarian differences when they fell to discussing the merits of their respective reapers. Was it the Buckeye, the Manny, the Champion, the Clow, the Plano, or the McCormick? I remember with amusement how, then as now, my sympathies naturally gravitated to the under-dog in the fight. Delicacy of adjustment, uniqueness of device, lightness and adaptability went with many other machines, while solidity, safety, thoroughness of construction and strength of material stayed with the McCormick, for the inventor in Cyrus McCormick promptly gave way to the craftsman, the business man, and the administrator. It is needless to say that my boyish enthusiasm went with the machines which embodied the newer devices.

Competition in America probably reached its high-water mark in the reaper struggle, and Cyrus McCormick was the most indomitable warrior of them all. He wanted to make all the machines that were to be made; he determined to hold the field against all enemies -- a field which he had so successfully pre-empted. His long years of brooding between the mechanical success and the first commercial reward toughened his sinews and equipped him for a life that was largely battle. "Meet Hussey in Maryland and put him down", was the closing of a letter which began with a pious recognition of a providence that "seemed to assist me in all our business".

The reaper tests in the Middle West in the nineteenth century took the place of the tourneys of chivalry in the Middle Ages. Here was fun, courage, strategy and oftentimes something less innocent. We are told that machines were secretly tested and slyly strengthened for special strains. Rival machines were chained together back to back, and pulled to pieces. When the Marsh harvester was being tried at Plano and the untrained farm hands in their new awkward situation pronounced it a "man-killer", declaring that no two men could bind as fast as the sheaves were placed on the table, the Marsh Brothers picked two vigorous German maidens, deft and skillful binders, put them on the machine and put the men to shame. At another test they took along with them a couple of trained men disguised as "Weary Willies". They put those hoboes on the platform and showed how even "tramps" could do it. One of the brothers achieved the marvellous feat of binding a whole acre himself in fifty-five minutes. After that their machines went like hot cakes.

Whiteley, the exploiter of the Champion reaper, has been called the Charlemagne of the harvest field. In an Ohio test, finding himself making no headway against his competitor, he unhitched one of his horses and went around with the other. His competitor did the same. Then this Hercules of the field shouted,

THE HARVEST FIELD: REAPING 95

"Take off the other horse!" and he put his own shoulders into the collar and cut a full swath. That ten minutes in a horse collar, the historian says, made him two million dollars. His competitor became his partner and they made common cause against all rivals. As high as one hundred and sixty thousand of those machines went out in a year. Two million "Champions" were made in Springfield, Ohio at a profit of eighteen million dollars. At the Philadelphia Centennial in 1876 this machine was exhibited, one quarter natural size, made in rosewood and gold. The next season a train of seventy cars, three quarters of a mile in length, hauled the output toward Baltimore alone.

I have said that McCormick the inventor soon developed into McCormick the business man. Here is a chance to glorify business, to crown the dollar with fame, and to call down upon it the benedictions of religion. If the combinations of capital and the organization of vast industrial units have made hardships for individuals, the method of combination has been wrong, not the principle. What is so right, nay, so inevitable -- economically considered, must be made ethically right.

When one Neighbor Ruff found the McCormick machine, way back in the experimental days in Virginia, rattling the heads off his wheat, he cried, "Hold! This will not do." Then the Honorable William Taylor, who owned the wheat field on the opposite side of the road said, "Pull down the fence on the other side; I will give the young man a fair chance to try his machine if I lose my crop!"

When in a severe test at the London Exposition in 1851, the neighbors urged an Anglo-Italian farmer, Mechi by name, not to allow the further destruction of his grain, he replied:

> Gentlemen, this is a great experiment. When a new principle is about to be established, individual interest must always give way. If it is necessary for the success of this test, you may take my seventy acres of wheat.

And the American McCormick swept in and won out. Horace Greeley was present at that test and thus described the scene:

> In seventy seconds McCormick had become famous; he was the lion of the hour. Had he brought five hundred reapers with him, he could have sold them all.[5]

The story of the American reaper as the conquering hero in foreign lands is as exciting as it is unique. Crowned heads came out to be amused, perhaps to scoff; they stayed to admire and, what is more to the point, to purchase. They dismounted to take the hands of the men in shirt sleeves. With their own hands they pinned their ribbons of honor upon the inventors and returned to their palaces to promote the sales.

Casson's Romance of the Reaper is illustrated with American reapers drawn by camels, oxen, mules, as well as by horses, with photographs taken in the harvest fields of Siberia, India, Japan and Argentina.

William B. Ogden preceded McCormick in Chicago. He was already a rich man when the Virginia inventor arrived. He welcomed the reaper man and put twenty-five thousand dollars into his hands to build the first

- - - - -

[5] Casson, Life of Cyrus Hall McCormick, p 128f.

factory. Here was a striking case of genius meeting capital and doubling the opportunity of both.

William Deering was a dry goods merchant from Maine. He came west looking for a chance to invest the forty thousand he had made behind the counter. He met an old Methodist elder from Maine, his former pastor, who had already abandoned the circuit in order to sell reapers. Gammon was his name. He persuaded his former parishioner to put his cash into the reaper venture, which he did. Deering, who was neither a farmer nor an inventor, said, "I will beat them by making a better machine", and his interest in money-making was speedily lost in a greater interest in machine-making.

At last, at the height of the merry war, there came a lull and then a great calm in the reaper market, as strange and unexpected as that which settled down on Vicksburg on the fourth day of July, 1863, when the white flags appeared over the bristling battlements. Four men -- stalwart warriors all of them, men who had delighted in competition, who believed profoundly in individualism, particularly in their own individuality, who liked the battle -- were corralled, imprisoned, entranced and then they surrendered to a new genius -- the genius of Combination. The managers of this genius did not dare put these fighters together in one room. Experts in the business of merging, those trained in the school of John Pierpont Morgan, flew from one room to the other until these stalwart fighters were coerced and persuaded to ground arms and make common cause with what were before rival interests. So in 1903 the International Harvester Company came into being with its one hundred and twenty million capital, its annual output of seven hundred thousand harvesters. The combine owns or controls its own ore beds, steel mills and forests, and now makes most of the machines and implements necessary to successful farming, from cream separators to threshing machines, from horse-rakes to steam engines. The democracy prefigured by this stupendous combination as it is may be far away, but it is coming, along the lines indicated by the words "International" and "company".

Time and space forbid giving the bewildering figures, the mere recital of which appeals to the enlightened imagination with as much power as a Shakespearian drama. Nothing in the poetry of Robert Browning or the fiction of Victor Hugo can parallel this Epic of the Reaper. Two hundred and thirty-five miles of leather belting, nine hundred and forty miles of cotton belting, four million pounds of wire, fifteen million pounds of nails are among the items which Casson gives in the expense bills of this combine for 1907. To the intelligent these figures fly out of the ledger, escape the trammels of bookkeeping! They are not only items in the world's economic life, but sentences in the great Declaration of Independence that releases the worker from the slavery of toil, the drudgery of the field, the fear of starvation. They glow as so many illuminated sign posts directing the way to liberty. They are stanzas in the great epic of bread which, when pushed a little farther and lifted a little higher, come to be psalms of the spirit, texts in the Bible of love.

Here again, the gospel of the farm parallels the Gospel of the New Testament.[6] These inventors and manufacturers were profound evangelists of the better life.

- - - - -

[6] A confusing sentence has been omitted.

THE HARVEST FIELD: REAPING

I have said that E.H. Gammon, a Methodist minister, persuaded his parishioner, Mr. Deering, to invest, that together they might become reaper men. Somewhere and somehow on the road, the wheat harvesting machine helped make Evanston, Illinois, a university town, and, by strange fitness and heavenly logic, the McCormick Harvester, the McCormick Theological School and the Emmons Blaine School of Education, are children of the same father. If they are sometimes slow to recognize their common paternity, we must be patient while the children are being brought up to their majority.

Casson traces the last and highest triumph of the harvester to the rather windy eloquence of a Wisconsin editor. Fifty years or more ago, "Pump" Carpenter[7], as he was called, was a noisy figure in Wisconsin politics, an agitating editor. In his political fights upon the stump he loved to dwell on the coming time when the grain would be bound by machinery and the drudgery of the harvest field would be lifted from the shoulders of men. Says Casson:

> It is a most interesting fact, and certainly not an accidental one, that the group of noted inventors who together produced the self-binders, all appeared from the region south of Madison.[8]

Withington of Janesville, Wisconsin gave to McCormick the wire binder, which worked well and held the field until Appleby of Mazomanie, gave to Deering the twine binder, which knocked out the wire binder of

- - - - -

[7] Stephen Decatur Carpenter (1821-1906), inventor, politician and editor.

[8] Jones is in error here. This passage is not in the Casson books.

McCormick. We are left to infer that the brains of both Withington and Appleby were quickened by the oratory of "Pump" Carpenter.

While it is true that the final perfecters of the reaper -- many of them -- were farmers, the early inventors were dreamers of the study, men of the closet. The story of the reaper, like all the other great triumphs of man, in its last analysis is resolvable into spiritual power, and is best expressed in terms of human intelligence, will and consecration.

The upshot of this study of the harvest field is that the problem of garnering is quite as much an element in the gospel of life as the problem of growing. Our plowing, sowing and hoeing are vain if we are not able to harvest the product. What avail fertile fields or even diligent tillage, if at the critical moment -- how critical only farmers in this northwestern latitude can understand -- the joint product of man and God be not promptly conserved? The law of the field is the law of mind; civilization depends upon harvesting.

The mighty mills of Minneapolis, the thousand elevators on lakeshore and railroad siding, transcontinental trains and the mighty grain ships of the ocean are all indispensable parts of the great feeding machinery of the world. They are not only the logical sequences but the logical necessities of the self-binding harvester. And it is these great harvesting schemes of humanity that are to make hunger, starvation and famine impossible; for the abundance in one harvest field of the great farmer, by adequate harvesting, can be promptly made to supply the deficiencies of the blighted fields elsewhere.

Libraries and laboratories, schools, colleges, churches, homes are only so many depositories of the higher wheat -- storehouses of that which nourishes the imperishable part, distributing stations where the wealth of the harvest is made accessible to the hungry souls of men and women, where the abundance of summer is saved to the needs of winter.

I have tried to lay hold of the last triumph of the farm and convert it into a gospel hope. The International combine -- what of it? Admit, as I fear we must, that its basis was largely greed, that its economies were material, I for one will hope and believe that that triumph on the lower field will inevitably bear us on to similar triumphs in the upper field. It is over this rough road that the Mount of Vision is to be reached and the victory of the spirit is to be won. Cooperation and not competition is to direct the industries of the future. Are the combinations of today tyrannical, relentless, building up vast fortunes and at the same time sinking great groups of laborers to a condition where they are inadequately fed, clothed and housed? The remedy is in more cooperation, not less, a more intimate combination of capital and labor, a shortening of the distance between the shops and the counting rooms. The interests of the consumer of farm machinery have been greatly advanced by the combinations; the farmer is buying better and cheaper machines than he could under the regime of cutthroat competition. If the makers of the machines, the toiling artisans and diligent "hands", are not also profiting by the cooperation, then the still larger combination represented by the state must see that a more equitable distribution is secured.

Robert McCormick, the Scots-Irishman of Virginia, could afford to buy shoes for all the children, but the wise mother of Cyrus decreed that he should run bare-foot in summer lest he be weakened by luxury. After the Chicago fire, when the great factories were all in ashes, Cyrus McCormick summoned his wife. He was already a man of millions. He had won out; it was a good place to stop. "What shall I do," said the halting man to the clear-eyed wife, "close up and retire, or rebuild?" "Rebuild," said the sagacious wife. "I do not want my boys to grow up in idleness; we want to give them something to do."

The boys and girls were given something to do. What are the children of these recent conquerors to accomplish? Is the combination which their fathers proved so economically feasible to be carried higher by their children? Are we to realize "great combines" in religion? Are rival forces, disputing sects and quarreling creeds to ground arms, recognize their kindred interests, confess their common duties, and together proceed to feed the hungry world, to humanize and civilize warring factions, brutal forces and blood-spilling nationalities?

This chapter originally appeared in the **Wisconsin Magazine of History** 67:2, and is reprinted here with permission.

VII

Along with Thanksgiving Day, Arbor Day was one of Jones' favorite holidays. It, too, was distinctly American, distinctly modern and oriented to the natural rather than the supernatural. This was his Arbor Day sermon to All Souls on 9 April 1905. He printed it the week following in <u>Unity</u>.

He draws heavily on a single written source for his material, and characteristically quotes extensively from it, not even trying to draw any "lessons". His retelling only adds color and underlines the important elements. For him the "bold reality", "the plain simple story" of John Chapman is enough. The life of a saint needs only to be told, not moralized on.

He does introduce a celebration of the apple as an attempt to expand on his point, but it is not much developed. The man, John Chapman, draws him back very quickly.

The poem Jones selected as a preface to this sermon was "The Banyan Tree" by Rudyard Kipling - a rather strange choice.

JOHNNY APPLESEED

> And Jehovah planted a garden eastward, in Eden; and there he put the man whom he had formed.   Genesis 2:8

In a beautiful public park in the city of Mansfield, Ohio stands a modest marble shaft which bears the following inscription:

> In memory of John Chapman, best known as "Johnny Appleseed", pioneer nurseryman of Richland County from 1810 to 1830.

John Chapman has already passed out of history into legend; the humble nurseryman has become a fanciful myth. His story bloomed into quaint legend and grotesque traditions. Three times at least has he been woven into the pages of fiction and made the hero of a novel. <u>Philip Seymour; or Pioneer Life in Richland County, Ohio, Founded on Facts</u> by Rev. James F. McGaw is a story saturated with the local traditions of central Ohio. It has been edited and re-published with historical addenda by the Richland County Historical Society. In this story the experiences of certain pioneer families and personages well known in local history are woven into a romance by a country school teacher and rural preacher. Johnny Appleseed moves in and out among these characters in such a way as to give satisfaction to his old neighbors who knew and loved him. The Rev. Newell Dwight Hillis, pastor of Plymouth Church, Brooklyn, has written a more ambitious novel, entitled <u>The Quest of John Chapman: The Story of a Forgotten Hero</u>. Still a third well-elaborated novel is <u>Johnny Appleseed</u> by Eleanor Atkinson. I have read all of these books, but believing that here, as elsewhere, truth is stranger than fiction when there is adequate insight to understand and appreciate the facts, I have confined my studies to the historical data available rather than to the creations of the imagination kindled by the story.

The fictitious stories of Johnny Appleseed are not exaggerated history but inadequate history. These romance writers have tried to make vivid and real the story of the humble nurseryman, but there is reason to fear that they unwittingly obscured the sane, gentle, intelligent and devout lines that history gives to the face and career of this pioneer. At any rate the few pages based on the historical research of the Richland County Historical Society, published as an appendix to the story of <u>Philip Seymour</u>, move me more than all the pages of any novel that tries to bring to the surface the hidden heart-life of John Chapman. From these pages of contemporary history I prefer to draw my material.

At the unveiling of the John Chapman monument, November 8, 1900 in the city of Mansfield, General Brinkerhoff acted as chairman and made the opening speech. This is the General Brinkerhoff whose bright record on the battlefields of the Civil War is obscured by his brighter record as leader and sometime president of the National Association for Prison Reform. He was in his day an authority on crime and criminals and a student of those movements which ameliorate the hard lot of the sinner by such influences and instrumentalities as may reconstruct broken lives. On the battlefield, General Brinkerhoff showed himself a competent soldier in the interest of the Union. In his humanitarian work he proved himself a competent soldier in the interest of humanity.

In the opening address at these dedicatory services the presiding officer said:

We have met here today to dedicate a monument to one of the earliest and most unselfish of Ohio benefactors. His name was John Chapman, but to the pioneers he was everywhere known as Johnny Appleseed. The field of his operations, in Ohio, was mainly the valley of the Muskingum river and its tributaries, and his mission for the most part was to plant apple seeds, in well-located nurseries, in advance of civilization, and have apple trees ready for planting when the pioneers should appear. He also scattered through the forest the seeds of medicinal plants, such as dog-fennel, penny-royal, catnip, hoarhound, rattle-root and the like.

We hear him as early as 1806, on the Ohio River, with two canoe loads of apple seeds gathered from the cider presses of western Pennsylvania, and with these he planted nurseries along the Muskingum river and its tributaries.

About 1810 he made his headquarters in that part of the old county of Richland, which is now Ashland, in Green township, and was there for a number of years, and then he came to Mansfield where he was a familiar figure, and a welcome guest in the homes of the early pioneers.

All the early orchards of Richland county were procured from the nurseries of Johnny Appleseed. Within the sound of my voice, where I now stand, there are a dozen or more trees that we believe are the lineal descendants of Johnny Appleseed nurseries. In fact this monument is almost within the shadow of three of them.

As civilization advanced Johnny Appleseed passed on to the westward, and, at last, in 1847, he ended his career in Indiana and was buried near what is now the city of Fort Wayne. In the end he was true to his mission of planting nurseries and sowing the seeds of medicinal herbs.

To the pioneers of Ohio he was an unselfish benefactor, and we are here today to aid in transmitting to coming generations our grateful memory of his deeds.

The historical address that followed was made by A.J. Baughman, who was five years of age when, in 1843, this planter of apple trees made a last call at his father's house, upon whose farm were then growing two orchards which had been planted with trees bought of John Chapman. Thus, this local historian compiled his critical study from the immediate recollections and the well-stored traditions in his father's and grandfather's households. From this standpoint John Chapman appears as:

> a fairly educated man, well-read, polite, attentive in manner and chaste in conversation. His face was pleasant in expression; he was kind and generous in disposition; his nature was deeply religious; his life was blameless among his fellowmen. He regarded comfort more than style and thought it wrong to spend money for clothing to make a fine appearance.

It was the more sophisticated life of an after-generation that clothed with fantastic traditions the plain pioneer who went about his work barefooted, perchance bareheaded, who took old clothing in pay for nursery stock when there was no money to be had, who was sometimes seen at his work in a coffee-sack garment in which holes had been cut for his neck and arms, making of him the "wild man of the woods", a sort of wandering Jew of the frontier, a crazy apple-tree man. The plain simple story as compiled by the historian is something like this:

Born in the year 1775 in Springfield, Massachusetts -- a lover of plants and birds, a child enamored of the woods, he early became learned in the lore of the garden and orchard, and twenty-five years later either led or followed the emigrant wave westward. The first record of his appearance in Ohio goes back to the year 1800, when one day an old settler saw "a queer looking craft coming down the Ohio river in Jefferson county, manned by a solitary passenger". It consisted of two canoes lashed together. The pilot, captain and crew landed and said his name was Chapman, that his cargo consisted of sacks of apple seeds gathered at the cider mills of western Pennsylvania, that it was his purpose to plant nurseries along the river front and extend as he could his work into the interior of the state.

It was his custom, wherever he found a suitable place along the river banks, to cut away the underbrush, dig up the ground and plant his appleseeds, then build a brush enclosure around the spot to protect the young plants from the depredations of animals, wild and tame. These nurseries he would visit from time to time to care for his saplings -- weed them, hoe them, prune them, in proper season graft them. Then he would solicit orders, dig and sell them to the pioneers who were forming the great State of Ohio, making it not only the second mother of presidents but the famous orchard state of the Middle West. For many years he lived alone in a little cabin near Perrysville in Richland County. Later he made his home with a half-sister in what is now the city of Mansfield, where the oldest settlers well remember him. Meanwhile he went about tending to his primitive nurseries, soliciting orders and delivering his apple trees up and down the settlements. Far and wide did he go with his saplings, until "Johnny Appleseed" became a widely-known and much-beloved character in central Ohio.

Gradually but surely the adventurous spirit of the pioneer carried him westward. His habit of planting apple seeds and distributing nursery stock bore him within the boundaries of Indiana. He found lodgment in the neighborhood of Fort Wayne. When seventy-two years of age, during a temporary stay in the village, word came to him that cattle had broken into his nursery and were destroying his trees. It was a cold raw day in March with flurries of snow, but Johnny Appleseed loved his trees and so he started out afoot to look after his seedlings.

It was twenty miles of muddy road. He arrived cold, wet, hungry at a farmer's door -- one who was born in the Buckeye State and knew well the fame of Johnny Appleseed. He found cordial welcome, but the modest traveller, begging to be excused from sitting at the supper table, partook of his bowl of bread and milk at the open fire. The sun went down with a glorious promise of spring; there was an Easter prophecy of flowers which the old man observed as he stood on the doorstep looking towards the West. He declined the bed and begged for a quilt and pillow on the floor near the fire, but asked permission, as was his custom, to conduct family worship before retiring. He read the Beatitudes and offered a prayer, the traditions of which still abide in the family.

> He prayed for all sorts and conditions of men; prayed that the way of righteousness might be made clear and that saving grace might be offered to all nations. He asked for the guidance of the Holy Spirit and the comfort that comes to the truth-seeker and the truth lover.

The historian continues: "Not only the words of the prayer but the pathos of his voice made a deep impression upon those present."

Next morning the poor planter of apple trees was found with a burning fever; the exposures of the day before were too much for him. A physician was summoned, but pneumonia, that quick, sharp angel of death, had marked John Chapman for its own, and with a beautiful smile and a resignation of spirit which stayed with the physician and friends as a lasting revelation, the maker of orchards passed on to the beyond, leaving his nurseries to the tender mercies of his neighbors, his memory too much to the fantastic imagination of the frivolous, the skeptical and the superficial. Subsequent efforts of the Historical Society of Ohio have failed to locate the grave, though they have established beyond a doubt the graveyard wherein sleeps the dust of John Chapman.

In answer to an attempt to locate the grave, John H. Archer, of Fort Wayne -- the grandson of David Archer who set apart the private burial ground for the pioneers of Fort Wayne -- wrote:

> During his life and residence in this vicinity I suppose that every man, woman and child knew something of Johnny Appleseed. I find that there are quite a number of persons yet living here that remember him well, and enjoy relating reminiscences and peculiarities of his habits and life. The historical account of his death and burial by the Worths and their neighbors, the Pettits, Gonges, Porters, Parkers, Notesterns, Beckets, Whitesides, Pechons, Hatfields, Parrants, Ballards, Rindsells and the Archers, in David Archer's private burial grounds, is substantially correct. The grave, more especially the common head-

boards used in those days, have long since decayed and become entirely obliterated, and at this time I do not think that any person could, with any degree of certainty, come within fifty feet of pointing out the location of his grave; suffice it to say that he has been gathered in with his neighbors and friends, as I have enumerated, for the majority of them lie in David Archer's graveyard with him.

The first point to be noted in this story is the refreshing charm that goes with a man who has an individuality that marks him and sets him apart, a man to be remembered, one to be quoted, one who has achieved that nearest and, on that account, dearest pledge of immortality; he "though dead, yet speaketh", though buried, lives in the memory of his fellows, a man of whom those who saw him in their childhood will love to tell in their gray hairs.

John Chapman as he stands out in the few meager pages of history is a hundred times more charming than the Johnny Appleseed of the romancers. As one might expect, this grower of apple trees never killed anything, not even, says the historian, "for the purpose of obtaining food". He never carried weapons, not even for self defense. He was welcomed by the red man even in times of hostility. He was no mendicant -- the stories of his wanderings notwithstanding. Says Mr. Baughman in his historical address:

He was never in indigent circumstances. He sold thousands of nursery trees every year. Had he been avaricious his estate instead of being worth a few thousands might have been worth tens of thousands at his death.

In another place the historian says, "His usual price for a tree was a 'fip-penny-bit', but if the settlers had no money John would either give them credit or take old clothes for pay."

It almost goes without the saying that John Chapman was a devout soul. It must have been so. We would have been safe in assuming this truth even if there were no records to prove it, but it was universally known that the life of this gentle man was an ellipse drawn around two foci: one, an apple tree; the other, the teachings of Emanuel Swedenborg. Wherever he went he was a missionary of this poetic, mystic, spiritual faith. His mind was well stored with the teachings of the Scandinavian church seer. His pockets were well filled with the tracts of the Swedenborgian church, and his ripened thought on these subjects was appreciated only by the cultivated men of the settlements.

The monument at Mansfield was erected by the Honorable M.B. Bushnell. His father was Dr. William Bushnell, the good physician of the early days, of whom the historian says: "His scholastic attainments and intuitive knowledge of character enabled him to know and appreciate Chapman's learning and the noble traits of his head and heart."

This missionary of peace and good will, of course, was the reconciler, the benignant go-between of the red man of the woods and the white man of the settlement, and he often rendered high service in protecting life. We read that during the War of 1812 he often warned the settlers of approaching danger. One incident is told in detail. When the citizens of Mansfield were huddled within the protecting walls of the blockhouse in the face of immediate danger -- the protecting troops were thirty miles away and attack was imminent -- a messenger must be found to carry the message. The journey must be made in the night through the wilderness filled with hostile Indians. A volunteer was asked for and "a bareheaded, barefooted, unarmed, tall, lank man said demurely, 'I will go.' His manner was meek, but there was that expression in his countenance such as painters try to portray in their saints." It was another Paul Revere journey, only it was made on foot -- barefoot at that, and as yet there has come no Longfellow to sing the story for our school children. Quietly the unarmed man stopped in the depth of the night, gently tapped at the cabin doors along the way advising the settlers to flee to the blockhouse. The garrison at Mount Vernon was aroused and succor came with the day.

Surely a tender pathos gathers around personality -- all personality, but the pathos deepens and the glory heightens as that personality represents the love of nature, a passion to serve, devout trustfulness and an unresisting courage.

The story of John Chapman is the story of the apple tree. Where and when will the adequate historian of the apple appear? Who will tell us of the human investment in the Pippin, the Greening, the Baldwin, the Wealthy, the Ben Davis and the hundred other varieties that prolong the lives of forgotten ministers to humanity and unconsciously perpetuate the memory of the peaceful conquerors who heroically lived lives which an ungrateful posterity has reduced to mere names of apples which they buy by the barrel, grumbling at the market price? Who will tell the spiritual as well as the physical value of orchards? Who can count the civilizing power of the apple?

The upward rise of the race is traceable through the hunter, the herdsman, the cultivator of flowers. As the plowman is above the cowboy, the farmer above the herder, so the gardener is above them all. Horticulture is the fine art of agriculture. As the rose is queen among flowers, so is the apple king among the fruits, and the apple is largely a human product. The apple-man is the humble prophet of healthier, saner living.

John Chapman had an apostolic mission; he was the Paul of the new order of things in the valley of the Ohio. He was a conspicuous representative of a refining host that moved westward from the sterile hills of New England and the more fertile but still flinty valleys of New York and Pennsylvania, planting apple trees as they went -- arboreal John the Baptists preparing the way for school houses, churches, court houses and colleges. They knew the mystery, the beauty, the poetry of an apple tree.

We gladly read Bryant's "Planting of an Apple Tree" and recognize a humane and humanizing poem, but he who would learn the poetry of an apple tree in these days must take counsel not of the poet in his study, but of the scientific wonder-workers in their laboratories, chief of which is Luther Burbank, the California wizard, who out of five hundred thousand plum trees selected two by means of which he was to put new flavor and value into the old fruit -- if not indeed to create a new fruit. Out of one single seed grown under his intelligent hand came the three that offered thirty-six different varieties of apples, each one of which was a subtle contribution to the science of heredity.

The apple-man, as every pioneer in the Mississippi valley very well remembers, was a missionary of refinement. John Chapman is not so unique as the novelists would have us think. I recall in my own childhood the fame and influence of old Squire Geer, who never made a call without an apple in his pocket. In his old age he went up and down the valley neighborhood with his pockets full of sample apples. I have read Ruskin's eloquent discussions of great art masterpieces; I have heard musicians descant upon the quality of great compositions, but none of them exceed in delicacy of discrimination, in refined appreciation, in skillful adjectives and subtle analysis old Squire Geer's description of the peculiar flavors, tints, habits and aromas of his apple children. Blessed is the man who plants an apple tree!

But the apple-man is but a selectman in the larger guild of co-workers with God - the tree planters of the world, to whose high mission one loves to pay tribute. The day is coming when the tree planter will stand as a type of the noblest contributors to the growth of civilization - the world-makers, as the tree-destroyers stand for the destructive forces that denude the world and debase the men who must live therein. When King Asoka (250 B.C.) sent his own son on the missionary journey to bear the gospel of the blessed Buddha -- the religion that made Asia pitying -- to the far-off island of the sea, a sister soon followed after him, and she with womanly instinct took with her a cutting from the sacred Bo tree, under which the Buddha came to his illumination. She planted that cutting in the spicy atmosphere of the tropic seas; it grew, and successive generations of the faithful nurtured and watered it. As it grew aged they bound its branches with bands of iron; they terraced its trunks, and the Bo tree of Ceylon lived until 1889, and was at its death the oldest known tree on the globe. I state these facts on the authority of botanists, as well as of students of religion. Some leaves of this ancient Bo tree of Ceylon were presented to All Souls' Sunday-school in Chicago by Dr. Carus of "The Open Court".[1] These leaves, carefully preserved, were brought to the Parliament of Religion in 1893[2] by Mr. Dharmapala, secretary of the Maha-Bhodi Society of Ceylon and presented to Dr. Carus, who in turn presented them to the Sunday School. For at least twenty-one hundred years the leaves of this tree have literally been for the healing of the nations. Under the branches of that tree wayward passions have been controlled, unholy ambitions have been bridled, selfish desires and petty envies have been abated, and man has been made more conscious of his human brotherhood and his divine sonship.

This historic Bo tree represents the benignity of Nature augmented by the beatitudes of the soul, so it becomes the most venerable representative of that blessed enlargement of Nature that comes through the planting hand of man. Every planted tree is the bounty of Nature plus a human investment. God made the forest;

─ ─ ─ ─ ─

[1] Paul Carus (1852-1919) founded The Open Court Publishing Company and was an important agency for introducing the study of Asian religion into North America.

[2] The World's Parliament of Religion was part of the Chicago World's Fair of 1893.

man made the orchard. God gave us the crab apple; man gave us the apple. Nature leaves her fruit sour; man eliminates the sour and increases the sugar in the fruit.

I would be true to the story, though not true to the spirit of John Chapman, if I ended here and let this simple story of actual life rooted not in legend or myth but in reality, serve as my contribution to Arbor Day sanctities. May the spirit of John Chapman inspire a more adequate recognition of this recently founded holy day in the American calendar.

But I would not be true to the method of John Chapman if I stopped here. The heart, tutored by Emanuel Swedenborg, did ever see in every seed a spiritual counterpart. Every sapling was a parable and every orchard a sermon. And so I am quite true to the great orchard-maker of Ohio when I repeat for you a verse from the mystical hymn of creation with which the Hebrew Bible-makers introduced their book of revelation:

> And Jehovah planted a garden eastward in Eden; and there he put the man whom he had formed.

We may not all be planters of trees, though every man, woman and child should have a perpetual ambition to fill the waste places of the earth with growing beauty. No man, woman or child should be content to let a springtime pass without more or less directly causing at least one more tree to grow for the shelter and the nourishment of mankind. And everyone can become a planter of apple seeds in the garden of the spirit, a maker of orchards in the realm of mind, a grower of apples in the fields of thought. And what symbol more fitting, what analogy so searching to apply to the great work which we all have in hand - the work of making our own hearts bloom, making the community fertile, making our social life productive. Out of the refuse of the cider presses of western Pennsylvania, Ohio was made an orchard state. Seventy years ago John Chapman literally laid down his life for his apple trees. I deal in but cold science - exact history, what ought to be verifiable demonstration - when I say that those children of the childless man, those loves of the unwedded spouse of orchard trees are still bearing fruit a hundred fold. Not only could the orator at the unveiling of his monument say, "Within the sound of my voice are a dozen or more trees, aye, under the very shadow of the monument there are three of them, who are lineal descendants of Johnny Appleseed's nurseries," but fragrant trainloads of Ohio apples find their way every year to metropolitan markets directly from the nurseries of John Appleseed. For the cultivated apple tree, the developed fruit, the rarest variety, knows no death. There is but one tree to bear your favorite Pippin, or its rival the Baldwin. That tree is perpetuated; its life is prolonged; its area is extended by grafts and slips throughout an ever increasing realm. It is one tree striking root in many soils.

The perpetuating power of a great thought, the resources of a loving sentiment, the surprises possible in the meagerest orchard of the spirit cannot be shamed by the fertility of Nature.

Let us go forth, then, out of our loneliness, our weakness, out of our disappointments, out of our poverty, and sow our seed like John Chapman. If we sow as persistently, if we are as true to our best, as single-minded in our quest as he was, we like him may be branded as "queer", suspected of being "crazy", known by our idiosyncrasies. But that wanderer in the wilderness who carried his kit of cooking tools on his back when need be, wore his mush pan as a hat on his head that it might thereby serve the double purpose and have secure surer transportation, he whose wine was drawn from the forest spring, whose sleeping chamber was oftentimes the protecting arms of forest trees, whose bed was made of forest leaves was, by the most severe material tests, by the most gradgrind canons of practicality, perhaps the most potent pioneer, the greatest state builder, the wisest statesman and the most far-reaching patriot of all the brave band that converted the wild territory of Ohio into one of the richest and noblest states in the Union.

I have made several unsuccessful attempts to leave the apple trees of Ohio and the apple planter of the frontier, and go in search of spiritual applications - of ethical lessons, but every attempt fails. The story is so efficient in its bald reality; the blooming apple trees every May will fill the air with fragrance all the way from Mansfield to Fort Wayne and far beyond, will convert thousands of acres into bouquets as beautiful as the blooms of Paradise dreamed by Dante. These trees teach their own lesson, deliver their own message. They ask us to think more of planting and less of harvesting, to believe in seeds more than in trees, in cultivation more than in accumulation. Doing this we will find ourselves in the blessed line of planters, comrades of Johnny Appleseed.

VIII

Like "Johnny Appleseed" this is an Arbor Day sermon, preached at All Souls in April of 1895 and printed in <u>Unity</u> the same year.

Jones is here explicitly espousing a conservation policy at a time when few were. His concern for forests and bird-life, being devastated by human carelessness and greed fore-shadows the ecological concerns to become prevalent eighty years later.

His rather formless praise of trees, that accounts for over a third of the sermon, illustrates the wide reading that Jones did beyond ordinary "religious" subjects. It also shows the fascination that statistics of quantity and size held for him -- as they did for many liberals of his age.

It may seem like a too-obvious choice that the poem for this sermon was Joyce Kilmer's "Trees". In 1918, though, it had only recently been published and was not yet the cliché it has become to us.

TREE PLANTING

And Abraham planted a tamarisk tree
in Beersheba and called there on

> the name of Jehovah, the everlasting God.
>
> Genesis 21:33

Reading between the lines of those quaint and early records of the Hebrew people, we discover the story of civilization. Thinking of Abraham as a well-digger and as a tree-planter, we must think of him as a man far removed from the barbarian. We must think of him as one who had ceased to be a nomad, a wanderer on the face of the earth. He had already begun to strike his own roots into the soil and draw the nourishment of his life -- social, mental and spiritual -- from one locality. He had already become a home-maker. To think of Abraham as a tree-planter is to think of him as a man with a future. He has risen above the careless life of the savage, the hand-to-mouth life of the thriftless and the shiftless.

Tree-planting -- how the phrase suggests intelligence, forethought, skill. How long is the perspective here suggested, how wide the range, how profound the significance!

"What a great thought of God was that when He thought a tree," said Ruskin.

> There is nothing in vegetable nature so grand as a tree; grappling with its roots the granite foundations of the everlasting hills, it reaches its sturdy and gnarled trunk on high, spreads its branches to the heavens, casts its shadow on the sward and the birds build their nests and sing among its umbrageous branches

said Gen. Robert E. Lee while leaning against one of

TREE PLANTING

the great forest trees in front of Fredericksburg, under which his army was encamped.

The poets marshall themselves before us at the suggestion of a tree. How Whittier, Longfellow, Lowell and Holmes loved the trees! Hearken to them while they chant a few lines.

Says Lowell "To a Pine Tree":

> Thou alone know'st the splendor of winter,
> Mid thy snow-silvered, hushed precipices,
> Hearing crags of green ice groan and
>   splinter,
> And then plunge down the muffled abysses
> In the quiet of midnight.
>
> Thou alone know'st the glory of summer,
> Gazing down on thy broad seas of forest,
> On thy subjects that send a proud murmur
> Up to thee, to their sachem, who towerest
> From thy bleak throne to heaven.

Bayard Taylor in "The Palm and the Pine" thus describes the influence of these trees upon the Norse crusader who wooed an Arab maid:

> And stronger, as he grew to man,
> The contradicting natures ran,
>
> As mingled streams from Etna flow,
> One born of fire, and one of snow.
>
> One gave him force, the other fire;
> This self-control, and that desire.
>
> One filled his heart with fierce unrest;
> With peace serene the other blessed.

And Robert Browning in his "In Album" gives us this majestic apostrophe to an elm tree:

>Placidly full in front, smooth bole, broad branch
>And leafage, one green plenitude of May.
>
>O you exceeding beauty, bosomful
>   of lights and shades, murmurs and silences,
>Sun-warmth, dew-coolness, -- squirrel, bee
>   and bird,
>High, higher, highest, till the blue
>   proclaims
>'Leave earth, there's nothing better till
>   next step
>Heavenward!' -- so, off flies what has wings
>   to help!

But even the masters grow inadequate when they sing of a tree; the thing so outreaches the song, the sermon is necessarily so inferior to the text. Human history gathers around the story of trees. Man's achievements were accomplished under the shade thereof, and the story of these achievements are commemorated thereby. Indeed, there is but little marble or bronze on this earth whose antiquity is not ante-dated by some of the trees of the earth. The memorial places of the world are tree places. The Bo tree in Ceylon has already been referred to in these pages as having been grown from a slip of the tree under which Buddha caught his vision of the path of virtue. There is a cypress tree in Lombardy whose antiquity, established by documentary evidence, reaches back to 40 B.C.. Botanists believe that some of the olive trees still extant on Mount Olivet shared the sunlight with the great prophet of Nazareth while he was giving to the hungry peasant souls the lessons of the lily and the mustard seed. Professor Gray estimated that the Sequoia of California are as old as Christianity, and certain palm trees are supposed to be as venerable as the pyramids. General Brisbin in his book, Trees and Tree-Planting[1], speaking of the African Baobab tree as the oldest and largest specimen of vegetable growth in the world, says:

> Adenson saw one in the Cape Verde Islands within whose trunk, overlaid by three hundred close layers of wood, he discovered an inscription carved by two English travelers three centuries before, and he estimated the age of the tree at 5150 years. They still show in Mexico the cypress of Montezuma; when this hero entered in 1520 it was then a tree of forty feet in girth and one hundred and twenty feet in height.[2]

Amid all the wreck and ruin of Babylon there survives, it is reported, a willow tree that is supposed to be the sole relic of the glory of the reign of Semiramis. A linden tree near the city of Neustadt was the object of municipal care and protection for hundreds of years. It antedated the city, which was nearly destroyed in 1229. In 1408 a poem described its branches as being propped by sixty-seven stone pillars; in 1664 the pillars were increased to eighty-two, in 1832 to one hundred and six. At that time the trunk

― ― ― ― ― ―

[1] James S. Brisbin, Trees and Tree-Planting (New York: Harper and Brothers, 1888).

[2] Brisbin, p 282.

measured thirty-seven feet around, six feet from the ground, and the terrible storm that wrecked it broke down the monument of eight hundred years. Brisbin is my further authority for saying that there are oaks still living in England planted before the Norman conquest of 1066. The yew trees at Fountain Abbey and Ripon are still older, and one in Kent, it is estimated, has reached an age of three thousand years. The walnut carries its history in its name, for the early English fathers called it the "gaulinut" -- the nut introduced from Gaul. Paris has an elm tree planted in 1605. Our own Charter Oak, which held concealed the charter of the city of Hartford, placed there in 1687, went down before a storm in 1854, with its six hundred years or more upon its venerable head, furnishing material for what would doubtless amount to several car-loads of walking sticks, pencil boxes, or sign boards. The Peace Elm, under which William Penn closed his famous treaty, was two hundred and eighty-three years old when it fell in 1810. Washington's elm at Cambridge still bears witness to the great first President, though its leaf is faded. But even when life is gone, the substance of the tree abides; Egyptian timber ties are found over four thousand years old, and they are still sound.[3]

Quite independent of the human element in the story of the tree, how marvellously interesting is a study of individual subjects. I have mentioned the Baobab tree with its historical record three hundred years old, but this is the tree that gives the name to Cape Verde - the green cape. In some respects the

- - - - -

[3] The material of this paragraph is taken from chapters 6 and 7 of Brisbin's book.

TREE PLANTING

Baobab tree stands foremost among the remarkable products of the vegetable world. Its main stem is only about twelve feet high, but it often measures thirty-four feet in diameter, lifting its branches sixty feet high. The natives call it by a name which indicates "a thousand years".

The story of our own great trees on the Western slope has been told in figures and in picture so that even our children are familiar with it: the tree in whose hollow miners encamped at a point that would have been three hundred feet above ground; the tree through which a man can ride on horseback for seventy-five feet and turn around and return.

A banyan tree in Ceylon throws a shadow over four acres of ground, and I have read that the eucalyptus forests of Australia lift their straight, slender and, for the most part, naked trunks five hundred feet high -- as high as the Washington monument, higher than any structure made by man before the erection of the Eiffel Tower.

But what need to specify? Any tree -- every tree -- embodies in itself an epitome of the miracle of life. Here on a grand scale is ever being constructed and maintained one of the high bridges of evolution, the bridge over which matter passes from the inorganic into the organic realm; at its feet are the stolid substances of the mineral world, around its head the subtle and fluid gases of the same realm. Whether as solid, as water or as air, matter yet is insensate, unyielding, inorganic. But the tree lays hold of these substances and, by some divine alchemy which no one has explained, in the secret laboratory of the leaf the mighty transformation takes place. Then matter becomes alive. Matter is there transformed so that it is evermore the store-house of life — abounding, progressive, aggressive, increasing life. The cycles of evolution are traceable from the clay at the root of the tree, meeting the rain and the sun in the leaf, back again to grass, up again through bird and quadruped into the manchild glorious. The final efflorescence of the tree is a Shakespeare, an Edison or a Lincoln.

But the study of the individual tree pushes us in every direction to the study of the tree as a member of a community. There is a commonwealth of the woods, magnificent and sublime. There is a new science recently come into prominence, the science of forestry — a science of such proportions that on the economic side it challenges the attention of governments and arouses the concern of the industrial world. The trees blanket the earth in winter. They shadow it in summer. They conserve its moisture. They feed its springs and replenish its rivers. The trees preserve that delicate balance of nature with which reckless and foolish men so often interfere. That which is poison to the animal is the food of the tree. Forests purify the air, lay hold of the noxious fumes from mine and from city, rob the breezes of the pestilence and give them back in refreshing and invigorating draughts. A good-sized peach tree, it is said, gives off about two gallons of moisture in twelve hours. Plant a grove and you have modified the climate for the benefit of man. Chop down a grove and you have rendered a tract of nature less hospitable to man. Persist in your chopping and you convert the habitable land into a desert, as has been done with millions and millions of square miles on this earth's surface.

The island of St. Helena, when first discovered, was beautifully wooded, fertile and well watered. Then

TREE PLANTING 129

man came with his ax and fire to chop down the good trees and to burn the poor ones. He brought his large herds of goats to browse down the young trees, and in two hundred years the island became parched and barren. Since 1700 some governmental attention to the replanting of trees has been gradually bringing back its fertility.

The barren desert, the waste lands from the Mediterranean to the Euphrates, now the home of marauding nomads, where even foxes and wolves find but uncertain living, have been made so by the vandal hand of man. Degenerate Spain[4] is brought to her present pitiable plight economically and morally by the high-handed infidelity that for centuries defied the laws of God which are the laws of nature, by stripping her hillsides and devastating her valleys of nature's protection, her fertilizers and her guardians of life and peace. The unguarded fires of the American Indian perpetuated and made permanent, if they did not create, the vast prairies of Illinois, Iowa, Minnesota, the Dakotas and Kansas. The reckless fires of Brazil that are allowed annually to sweep over her fertile plains are said to be rendering what once was a land wonderfully hospitable to man an arid and desperate home for thousands of settlers. Professor Marsh in his book, <u>The Earth as Modified by Human Action</u>, says:

> In some of the Alpine regions of Northern France this vandalism has been carried on to such an extent that man at last retires from the fearful desert. In the year 1843 I

- - - - -

[4] This reflects the American view of Spain in the years leading up to the Spanish-American War.

> found not a living soul in districts where I remember to have enjoyed hospitality thirty years before.[5]

I will not attempt to present the economic importance of forestry, because I am inadequate to the task. But two great facts on the economic side can be easily established. One is the large dependence of modern arts and industry upon trees. <u>The Journal of the Society of Arts</u> in London in 1889, said that "six of the leading railway systems of France reached an annual consumption of 3,650,000 sleepers" (ties we would call them in this country). This, it is estimated, required the cutting of one thousand fine trees every day to meet the demand of the French railways. The estimate for Great Britain was put at fifteen million per annum, or an annual stripping of 197,600 acres of forest. And this is but one of the smaller items. It has been well said that the invention of a passing toy for children implies the destruction of thousands of cords of wood. Who can convert the annual output of the Diamond Match Company back into its primal condition in the forest? It is a well known fact that the great pineries of the North are practically exhausted. Long since, the centre of our lumber trade has shifted to the Southward and to the far Northwest. Wood is already too expensive for fencing, and in many places for fuel. Some one has estimated that the fences of the United States have cost more than the land. It has been estimated that about three hundred square miles of land are being stripped in one year to supply the Chicago market with lumber.

- - - - -

[5] George Perkins Marsh, <u>The Earth as Modified by Human Action</u> (New York: Scribner, Armstrong, 1874), p 254. (Jones quotes the material inaccurately.)

TREE PLANTING

The chief of forestry at Washington estimates that if Connecticut were turned into a woodyard it would hardly be large enough to yield this one year's supply. When we remember how slowly the great trees grow and that it takes from fifty to a hundred years to grow a respectable sawlog, we realize how recklessly we are bargaining for a relentless, hopeless famine. Unless there comes some infusion of wisdom, some interposition of sense, some application of the law of morals to this great bounty of God, we are by our haste and our selfishness rendering our fruitful land inhospitable if not uninhabitable for man. What right has a lumber king who by enterprise or fraud has secured, through tax title or otherwise, a paper deed to these precious acres, the great storehouses of vegetable history, thus to break into the treasure house of nature, make personal wealth out of the commonwealth of God, a wealth which man did not create and cannot replace?

The other fact is that here the law of thrift is more flagrantly defied than almost anywhere else. Out of the eight million acres of trees that are denuded annually, less than one million are replaced, and much of the waste is wanton. The impulse to destroy is one of the strongest impulses in primitive man. The impulse to plant, to conserve, to protect, to co-operate with nature is one of the slowest and latest movements of civilization. How much man has done to disturb the delicate balance of nature, to man's immeasurable loss let the abandoned provinces of Asia and the wasted fields of Virginia, the torn and eroded cotton fields of Mississippi and Alabama, the rabbit pests of Australia, the sparrow pests of America, show.

Undoubtedly man is the greatest enemy of the

forest, but it has other enemies -- the endless legion of insects, canker worms and caterpillars which make war not only upon our orchard but upon our forest trees. What is known as the "Pine Spinner Caterpillar" has destroyed whole pine forests in Germany. But nature in her determination to preserve the balance of life has her army of birds, large and small, which are at work, in season and out of season, ridding the forests of their foes, stripping our orchards of their pests. But here comes the woman first with wanton thoughtlessness, but later with well-formed defiance to disturb this balance and interfere with this protection that her bonnet may be trimmed. Flora J. Cooke of the Chicago Normal School compiled some interesting and accusing figures of this kind. Every time a woman bargains for a chickadee for her hat, she bargains for the life of 138,750 canker worms, which is the average number of canker worm eggs which that chickadee will destroy during one season of twenty-five days in which the canker worm mother lays her eggs upon the trunks of trees.

  The cuckoo will eat one hundred and seventy good-sized caterpillars in a day, each of which will, if allowed to reach the butterfly stage, lay five hundred eggs. Thus the cuckoo stands between the trees and eighty-five thousand caterpillars. The woman breaks down this fence of nature, lets eighty-five thousand caterpillars push their devastating work, that she may wear a "love of a bonnet". The United States Agricultural Report credits to the woodpeckers more than to any other agency, the preservation of our timber from hordes of destructive insects, but the woodpecker is, alas, a "perfectly lovely decoration for a woman's hat".

But man slowly is learning his lesson. After paying the bitter price of stupidity, he begins to realize the value of a tree -- that is, some men do. There slowly dawns upon the intelligent the conviction that man may do much to restore his lost estate and do more towards avoiding further disasters in the future, hence the great science and art of forestry which is enlisting the interest of scientists, economists and legislators the world over. The forestry laws of Europe and America are constantly growing and are among the most prophetic and consequently the most ethical laws upon our modern statute books, for they look toward restoration not destruction, toward creation not desecration. The elaborate reports with their costly and beautiful maps and other exhibits published by our state departments are full of interest, but of them I cannot speak.

That special form of forestry legislation which seeks to educate the children into love of trees and to lay the foundation of a life-long habit of planting and protecting instead of mutilating and otherwise destroying is of particular interest. Most of the states in the Union now provide that the governor shall set aside one day in the year to be observed in the public schools and other educational institutions as Arbor Day, on which day with fitting accompaniment of song and speech and recitation, school grounds, public parks and highways will be enriched by the planting of trees, shrubs and flowers. The superintendents of public instruction in many of the states honor the day by publishing special annuals for the use of school children, pamphlets enriched with song and story, parable and scientific fact. Who can measure the far-reaching influence of such days? What fundamental work in religion is done by these servants of the public when they teach the children to appreciate the delicate conditions of life, to familiarize themselves with the laws of reproduction and growth, when their sympathies are sent out on lines so long that they outreach the utmost limit of their own earthly career.

James Russell Lowell is remembered as saying, a short time before his death, while leaning his trembling hand upon the trunk of a magnificent chestnut on his lawn: "I planted the seed of this tree and my father was standing by to show me how." He who plants an elm plants for his grandchildren. The child who puts a willow slip into the ground is throwing shade over cattle that will give milk to generations unborn. The child who is taught to deal with the germ-life of the maple and the hickory is unwittingly brought into co-operation with the most lasting of forces and the most imperishable of earthly organisms.[6]

Leaving still open the disputed question as to whether any seeds found in the Egyptian mummies have actually been propagated after their thousands of years of sleep, there is no doubt of the marvellous vitality that goes with the germ of plant life. The desert of Sahara needs but to be watered and the waiting germs promptly rise up, witnessing to the pre-Adamic parents who once peopled thick the burning sands. The dirt drawn up out of deep wells and exposed to the conditions of growth have brought forth extinct forms of vegetable life. Professor Houston quoting from Lindley, the English botanist, says:

> Melon seeds have grown when forty-one years old; maize when thirty

- - - - -

[6] The next sentence was omitted as a digression.

years; rye when forty; the sensitive plant when sixty; kidney beans at one hundred. Clover comes up from soil in which no clover has been known to grow, since the memory of man.

Says the botanist:

I have at this moment three plants of raspberries before me, raised in the garden of the horticultural society from seeds taken from the stomach of a man whose skeleton was found thirty feet below the surface of the earth, at the bottom of the barrow which was opened near Dorchester. He had been buried with some coins of the Emperor Hadrian and it is therefore probable that the seeds were sixteen or seventeen hundred years old.

This vitality is as expansive as it is enduring. The magnificent maple is borne upon the wings of the wind when it is in the seed. At this beginning, the child carries the king of the forest in his hand and makes fairy tea-cups of the acorn saucers. From the single seed of a wild cucumber vine in the short summer at Westhope Cottage on Tower Hill, the subtle chemistry of sunlight and air wove a vine seventy feet long, decorated it with leaves and gloried it with uncounted flowers. It is with such suggestive material that the children work on Arbor Day. These nature parables prove the far-reaching significance of little things, the enduring vitality of real things.

Perhaps I cannot work it out in detail, but I have a feeling that somehow the problem of forestry is wonderfully allied to the problems that present themselves in our human husbandry. The human continents have been devastated by the selfish iconoclasm that has laid hold of all the available outgrowths of the human heart to advance the interests of the hour and enhance the pleasures of a day. We have cut off that benignant forest growth that would shelter the tender plants, keep moist the soil and make fertile the fields. Thousands of souls about us are in the condition of burned-out Palestine. The trees have been cut off, the springs of reverence have dried up and there are no rivers of emotion flowing with their refreshings through the spaces of life. Nothing will save such a soul but some more tree planting, tree nurturing -- a gradual restoration of the forests that again will prove the divine resources by present growths, establishing heavenly connections with the life that now is.

Let us plant trees by the roadside, in the front yard, along the alley; plant oak and elm, pine and maple, basswood and birch, any tree so that we plant indigenous trees. There is an economic value in anything that grows.

In thus pleading for tree planting, it is hardly clear whether I am pleading for trees material or trees spiritual. It matters little. The difference is not so great as it seems. The one will produce the other. In teaching our children the value of the one, we will teach them the value of the other.

Garibaldi wrought for the liberty of Italy, and Garibaldi planted great groves of eucalyptus trees in the malarial sections of Rome; Garibaldi was magnificently successful in both ventures. Let us plant the eucalyptus where the moral malaria festers. It probably contains no mystic virtue, no specific or peculiar value. It is simply a great grower, a rapid transformer of muck into protoplasm, a splendid absorbent of mud and moisture which it promptly transports into the great laboratory of green leaves high in the air where the miracle of creation continuously takes place. What is the transforming power there? There is a stage in the development of science when a solution seems to have been reached by calling this power "chlorophyll". But what is that? Nobody knows. It is a name with which we cover our human ignorance. It is another word for the divine mystery.

I am giving you the raw material. Work it out, as the forests are worked out, in silent, persistent elaboration. Work it out so that evermore a tree will be somewhat more sacred, and the hand that plants a tree be somewhat more revered, and the problems of morals and religion, individual and collective, may become more and more but different phases of the forestry problems. Our human work is the reforestation of the desolated fields of life. We must preserve what we have, restore what we have lost and utilize our gains. In 1860 France published a famous code for the reforestation of mountains by which its citizens are encouraged to work for the general good. That, I take it, is the kind of missionary work that is true to nature. Let us plant trees for the general good. Let us multiply the Arbor Days of the spirit. Like Abraham, we must cease to be vagrants, despoilers of the ground, wandering bands of spiritual gypsies, profiting by what others have planted, devastating those who are to come after us by leaving a waste where we found a grove. Like Abraham let us plant a tree in the name of the Lord, with a thought of the everlasting God in our hearts.

IX

"The Tower Hill Pleasure Company" was formed in 1889 by Jones, Henry Simmons, William Channing Gannet and Jones' brothers, to develop the derelict site of "Old Helena" across the river from Spring Green, Wisconsin, as a vacation grounds for themselves and Jones' Chicago congregation. Shares were sold, improvements made and it became a going concern.

This sermon tells the story of what happened to the hill itself during the first six years of its use as a resort. Perhaps better here than most places Jones is able to draw his lesson smoothly from his factual data. The re-clothing of the hill was the model for the development of human goodness.

The congregation of All Souls first heard this as its after-vacation sermon on 18 September 1895. It was repreached in the autumn of 1898 and published in Unity on 29 September of that year.

The prefatory poem for this sermon is noted as "From Horeb's bush the Presence spoke -- Browning". No such line is found in any poem of either Robert or Elizabeth Browning. Since Jones was the founder of the American branch of the Browning Society, the lapse is puzzling.

THE REFORESTATION OF TOWER HILL

There are no vacant spots in nature. There are no vacancies in the life of the world. The term "vacation" is misleading. Life and death, peace and war, joy and despair fill to the full the measures of time that intervene.

It is not my river, nor the bird, nor the tree, nor human event, nor personal incident that will occupy this after-vacation study. Rather let the Old Tower Hill itself send to you its message. For two months and more these many summers I have nestled in its bosom. Asleep and awake, in daylight and in darkness, through sunshine and moonshine, the "Hill" has ministered unto me. It is true that ever and anon the human forces which gathered at its feet and traversed its brow were rallied and precipitated in this interest and that. The human parasites have tried to do something for themselves, for others and for the hill. It has witnessed an output of mind and will, a manifestation of what we in our conceit call "civilization" on that hill[1], but the truth that stands out above all others is the truth that there was a force beyond and behind the human -- working upon human life -- and more mysterious than any conscious force that man could bring into action. In other words, the hill was more creative than its inhabitants; life revealed itself most persistently and abundantly in the sub-human and super-human forces at work on and around the Hill.

I would illustrate rather than state what I mean.

- - - - -

[1] In addition to merely vacationing, by this time Jones had begun a Summer School on Tower Hill that was to become an important institution by the time of his death.

THE REFORESTATION OF TOWER HILL

Our hill is not wanting in a human investment that is interesting. The story of its men and women, traceable through seventy years or more of mortal time[2] has its hidden wealth and pathos, its comment "on the world's seemings and realities".

Tower Hill is one of the countless bluffs moulded by the eroding fingers of the Wisconsin river which quietly flows at its base, two hundred feet below its summit. It was a landmark to the early navigator of the waterway, when the river was the highway of territorial commerce. Twenty miles to the southward lay the once-famous lead regions of Wisconsin. At that time Tower Hill was the "Shot-Tower Hill". Through its bold face was bored in 1836 the perpendicular shaft through which the molten lead was dropped into the water waiting below to fix the little spheres. A horizontal shaft carried the shot out into the daylight to the "finishing-house", from which they were loaded directly onto the boats that carried them to the St. Louis and other down-the-Mississippi markets. At that time Shot-Tower Hill had a commercial significance. Its value was rendered in terms of trade. Its sloping sides were early denuded of the stately pines for their lumber-making values. The houses of the operatives flecked its base, and the boys and girls of a thriving village made excursions to its summit to see the "works".

Then the railroad came and changed the commercial front of the country. The lead regions were exhausted. The thriving village vanished. The portable portions of the shot-tower plant were moved to Chicago and be-

- - - - - -

[2] Jones' niece, Jane Porter, wrote and produced an historical pageant on Tower Hill in 1927. The script is among the Jones' Papers at the Joseph Regenstein Library, University of Chicago.

came a part of the West Side shot tower. In a few years Helena, as the neighbors called the town, became less than a deserted village, and there was nothing left of the shot tower but the holes in the bluff. The hill became waste land not worth the taxes. It was exposed to the annual or semi-annual devastations of fire. It became the unfenced land that was the rendez-vous of the tramp steers, the vagrant sheep and the long-nosed pigs that belonged to that far-off primitive farming when hogs had to root for their own living. It became the abandoned lot, marked with blackened stumps and tangled briar. Here the barren sand was seamed with irregular cow paths lined in the autumn months with the formidable sand burr which the Agricultural Department at Washington cited in one of its Yearbooks classed among "the twenty-five most harmful weeds", and which science well calls the <u>Genchrus Tribuloides</u>, for who has ever come within touch of its insolent familiarity and not known tribulation? So utterly abandoned, unprofitable and disreputable had this hill become that the neighbors of that countryside smiled a sickly smile of sympathy for the city parson who wasted even the little money required to secure a tax title to the worthless, apparently fruitless and abandoned, sun-burned hill. The sickly smile gave way to an open laugh when around and upon this tax title, three parsons proposed to organize the Tower Hill Pleasure Company and to make it a retreat for the tired, a resting place to weary nerves, a shelter to the footsore travellers on the pilgrimage of life.

This was in 1890. During the next eight years the old village was again re-platted; cottages, dining-hall, pavilion, "long-houses", ice house and snow white tents rapidly took possession of the hillslope. Through the shaft where once the molten lead dropped on its way to murder, the wind now lifts the purest of water from the cool heart of the Potsdam sandstone, the earliest of stratified rocks, close to the granite backbone of the pre-Adamic island.[3] The fresh water is deposited in a rock-ribbed reservoir on the top of the hill and distributed through hydrants that almost justify the urban title of "waterworks".

During these eight years there was some unsystematic tree planting. A few score of elms and maples, birch and basswood planted by men's hands are getting a start. There has been some seed-sowing and a little sprinkling in midsummer, some planting of flowers, but the planted trees were slow in starting, the so-called cultivated flowers for want of early tending were often sickly, and still the hill even to those who knew it in its fallen estate promptly became confessedly pretty; and to the learned eye it grew increasingly beautiful.

After eight years of occupancy -- at the time of this study -- it has become, as the horticulturist tells us, a marvellous nursery of forest trees. Its breast is matted with baby oaks, maples and ash. Thousands of little pines -- two, three, four years old -- are pushing their evergreen spires upward on the very places where their fore-elders fell in their majesty before the devastating ax of man, half a century and more ago. Now, where the graceless <u>Tribuloides</u> held their burrs in waiting to throw the city matron off her dignity, little children roll on the white clover

-----

[3] The next sentence disrupts the sequence of thought and has been omitted. It reads: "The 'Old Hill' deserves the name for it is the part of geologic Wisconsin which was the first to lift its head above the ocean wastes in all of what is now the Mississippi Valley."

swards, and the neighborly farmers, cordially rejoicing in the truth, tell us of the wonderful change we have wrought on Tower Hill. Change there has been, but the interest culminates in the inquiry, "What has brought about this change?" The point of this chapter will be found in the attempt to answer this question.

The seeding, the planting and the sprinkling are but small, insignificant and relatively unnecessary elements in the change. The great thing that was done for the hill on the human side was the mere negative work of throwing a barbed-wire fence around the seventy acres to keep out the denuding hordes of cattle, the browsing sheep and the rooting hogs, and to give it that protection which for eight years has saved the hill from the annual holocaust of devastating fires. In other words, we simply defended the hill from human interference, and nature was allowed to do her work. The cottagers have planted a few vines and they are doing well. They may boast of their morning glories and summon men and women to the early revelations, but nature has twined her trees with ivy, groined forest arches with the grape vine and interwoven the whole hill-slope with the magic tracery of twisted and climbing things -- the delicacy of whose foliage and the grace of whose drapings enhance and interpret the high achievements of the women-trained vines in their grace and glory. The women have done best when they have taken counsel of the hills and have re-planted only what nature has already planted there. They have been somewhat successful with the nasturtium, and the geraniums have been faithful as they are everywhere to human guidings, but the hill itself has grown, to the delight of its dwellers, great wealths of columbine and painted cup, spider wort and milk weed, scouring rush and

THE REFORESTATION OF TOWER HILL   145

purple vetch, lobelia and cardinal flower. Tower Hill has a garden which does splendidly with its parsnips, carrots and cabbages, its peas, its beans and its melon -- as the boarders gladly testify, but the hill grew, without the gardener's touch, catnip and spearmint, smartweed and boneset. It had its ornamental shrubbery in the way of button bush, spirea and silver weed. Man had but to keep down the fires, keep out his cattle, and then the hill gave to him harebell and evening primrose, sunflower, gerardia, marguerites and half a hundred other plants that need only rarity to make them the pride of the florist as they are already the joy of the botanist. We kept the fires off the hill and junipers matted the hillslopes with their evergreen saucers thirty feet in diameter and five feet high at the rim. Gracious cedars confidently lift their little heads in front of our cottage doors. Their tops now range from the height of a child's knee to the level of a man's eye; they have started out on the patient growth that will see them a hundred years from now, if allowed to grow unmolested, become the stalwart elders of the forest. If man keeps his fire out and protects them from the browsing goat and his kind until they are strong enough to take care of themselves, they will rise to the dignity of the cedars of Lebanon.

Seated in front of Westhope cottage, I counted one day within distinguishing range of the eye -- a radius of perhaps sixty feet -- a variety of thirty different plants and grasses without including the trees and cultivated varieties. Whence comes this fertility, this splendid fecundity even of an abandoned hill?

The first answer is a most comforting one. This much at least we are sure of, that most of them --

lovely plants and gracious trees -- were not man-sown. Nature is fecund from the center to circumference. Every yard of earth, every cubic foot of air, and every pint of water is full of undeveloped possibilities -- a mighty storehouse of living germs impregnate with life. Give any one of them a chance, keep out the devastating forces, and lo, they burst into life. Potential forests slumber in the close-cropped pasture lots. The abandoned hillslope of which you can secure possession with a tax title is in possibility a great arboretum where the student of trees may revel in lore, independent of college or professor. One of the Vanderbilts has made himself a benefactor to his state by setting apart Biltmore, his great forest park near Asheville, North Carolina, for a school in forestry, whither the young men of the nation may go and prepare themselves for the rising profession of forestry. But there lies a possibility of a Biltmore, a school in forestry, anywhere -- on any of the bluff sides of Wisconsin, in any of the hollows and pockets formed by the tributaries of the upper Mississippi, if only the fires were kept off and nature were given a chance.[4]

This fecundity of nature, this tendency of old Mother Earth to reclothe herself in becoming habiliments, is of an immense economic significance which the governments of the world are all too slowly realizing.

Forestry is as I have said a growing term in economics, engaging more and more the attention of statesmen and scientists. Our country is beginning to waken up to the fact that it must take warning and instruction from the older countries of Europe and

- - - - -

[4] Jones' widow donated Tower Hill to Wisconsin for a State Park in 1927.

THE REFORESTATION OF TOWER HILL 147

protect its forests. The department at Washington estimates that the existing supply of timber would be exhausted in sixty years, but that forests may grow into fuel-supplying size in fifteen to twenty-five years and into timber-yielding dimensions in from seventy-five to a hundred years. Much has been written concerning tree planting. J. Sterling Morton, Secretary of Agriculture under President Cleveland, won for himself sure fame and national immortality in establishing Arbor Day and giving to Nebraska the name of "The Tree Planting State". But it is quite apparent now to the student that the production of forests is not so much dependent on artificial planting as it is on the protection of nature's planting. Much of the semi-desert country of the East, including all of Palestine and much of Turkey, simply awaits the protecting, not the producing, hand of man. The far-seeing legislators of Wisconsin, Michigan and Minnesota have long tried to devise some method by which the State can re-possess itself of the pinelands which once seemed to have been rendered worthless by the denudation of their forests. Now it is clearly seen how short-sighted was the State that sold the land instead of selling the timber on the land. If it had only held its right to the realty, the great grand-children of the proud pine barons, made rich by appropriating to private uses the great public providence deposited in the forests of earth, might again reap another golden harvest, if indeed the State had not meanwhile learned the lesson that forbids it to sign away for a nominal consideration the great natural bounties of God that constitute the natural wealth of all the people.

But I have not called attention to this nature triumph on Tower Hill in order to point an economic lesson, though surely there is here a profound lesson for the economist and the legislator. I have told the story chiefly for its spiritual significance. The reforestation of Tower Hill teaches a lesson as true of soul fields as of physical fields. Children's lives are often desecrated by the wanton hands that destroy the tree-growths in their infancy. Hearts are devastated by the consuming fires of passion in its many forms. Minds are prostituted by the interfering and intrusive hands of others.

This parable of Tower Hill leads us to some very subtle and sober problems in child rearing, character making, home planting. Something can be done in the planting of seeds, in the cultivation of exotics, in producing what might be called a man-made crop in the fields of the spirit. To this end we establish schools, lectureships and churches. To this end we organize classes and clubs. All this is very well. Let the good work continue. But there is a higher work in protecting the seeds planted deep in the constitutions of our children by an unrecorded ancestry. Our greatest work is to keep out the fires, protect the tender buds while they are still tender, nurture them until they become self-reliant and self-assertive forces in the spiritual realm. A vagrant goat may nip off the terminal bud from the pine seedling when it is but a foot above the ground, and the tapering axis that would have climbed straight as an arrow eighty or a hundred feet into the air, is made forever impossible. It may grow, but it will be through lateral branches. It will be forever a crooked tree. "Just one pebble at the root mars the straightness of the Pine."

So it is in the life of the child, in your life and mine. Our highest concern should not be to fill our minds with transplanted growths, but to protect and bring to completion the germs that are already planted there. The splendid fecundity of Tower Hill, never noted for its fertility, is a symbol of every soul. There are possibilities within all of us that we ourselves know not of. The germs of pine and oak lie slumbering in our souls. Give them but a chance, keep off the fires -- the distracting interferences, and in ways we know not and in times we dream not these germs will venture into life, climb into vigor and become in God's own good time mighty towers of strength and beauty.

Darwin in the later years of his life bemoaned the fact that in the absorbing studies of his mature years he had neglected poetry and music, and had thereby lost to a great extent his power of enjoying them. But Darwin himself was at the very time making poetry for the generations that followed, gathering material that is convertible into song and into literature and morals as well as into science. He needed but to give his soul a chance, secure for it a little leisure, build around it a little fence to keep out the intrusive studies and the carking cares, and the song-seed and the poetry-germs lying dormant there would have been promptly quickened and have burst into life in due time to bloom and bear fruit.

John Stuart Mill, the tireless philosopher, came to a period of soul barrenness, a time when the world seemed to him flat and unprofitable and his heart was depressed within him. This fell spell was broken when one day he discovered himself weeping over the sorrows of an imaginary heroine described in a work of fiction. The seed was there; all it needed was the opportunity, the favorable condition, the quickening circumstance.

Have you a child that seems to have grown indifferent to the holy things of life, blasé to the sanctities, stolid in the presence of the duties and the beauties of being? Study the case carefully and you will probably find that the soul-field of the child has been invaded by outside influences and interferences. It has been burned over by the passion of publicity, idle curiosity and social sensation. Try to retire it; throw a fence around it, protect it from these wild and shallow dissipations, and the process of reforestation will promptly follow. A skillful mother argued the other day that any child taken young enough could be made a good child. Yes, perhaps, under the protecting guardianship of such a mother. Not what you teach your child, not what you do for it, but what the child is allowed to do for itself, particularly the life it is allowed to live by itself and of itself, is of most importance. Said the experienced forester to the Tower Hill directors, "Let the hill alone. Cut no underbrush. Let the matted thickness be. Let the fallen leaves decay where they fall. They hold the moisture, retain the snow, shelter from the scorching sun, and trees will grow thus fostered that would otherwise die under your cultivation."

I would not push my illustration too far, but I do believe that there are boys and girls all around us whose souls are withered and dry and growing barren from over-interference under the name of "cultivation". The Nebraska tree-planters have found that their pines grow better when planted thick, and that the best results are secured when the young conifers are furnished with nurse trees -- quick-growing deciduous trees planted between the rows. The rapid-growing locust or soft maple nurse in their youth the baby pines that will outreach and outlive their foster mothers.

THE REFORESTATION OF TOWER HILL 151

Let us take the problem a little deeper into life. Here is the man to whom business is a necessity and to whom books are a burden, a man whose life is expressed in figures, market quotations and percentages. Once that man loved poetry, once he was genial company, once he could sing, had an eye for flowers and time for music. Are all these forces driven from the soul? No. He is a case for re-forestation. Keep out the fires and keep off for a while the browsing quadrupeds, and nature out of her abundant breast will again send forth a new mantle of green -- a new output of spiritual vegetation.

Our hill has a lesson for communities as well as individuals. Here perhaps we discover the philosophy of so-called protective legislation. What did the wise founders of the village of Hyde Park[5] do for us? With what great spiritual advantage did this territory come within the city limits of Chicago? What is meant by the "prohibitory district"? Simply a barbed wire fence which kept out, and still keeps out, the devastating fires, the consuming and denuding conflagrations of inebriety.

What is the church in its best estate? A place where souls may find shelter, may flee from the impoverishing and drying distractions of the world, where the heart may sequester itself and give to the germs of goodness slumbering in the seed a chance.

In conclusion, then, the sum of it all is that the potencies of life are abundant. Nature's resources are exhaustless. It is the province of the economist and the moralist not to create but to protect and

- - - - -

[5] Hyde Park is now a section in South Chicago, adjacent to the University of Chicago. All Souls Church was located near its boundaries.

direct this mighty power not ourselves, that makes for beauty and righteousness, for truth and duty. It is the province of the church, the school and the state to enter into co-operation with these mighty forces which are always lifting and always pushing. From beneath comes the mighty ground swell of progress. Out of the unseen, the intangible burst the revelations of the eternal. The big cities are devastated with greed and passion, the prairie fires of ambition and speculation.

The largest function of the church is to become a quickening power among men and women whose hearts are dried out, whose brains have been scorched with selfishness and outwardness, to make a Tower Hill of the spirit, a camping ground of the soul, a playground of the mind, a place where children will be restored to childlike simplicity, where men and women will be renewed in their domestic loyalties, their fireside enjoyments, the neighborly helpfulness -- where citizens will be snatched from the blistering winds of partisanship, carried from the arid sand beds of prejudice and distrust to be revived in the gracious shades of principle under the protecting limbs and the leafy bowers of dis-interested loyalties, international sympathies, cosmopolitan enthusiasms, and humanitarian devotions.

There is work for all of us to do -- for the children whom we inadequately control, for the lovers who imperfectly love, for the fathers and mothers who are raising orphaned children in the very laps of those who gave them being, because neither parent nor children have touched the soul-depths or quickened the soul-germs that God has planted there. Oh, there is work for us to do. Not to import into this garden of

THE REFORESTATION OF TOWER HILL   153

the Lord any delicate exotics, not to transplant the doubtful growth of other climes, but to develop what is already planted here, to uncoil the forces that have been coiled by the hands of the Infinite in our souls and to let the springs of action loose so that we may become as individuals and as citizens, co-workers, protectors and exponents of that

>   Energy that searches thorough
>   From Chaos to the dawning morrow
>   Into all our human plight,
>   The soul's pilgrimage and flight;
>   In city or in solitude,
>   Step by step lifts bad to good,
>   Without halting, without rest,
>   Lifting Better up to Best;
>   Planting seeds of knowledge pure,
>   Through earth to ripen, through heaven endure.[6]

- - - - -

[6] Taken from the poem "May Day" by Emerson.

X

This companion sermon to the previous one on Tower Hill was likewise an after-vacation sermon. The original manuscript is missing, but was probably preached in mid-September 1916. It was printed in <u>Unity</u> on 28 September.

The optimism of The Tower Hill sermon of 1895 is tempered by the experiences of his years, the viewpoint of a man in his seventies and the shadow of The Great War. The confidence in life and humanity is still present, but the negative side is more clearly seen and a critical tone dominates.

For Jones, this is a short sermon. He narrates the story which is his "text" in fairly brief terms and confines himself to drawing a single "lesson". As a consequence, the sermon is more unified and easier to follow than most of the others in this collection.

No poem is indicated to preface this sermon.

TOWER HILL TWENTY YEARS LATER

Twenty years ago I told the story of the re-forestation of Tower Hill. It was the story of how a fire-swept, ragged, torn and apparently barren hill had been reforested through human care, enterprise and devotion. It was a story of sowing and planting, a story to stimulate thought for it showed that even the barren fields of earth may be made to bloom as a garden - that roses may take the places of thistles and apples supplant the briar bush. It was a real story, taken out of real life.

Now I have a story not so in line with our ambitions and our energies. Nature at Tower Hill has responded all too willingly to the human care there bestowed. At the end of twenty years the twig we planted has become a sapling, and the sapling has become a tree. The seedling we held in one hand while we pressed the hospitable soil around the tender rootlets with the other has grown into umbrageous proportions, and we sit in the shade thereof.

The score of years has brought another problem to Tower Hill - the problem of <u>de</u>-forestation. For, alas, the trees have grown so as to obstruct the views they were to embellish; they blur the picture they were meant to enframe. Many of them are engaged in profitless battles with one another. The once sun-blistered side of Tower Hill has become over-crowded and over-shaded.

"Re-forestation" - the reclamation of this bit of waste land - was my theme twenty years ago. A study of the Tower Hill of today brings to us two or three very suggestive parables of the better life. Emerson says, "The laws above are twin sisters to the laws below." Surely the conditions of good tillage, the law of the garden and the park in the end become the law of society, the condition of the higher life.

The first lesson that comes to us through this Tower Hill experience is that we planted not well when we devoted ourselves to the short-lived products of nature. Throughout the West we have been too greedy for quick returns from the soil. The prairie folks were too impatient in their hunger for trees. Travel anywhere through our prairie country and you will see hundreds of miles of ragged wayside where the Lombardy poplar and the locust have served their day and have fallen into decay, giving us dishevelled streets and bedraggled roadways. The "box alder", as we call them in Wisconsin, was the favorite of the early farmer because he was told it would grow rapidly. Many farmers undertook to make windbreaks out of soft maples, locusts and "alders", which matured in fifteen years and became ragged in twenty.

It is appalling that we still spend our days in nursing annuals where perennials might grow. Poppies may decorate the lawn for the summer, but roses abide for many summers. Tower Hill now needs the woodman's axe to remove the transient, unenduring products which nature has given in response to our unwise planting.

In the second place we find that planting was overdone. We were too distrustful of nature; we planted too thickly. The trees are interfering with one another. A once-symmetrical clump of evergreens planted at the foot of the Hill has become a tangle, and we have not yet had fortitude enough to cut down half the pines and cedars in order to give the other half a chance to come into their full beauty. In the little sixty-foot triangle just south of Westhope Cottage there grows today a promising basswood, a beautiful pine, an elm, an ironwood, an apple tree and an oak - three out of the six hand-planted. There is room for only one or two of those trees to come to their maximum glory. The hand that planted in the days of dreariness reckoned not on the expanding power of a noble tree. But as yet we have not had the hardihood to use the axe. So the trees are left to quarrel with one another and eventually to disfigure one another. Every day on my way down the hill, I pass what is otherwise a splendid elm, but it is lopsided, imperfect, and it will remain so through a long life, accusing the forester who permitted in its younger days an oak - scrub oak at that - to mar the symmetry of the elm to which nature would have given maternal arms graced with beauty and charged with hospitality. To destroy that which you planted, to clear the earth of the tangle you invited, in the interest of the larger beauty, the permanent growth, is a task reluctantly undertaken.

Time was, on Tower Hill, when we delighted in anything that covered the barrenness of the hillside. Clumps of hazel bushes, dogwood, sumach and prickly ash sprang up as if by magic to hide the nakedness, and we delighted in them. But sumach, prickly ash, dogwood and hazel bushes have been compelled to retire through the supremacy of the trees that have claimed the ground. Weeds have given way to grass and grass breeds into fragrant white clover.

This, then, is the lesson from Tower Hill. Deforestation is often necessary in the interest of a better forestation. Cut out the underbrush; cease cultivating annuals where perennials are needed.

The analogies in human lives are evident. Our homes are bordered with ragged poplars and wayward locusts which defeat the possibilities of elms and maples and stately oaks. But God cannot make such trees for us if they are planted too thickly. His creative energy is thwarted by too much and too cheap interference.

In our early enthusiasms we planted on Tower Hill some apple trees among the native tree growths. For many years I have watched one of these, over-shadowed by larger trees on either side, defy its culture-habit and push itself upward and upward and upward toward the sunlight until it became a slim, aspiring, but deformed, tree. A few years ago one of these overshadowing trees had to come down, thus giving the apple tree for the first time a chance at the sun. The next year it flushed pink and reddened into the luscious apples nature meant it to bear.

How many apple trees do we plant in the shadow of growths less fruitful and subject to destinies less noble! How much first-class enthusiasm is given to secondary causes; how much high effort is bestowed on low issues; how many lives are wasting their energies in tending to the fleeting gardens on the hillsides of society.

The question of what to cut out is an important question in forestry. It is as vital a question in life. In mathematics we arrive most promptly at the equation by a process of cancellation. Throw out the unnecessary factors and the problem becomes simple. Achievement often comes through elimination. The larger and permanent issues – the cause of woman, of sobriety, of industrial justice, of peace – are not best served by the transitory undergrowths of human organization nourished out of hasty enthusiasms.

The question of deforestation is not simply a question of elm versus locust, or pines versus Lombardy poplars. There is something even better than a noble tree in your front yard. It was meant to harmonize with the view not to interfere with it, to enframe the picture not to blur it. On Tower Hill, as I have already said, the axman alone can save many of our finest views.

Many years ago, "Aunt Mary" used to send me the juicy plums from her favorite trees. I ate the plums and threw the pits onto the hillside. The pits I threw away grew and flourished. Year after year I watched the appearance and growth of these seedlings. At last they rewarded me with a few not-very-luscious plums. But those scrub plum trees have screened my view. Twenty-five years ago I put my bed on stilts that I might command the river view as I rested, but Aunt Mary's plum trees have hidden the bridge, and I must henceforth sleep behind the screen of plum trees, unless I sacrifice the plums in the interest of the view. What shall I do? I have not cut down the plum trees yet, but my judgement tells me they ought to go. I should let no near growth, however interesting, interfere with the view, the farther prospect. Beyond the trees is the horizon line touched with beauty by the rising sun, reflecting the glory of the departing day, promising continued life, the life of the day to come and the life that is ever beyond the farthest reach of human vision.

The question of forestation is interesting to the scientist and of great importance to the economist. Through the slow, struggling millenia nature found the way of cushioning the rugged rocks with fertile soil, padding the hillside with grass, shading the valleys with trees, making the world a possible home for man that, despite his weak fingers and unshod feet, he might by his wits utilize the resources of nature and enhance its beauty.

Following the forestation by nature came the deforestation by human nature. Pineries were spoiled;

the forests were denuded; the fields were robbed of their fertility by the wanton hands of man, and a second nakedness ensued. Then man took thought and realized that he must economize the bounty of God if he would live in a bountiful universe, and he began re-foresting.

Now it has come to pass that this re-forestation demands a second de-forestation that the view be not interfered with, the vision be not blurred, and that souls be not cramped, even within the walls of beauty. Life must not be thwarted, even by good causes, when the great fundamental causes of love, of life, of human freedom are at stake. Good trees must often be sacrificed if life reaches its fullest power and highest beauty.

Dare we devote ourselves to this high work of de-foresting our lives – cutting out the underbrush, that room may be given for the elms and oaks and pines. Nay, if need be, to cut down some of these great trees that the far view may be preserved, that the hilltops of God may still allure?

I have glorified the tree. I have exalted the elm over the poplar. But there are things and issues far greater than trees. There are times when the best trees must come down in order that the soul may not be hemmed in. The call is for high endeavour along lines where life is tested not by things done, not by majorities, not by achievements, but by the largeness of life and freedom of spirit which alone give glory to the city, beauty to the home or peace to the soul.

Gray hairs are a reproach, tottering limbs are a disgrace if they bring halting courage, waning enthusiasm, lost faith in things intangible -- a missing of the uplift that comes only from the hills of the Lord.

Yet there is an old age possible to all of us that is ripeness not decay, maturity not tracked from the great highways of God, who have not wasted life's most precious oil on incidental things.

The church, if it stands for anything, stands for the far-horizon view. It stands for the glory of the hill-top. If the place of prayer is to be of any service to human souls, it is because with its help they can at least occasionally climb towards the top of the hill where they may catch again the glory of the longer horizon that reaches across the centuries, the view that takes in the continents, the mountains of God, made resplendent with the words and lives of the world's saints and sages. Is the cause of untrammeled fellowship, the cause of free inquiry and open comradeship, to be made subordinate to little things which occupy the front of the stage today but will be forgotten tomorrow?[1] Noble is the height from which we catch a view of the mountain peaks of humanity - Confucius and Zoroaster, Socrates and Buddha and, chiefest of all, the carpenter's son who climbed from the Nazareth valley to the Calvary heights.

Indeed, we have many "chores" to do! There is "work" to be done - much of it. But not at the cost of the hunger of the mind or of the life of the soul. I resent the implication that the church is chiefly an "institution" for human benefactions. The words "Settlement" and "Center" carry with them great connotations, but they also carry with them great dangers, for they may bring weakness and not strength, into the

- - - - -

[1] This sentence seems to refer to the schism in the Western Unitarian Conference which had taken place 34 years earlier. Even though this was a crucial event in Jones' life, it is somewhat out of character that he is still fighting a long-finished battle.

lives they would serve. Unless through all our bread-doling helpfulness and hand-directing activities, there stream great floods of thought and life, of science and poetry, we have misdirected high energies to ineffectual activities. The golden key of conservation is discrimination between things more important and things less important. There is a spiritual economy as well as a physical economy. "Seek ye first the Kingdom of Heaven and all these things shall be added unto you."

Reform? Yes. But formation is better than reformation, and the highest task of the church is to render the reformation unnecessary by never allowing life to degenerate into selfishness, weakness or the fruitless indolence of unthrifty activities, the wasting of prime energies on secondary causes.

Heaven help our age in this high task of deforesting the Tower Hills of religion and morals when deforestation is necessary to promote the continued growth of perennials, to preserve the heavenly vision without which life is stale, flat and unprofitable.

XI

In "Road Making", the fifth of the series written for Hoard's Dairyman, Jones returns to the history of technology for his subject. The origin and development of roads and the situation of roads in 1917 are given about equal importance. He has very little need to draw any "lessons" from the material. Roads themselves and the effect of good roads on rural communities are quite "religious" subjects to Jones. The sermon comes to be a plea for highway development.

This is one instance where his challenge to action was really fulfilled by posterity. So much is this true that it takes an exercise of imagination to see the problem he was addressing.

Jones takes the familiar passage from Isaiah as a text and treats it on an unfamiliarly prosaic level. When Isaiah speaks of highways, Jones takes him at face value.

The poem to preface this sermon was to be Walt Whitman's "Song of the Open Road". The poem is too long to be used in full, but he gives no hint as to which part he meant to use.

"Road Making" was first preached at All Souls on 13 June 1909. It saw print in Hoard's in two parts, 20 and 27 May 1910.

ROAD MAKING

> Prepare ye in the wilderness the way of Jehovah; make level in the desert a highway for our God
>
> Isaiah 40:3

> The voice of one crying in the wilderness, Prepare ye the way of the Lord, make his paths straight
>
> Mark 1:3

These words first quoted from a then-ancient prophet were seized upon by the grim reformer of the Jordan as the slogan of a new revival which was to usher in the mightiest religious movement known in history.

Judaism had run to seed; her prophets had been largely overlaid by her priests; the free inspiration of her bards and civic leaders had been supplanted by the formal requirements of the law, the formulas of the ritual.

Clearly, in the mouth of John the Baptizer this cry of a prophet, as far away from him in point of time as St. Francis is from us, was high symbolism. It was to John a parable of the spiritual life. He would build a highway through the social realms, leading to the goal of spiritual awakening, civic righteousness and religious reform.

But it is altogether likely that the great unknown prophet of the Captivity -- the comforter of exiles, the psalm-singer of monotheism to the disconsolate children of Israel who had "hung their harps on the willow trees" by the rivers of Babylon, finding it impossible to sing the songs of faith in a strange land -- had his eye fixed on far-off Jerusalem. He may have been thinking of the sandy stretches, the rugged mountain passes, the trackless wilderness that lay between the exiled colony and their home-land, six hundred or more miles away.

This brave bard had fixed his prophetic heart on a return and his call was, as it were, to a road-making band. "Repair the trail, make level in the desert a highway for the people of Jehovah, a great broad road for our God!" was his cry. In his high confidence in the future, his abiding faith in God, he saw the valleys exalted, the mountains and hills made low, rough places made plain, in order the "the glory of Jehovah might be revealed and all flesh see it together".

What to John, the hermit preacher of the Jordan wilderness, seemed pure rhapsody, a celestial vision of the kingdom to come, may, in the mouth of the more accomplished statesman of the Captivity, have been a problem of statecraft -- a political issue, a question to be discussed by "The Department of the Interior", as a passage over the Rockies or a deep waterway from lake to gulf has engaged the attention of the far-seeing statesmen of the United States.

Be this as it may, we know from other sources that just this problem did engage the State Department in that far-off time and country. We do know that Cyrus, under whose more liberal administration the captives were allowed to return to the homeland, was a road-maker, a guardian of highways, a patron of commerce. Indeed, commerce is possible only where roads are, and its extent and quality are determined by the facilities of transportation.

Prof. N.S. Shaler, in his interesting work on <u>American Highways</u>, finds in the "pack train" the first step out of the savage stage. He tells us that "more than half the inhabited world is still, as regards its transportation, in the pack train state". Asses, camels, elephants, oxen, mules and horses still carry, largely as of old, the traffic between tribes that are too low or too indolent to make the roads over which wheeled wagons may travel.

Professor Shaler thinks that the first advance beyond the packing stage was made in the regions around the Mediterranean about ten centuries before the Christian era, and that

> the initial step towards the wheeled vehicle was attained in the hard task of moving on rollers the large blocks of stone necessary to the construction of the great pyramids in the Nile Valley.[1]

He is inclined to think that the Romans were the first road builders on any extensive scale, and that the great Appian Way, built about 300 B.C., represents their high triumphs in this direction.

Emerson describes a western road as beginning in a broad highway, narrowing into a wagon track, again narrowing into a cow path, which ultimately narrows into a squirrel track and runs up a tree.

The beginning of the road is as obscure as its ending. Away back in the dim twilight of history, the nomad tracked his game, left behind him his trail, which ripened into a by-path over which the woman - the wife, the weaver, the home maker - laboriously carried her faggots and led home her cow. In many instances

− − − − −

[1] Nathaniel Shaler, <u>American Highways</u> (New York: The Century Co., 1896), <u>p 3</u>.

ROAD MAKING

the cow was the early surveyor. Her zigzag route up the mountain side was the overcoming of altitudes which finally culminated in the switchbacks that enable the locomotives to haul transcontinental trains over mountain ranges.

L.W. Page, in his article on "Roads", in the Cyclopedia of American Agriculture[2], carries the pyramid-building roads back at least to 4000 B.C.. He quotes Herodotus' account of King Cheops employing one hundred thousand men for a period of ten years on the way leading from the great pyramid to Memphis, a paved highway lined with temples, mausoleums, porticoes and statues.

Strabo says that the streets of Babylon were paved two thousand years before Christ, and that great thoroughfares radiated from Memphis to Suza, Ecbatana and Sardis. Herodotus tells of a great royal road three hundred and twelve miles long, from Suza to Sardis, with little stations from eighteen to twenty-five miles apart, where the carriers could change mounts as they made from sixty to one hundred miles a day. The books tell us that asphalt was used for pavement in Babylon as early as 2000 B.C.. We know that Carthage reached and held her supremacy by virtue of her military roads. When at last Rome, her fatal rival, rose into power it was because she had become the great road-maker in history. Under the sagacious direction of her great road masters, the predictions of Israel's prophet were literally fulfilled; the valleys were exalted, the mountains were made low, the uneven places level, and the rough places plain.

Mr. Page tells us further that no less than

- - - - -

[2] "Roads and Canals", Vol. IV, Chapter 7.

twenty-nine great military highways radiated from Rome in its supremacy; she caused thirty-two thousand miles of improved roads to be built in Gaul and twenty-five hundred miles in Britain. Roman military roads crossed the Alps and penetrated into Gaul, Spain, Austria and the regions of the Danube. Even Africa and Asia were included in its great highway system. So skillful were these road-makers that the Appian Way, constructed three hundred and twelve years before Christ, was in good repair eight hundred years after its construction. It well deserves its title of "Queen of Roads". It was estimated that to construct that way even under conditions prevailing before the present war prices, would cost two hundred thousand dollars per mile. The three hundred and seventy-two great roads which traversed the one hundred and thirteen provinces of Rome, totalling a length of fifty thousand miles, would have cost under modern conditions some five billion dollars.

The story of the rise of modern France is the story of road-making. In 1661 it had fifteen thousand miles of hard roads constructed. The rise of England into power is again the story of road-making. Historians dwell upon the impassable character of English roads during the dark and trying days of the seventeenth century. The first way out of its muddy depression was by private enterprise. In the first seventy years of the eighteenth century five hundred and thirty Turn-Pike Acts were passed, permitting private capitalists to construct toll roads. As late as 1840 England and Wales had 104,772 miles of turnpike, the travel upon which necessitated such burdensome toll-paying that armed mobs of discontented peasants arose to destroy the toll gates. As late as 1870 we are told that five thousand persons were engaged in the mere task of collecting tolls on the highways of England, Wales and Scotland.

Were we not so close to it, we should see that the story of roads in these United States is as full of romantic as it is of economic interest. The deer tracks, the buffalo runs, the blazed trees of the Indian and the pioneer, the logway, the corduroy road and the all-too-few military roads built by the national government lie beneath our city streets and connect our farms. They lead to, or parallel, the transcontinental railroad lines. Boston is not the only city whose streets are but the improved calf-paths of pioneer villages. It took much courage and time before the pioneers of the West dared turn their backs on the waterways. The main streets of the pioneer villages fronted the rivers of the West, which have, in the change of front, too often become the unseemly dumping places that disfigure the back yards of our western river towns, menacing health and offending the eyes and noses of the inhabitants.

In 1892 the "Office of Inquiry" was established by the Department of Agriculture at Washington, and an appropriation of ten thousand dollars per annum made for the purpose of investigating the conditions, management and best methods of constructing roads. Now the office of Public Roads at Washington employs a force of nearly one hundred thousand men, making an annual expenditure of over five million dollars. Its bulletins, published from time to time, contain much material that will interest the historian, the poet, the sociologist and the moralist, as well as the pathmasters, road commissioners and contractors.

I would rather interpret the Bible texts quoted above from the standpoint of the later Isaiah than from that of John the Baptist. If our business men, legislators and voters could only be adequately impressed with the tremendous economic importance of good roads, if they could only realize the awful waste, not only of horse flesh but of man flesh, the profitless exhaustion of human nerve, muscle and brain incident to our neglect of the primal political economy of the highway, much of our present fuss over tariffs, corporations, railways, waterways, banking laws, even our concern for the educational and religious interests of our communities, urban and rural, would pass away. Many of our blustering reforms sink into insignificance compared with the primal importance of roadmaking -- just plain wagon roads at that.

Roads constitute the primal commonwealth of the community. Upon them rests the fundamental claim and right of "eminent domain" of the common law. How vast is the public estate represented by our highways! The Secretary of Agriculture in his report for 1917 shows that the public roads of the United States would encircle the globe at the equator with ninety parallel lines. In other words, there are 2,455,761 miles of road in the United States. Of these in 1917, 287,000 miles, or 11.6 per cent, were surfaced roads. The surfaced roads are now increasing at the rate of 15,000 miles per annum. In 1904 eighty million dollars had been expended upon these roads. It is estimated that there is now expended in the United States anywhere from $200,000,000 to $250,000,000 annually on roads. In 1916 $272,634,424 were spent on rural roads and bridges, exclusive of the value of the convict labor employed (estimated at $15,000,000 additional).

In 1904 the average haul to the station of all the railroad freightage of the United States was nine miles; the average cost was estimated as 25 cents per ton for each mile. The cost of hauling the same over a good broken-stone road would be but eight cents per ton per mile, while on earth roads, containing ruts and mud, it would cost 39 cents per mile and on dry, sandy roads, 64 cents. It was claimed that if our roads were brought up to the standard of those in Germany, France and England there would be a saving of fifty-one million dollars per year in the hauling of the field crops of the United States to the stations. Mr. Page illustrates the burden of bad roads on the producer as follows:

> The mean charge for carrying wheat by steamship from New York to Liverpool, a distance of 3100 miles, is 3.8 cts. per bushel, which is 1.6 cts. less than the cost to the farmer to haul his wheat 9.4 miles from his farm to the neighboring station. As it is, much of his produce cannot be delivered over existing roads except at certain seasons of the year, while good roads would make the market available to him all the year round.[3]

Mr. Page further estimates the cost of bad roads in the wear and tear of teams and wagons. He numbers the mules and horses of the United States at 23,500,000 valued at $4,423,697,000. Six hundred thousand wagons are manufactured each year. He estimates that an improvement in the roads would readily add one year to

- - - - -

[3] Page, p 324.

the life of the wagon and save one-tenth of the feed of horses, to say nothing of the great gain in the value of lands incident to the improvement of roads. He tells us that Jackson county, Alabama, by constructing one hundred and twenty-five miles of macadam road, increased the price of its land from four dollars and eighty cents to ten and twelve dollars per acre.

Notwithstanding the advent of the automobile and the greatly improved roads of today, these figures offered ten years ago by Mr. Page have still great economic significance.

But the kingdom of God comes not by dollars and cents. It is poor teaching that is content with money figures. The moral law and the spiritual life rest on something more profound than the figures in a ledger, or even bread and butter and roast beef. The dollar and cents value of good roads is but a trifle in the problem. The isolation of the farmer, the monotony and drudgery, the listless and uninspiring quality of much of the life on the farm can be dissipated only by better roads. According to the Bureau at Washington, of the 95,647 miles of public roads in Illinois in 1917 only 13 per cent of the same, or 12,400 miles, had been improved. There were then 1.6 miles of road for every square mile of land, or one mile of road for every fifty-one inhabitants, but less than 2 miles of improved road for every six hundred and eight inhabitants. This left the bulk of the population of Illinois wallowing in mud from three to four months in the year. No wonder that Illinois politics still represent dirt-road civilization and that the legislative wagon is often stalled in mire.

Road-making is the first industry that ought to profit by the growth of the social instincts. There is cause to fear that this high interest is about the last to come into prominence in the co-operative life of the United States today. It has been estimated that from five to ten per cent of the country is in roads, while in the city thirty or more per cent of the land is in the streets, which are simply municipal roads. How much of public pride, spirit, anxiety and devotion should be centered upon this indisputable public territory!

Much of the making of and caring for roads, in many of our western states at least, has scarcely yet escaped from the method which made them too largely a matter of township management. Even the township was cut up into little patches with their "Pathmasters", who by courtesy are supposed to allow the farmers, as far as possible, to work out their road tax on that portion of the road connected directly with their own barnyards. Says Shaler:

> There is no situation in which the American workman makes so unsatisfactory an appearance as when he is endeavoring to do the least possible amount of labor which is to count as a day's work on the highways of his district.[4]

I well remember in my boyhood days that "working on the road" was regarded as a sort of picnic occasion. The men went late to their job and quit early; they took their well-filled dinner pails along and ate very leisurely. It was a gala day, filled with neighborhood gossip. This old feature in the forced labor system on the highway has come down to us from medieval France.

─────

[4] Shaler, <u>American Highways</u>, p 24.

"Corvee" represents the enforced labor which villeins were compelled to render to the landed barons.

In the force of stolid conservatism and more stupid indifference, the movement for better roads is making slow but sure headway. The township system is giving way to the County Commissioner of Roads, and state legislators are beginning to recognize the great opportunity of increasing the value of property and improving the life of the state by subsidizing not only railroads or ship canals, but common, plain highways. We read of the talk in Europe of "international commissioners of highways". The wagon road, the connecting link between neighbor and neighbor, is the last hope of democracy, the noblest asset of the commonwealth. In rural districts, the road is the incipient public park; it should readily become the joy of the humble, the playground, the shelter, the thing of beauty, fringing every farm and decorating every front yard. The right of way on the public road, by common consent as by common law, is accorded to the loaded team, while, by the same token, the public road is primarily the right of the common toiler, of the man on foot or in his lumber wagon, more than of the man in the automobile.

The line between public and private ownership is hard to draw. Where the right of the individual ends and that of the community begins is a problem which calls for careful science and high statesmanship. Here at least the line is clear; there can be no doubt as to the absolute right of the public to the highways of civilization. Private ownership may, under proper restrictions, assert itself in field, orchard or garden, but public ownership must be guarded with unwearying severity in the land set apart for the common travel of society, the meeting places and passing places of citizens.

Here we come upon a possible solution, at least for a time, of many of the vexed questions in politico-economics. The trail has given way to the wagon road; the wagon road has grown from a rutted track into a graveled, macadamized or paved highway. The old guide who carried the mail on his back, following the rivers and sleeping under the stars, gave way to the pony express; the pony express surrendered in the interest of the four-horse stage; the stage to the postal car; and now the farmer draws aside his horse to let the trolley go by, and the "honk" of the automobile clears the road for the United States mail.

The logic of the situation seems to point to the ultimate development of the public road, by the public, for the exclusive use and profit of the public in its highest as well as its simplest developments. The control by the public of everything that must serve the public through its highways, whether it be telegraph wires above or water-pipes beneath the surface, must never be relinquished to the uncertain and selfish grasp of individuals or private corporations. The old toll-gate road is abolished. The wisdom, economic necessity and public spirit that took possession of the private turnpike and converted it into a public highway must eventually, by the logic of the situation and the trend of civic science, first control and then own the elongations and amplifications of the highway that sends its burdens over the railed turnpikes, where the load is drawn by steam. It must also own the wires on which the messages of the people are sent and the apparatus by which they are flashed through the wireless air.

In these studies of the Gospel of the Farm I have tried to call your attention to the names of neglected heroes, the unhonoured civic conquerors. Jethro Tull, the hero of "horse-houghing" devices, Oliver, Deere and Parlin, perfectors of the plow, McCormick and his associates, perfectors of the reaper, are names that will be better known by the children of the last decade of the twentieth century than by those of the second. Among these neglected heroes, the real fathers of modern civilization, true prophets of developed society, will be found the name of John Louden Macadam, the Scotsman of Ayr, who in 1815 became Surveyor General of the roads of Bristol, and who in 1827 was made general surveyor of the roads of England. This man spent several thousand pounds of his own fortune, which, to the honor of England be it said, was ultimately returned by the magnanimity of the government which recognized the great value of his work. Macadam's name has passed into the dictionary as a common noun, and, in its adjective form, into most of the modern tongues of Europe. Most intelligent people know what we mean when we speak of a "macadamized" road, or the use of macadam in the making of roads. But these words suggest to most people only crushed stone, specially treated, for the making of roads. Few of these "intelligent" people know of the man who grappled with the problems of road-making in the spirit of modern knowledge with the inspiration of a scientist and the devotion of a patriot. His triumph is one more illustration of how great truths and simple and divine revelations are to be found in things lowly.

The Romans built their road beds in layers of massive stone, carefully hewn into symmetrical forms. Great stone flags were laid in successive layers and top-dressed with earth or smaller stones. The great discovery of Mr. Macadam was that small fragments of stone make the best road bed. The massive blocks, the pride of the Roman road maker, he crushed into fragments, the maximum weight of which he fixed at six ounces, rejecting all that were too large to pass through a two-and-a-half inch ring. The man sitting by the roadside with his little hammer, cracking stone, became a familiar figure in the English landscape, and is yet in evidence along the beautifully paved, hedge-guarded roads of England.

The old Romans paid the price of ignorance by doing the right thing in the wrong way. They accomplished their high ends in the hardest manner. Their idea of art and efficiency required that their roads should run straight through, over or under all obstacles. The modern man has learned to go around the hill, if possible to avoid the swamp and to make more lasting than Roman skill could, the roadbed out of the chips of the quarry and crushed rock. Macadam ushered in an era of dominion greater than that of Rome, but a dominion which -- like that of Rome -- will rest upon the highways of the nation.

June is largely the month for the road-repairing in the West. Strike out into the country anywhere during this sunny month and you will find men more or less diligently - perhaps I had better say more or less leisurely -- working on the roads, making them for the time being distressingly uncomfortable.

No one summons me to work out my poll tax on the road, so I offer this study as my contribution to the fundamental conditions of civilization. I will be content if it but contributes a little to fill up a single mud-hole or to level up an obstructing hollow. I see this problem of roads leading out into finer lives and higher communities; it leads directly into happier conditions for man and beast. I hope to see the public roads leading to railway stations all through this country of ours, with their parallel lines of wagon track, automobile track and trolley line, bordered on either side with stately shade trees, punctuated every four or five miles (according to Shaler's prophecy) with drinking fountains for man and beast.

Upon these highways of the people the selfish greed of individuals or vampire corporations will not be allowed to place a little finger of their giant hands which now sink the five digits deep into the purses of so many communities. Already the states have begun to recognize their duty and to assert their rights here; until now every state in the union provides some form of state aid to local communities.

Massachusetts and New York, and perhaps other states, pay by state tax one-half, Ohio one-fourth, Pennsylvania three-fourths of all the money invested in the development of state roads. Illinois furnishes to counties and townships crushed stone free, prepared at its state institutions, and in 1916 its state funds paid three and one-half millions out of the eleven millions expended on the Illinois roads. Virginia and other states offer free convict labour for such counties as will use it in improving its roads.

The wisdom of the Department of Agriculture of the Federal Government far outreaches the public spirit or the intelligence of its servants and its citizens. That the federal government appreciates the importance of the public road is proved by the fact that its legislation is constantly improving -- the last being necessarily the best. In 1916 the new Federal Road Act was passed appropriating seventy-five million dollars and directing the Secretary of Agriculture to cooperate with each state in road-construction. Obviously this is but a beginning. The five million dollars that were available in 1917 will be twenty-five million in 1921 under the provisions of this act, and this fund is doubled by state requirements. In addition to all this, one million dollars is appropriated annually to construct roads in the national forests, which, with the advent of the roads, will become national parks - resorts for the tired as well as for those who would exploit the timber and promote the economic interests.

Surely there is a gospel to be found, not only by the road-side but in the road-bed. The devout may well take off their shoes on any public highway, for the place whereon they stand is holy ground. They who travel upon highways travel upon the roads that lead to the kingdom of God on earth, the community where men and women dwell together in unity and prosperity; not the streets paved with gold of the Book of Revelation, but the highways macadamized with crushed stone, lead more directly thereto. The spiritual highway for the building of which John the Baptist borrowed the words of the old prophet of the Captivity is not to be built, as the old Roman thought, of massive masonry, the solid blocks representing the aristocrats of the world, the aristocracy of money, of birth or of brains, but it is to be built of the small stones - the common people insignificant in their individuality, permanent, lasting, irresistible in their combinations. Road-making is first the science and then the practice of democracy.

The price of one battleship is, shall we say, at least ten million dollars. According to the prices offered by the Massachusetts Commission, this will build three thousand miles of good gravel road or five hundred miles of best macadamized road. Such an investment in any of our states would make life buoyant where now it is heavy, souls elastic where now they are saddened, boys and girls contented on the farm where now they are dissatisfied; and it would bring the gospel of the plow, the seed and the barnyard into its higher fruition.

When the roadsides bloom as gardens and the wagon roads are boulevards, with shade trees, flowing fountains, and concrete seats on which the foot-sore traveler will find rest and where lovers will tryst, then indeed will there be a highway for our God in what now are lonely places and dreary wildernesses.

XII

Jones devoted much of his summer holiday of 1908 to building a barn on his Tower Hill retreat. He drew on that experience for the after-vacation sermon that year. The barn whose construction he describes was still standing in Tower Hill State Park until a few years ago. It has since been dismantled, but the four-foot high stone foundation can still be seen.

The sermon begins as a pleasant description of the problems and processes involved in planning, building and utilizing a new barn. It turns, however, into an indictment of life in the modern city and a challenge to the congregation to be involved in reform work.

After Jones preached the sermon to All Souls (20 September 1908) he printed it in the next issue of Unity, 24 September. Governor Hoard read it and reprinted it in Hoard's Dairyman on 20 November. It inspired Hoard to ask Jones for the series of sermons on rural themes that became "The Gospel of the Farm".

No indication is given of the poem Jones intended to use as the preface to "Barn Building".

BARN BUILDING

> I have not where to bestow my fruits....I will pull down my barns and build greater.... Thou foolish one, this night is thy soul required of thee....So is he that layeth up treasure to himself, and is not rich toward God....
> Luke 12:17-21

I built me a barn one summer. The exigencies of Tower Hill, my summer home, require milk, and milk calls for cows, and cows must needs be sheltered. The interrupted farmer in me asserted himself in the days of my gray hairs, and barn-building became an interesting and, as I found, a profitable vacation pastime.

Sixty years ago in Wisconsin, as I remember it, a cow-barn was a very simple thing. A few boards or rails over which the straw-stack was built would suffice. Indeed, many cows were wintered on the sunny side of the straw pile or in side-hill excavations of buildings devoted to other uses. Not so now. How to build an up-to-date cow-barn is an academic problem. Experts in many departments must be consulted; materials from many sources must be assembled; patented contrivances and substances of intricate and mysterious manufacture must be used.

I was getting ready for at least two years for the building of this barn. The price of the plainest lumber climbed so high that it was simply prohibitive in my barn-building scheme. So the trees had to be found and felled on the place, and the accumulation of two winters' chopping was necessary before the travelling sawmill would deign to come and make a "setting". In my boyhood the problem of the countryside was to get logs to the mill; now it is the simpler, but quite as

BARN BUILDING

interesting, problem of getting the mill to the logs. The product of the sawing was a promiscuous pile of oak, ash, elm, poplar and basswood lumber - a rough output compared with the neatly piled, edged and planed product of the lumber yard supplied from the cypress swamps of the South, the great pine forests of the far West or the remnants of the pineries of Michigan, Wisconsin and Minnesota. But my lumber cost me four dollars and seventy cents per thousand for the sawing, while the prices at the lumber yard range upward from thirty dollars per thousand. And so my barn became possible.

The first story was built of stone that had to be brought from the quarry three miles away. The forethought that tried to arrange for the hauling of the stone in winter-time, when the roads were hard and the weather cold, miscarried, and much of the stone had to be hauled in the sweltering weather of the summer, incurring a free flow of sweat in men and horses. The upper story was to be frame, but suitable siding and shingles were priced too high, so, after the solid "sheeting" in rough boards from the home lumber yard, this barn was roofed and "sided" with felt paper - an innovation which awakened the distrust of neighbors. But my barn was small and was to be a preacher's barn; I could afford to experiment - nay, the missionary opportunity tempted - and so I ventured on the "paper barn".

But to build a barn as becomes one in the full light of modern science and academic husbandry is serious business. I was mastering a new science; I was taking at least a short course in agriculture.

Here I found the resources of the State ready to serve me. The agricultural architect of the University came, at the expense of the State, to show me how to build a poor man's barn that would carry with it the sanitation and convenience which the wealthy man's barn oftentimes misses. The first plans were furnished free of cost. Then came conferences, more or less non-commercial, with inventors, manufacturers and dealers, taking up questions of stanchions, mangers, ventilation - problems of intake, circulation and draughts.

There were economic questions to settle. Is it right or economically wise to patronize Chicago mail-order houses and save ten or twenty percent of cost, while the local dealers, the home industries, the village merchants - my old friends and neighbors - are thereby crowded to the wall?

Industrial questions were involved in the building of my barn. Would I build by contract or day labor? In finding an honest and skilful country carpenter, you find one of the most mechanically competent and industrially efficient workmen of modern times. I found such a one and trusted all to him, without contract or estimate. So there was no labor union to interfere, no walking delegate to watch me or be watched by me. It was all one to my barn builder and his men whether they shoveled sand, laid stone, mixed concrete, drove a team, connected pipes, painted, framed timber or laid a floor.

And so my barn grew, with its foundations of solid masonry. My good Welsh mason[1] would have none of the American twenty-inch wall - nothing less than twenty-four inches; and the stone must be laid in

- - - - -

[1] David Timothy was a local craftsman who did much stonework in the neighborhood, including Hillside School, now part of Taliesen, and Unity chapel. He is buried in the Unity chapel graveyard, not far from Jones himself.

courses, hewn and true, such as would befit a cathedral wall. He wrought like the workers of old:

> In the elder days of art,
> Builders wrought with greatest care
> Each minute and unseen part;
> For the gods see everywhere.[2]

The upper structure is paper-covered and elm-lined, with its well-lighted and ventilated mow for thirty tons of hay, and its hay-fork and track to be handled by horse power. Below is the cow palace with adjustable stanchions, gas-pipe stalls, swinging metal mangers, separating-room and gasoline engine-house. Wooden slat platforms, upon which my lady cow is to lie, protect her from the chill of the cement floor just below.

All this for eighteen cows, the maximum capacity. For the building of this cow-barn, forces had been directed, materials had been assembling, plans had been maturing -- and extra dimes and dollars had been surreptitiously snatched from the current outflow and set apart in a barn-pocket -- for over two years. This barn represents the conscious effort, the deliberate planning of many minds, but who can tabulate the unconscious forces that culminated in this bit of paper-covered, gambrel-roofed barn, built amid the bluffs in an out-of-the-way corner of Wisconsin?

The materials took shape and form within the limits of a summer vacation, but the lines that center in that cow-barn reach back through the architectural struggles of history. The purline plates, rafters and jack rafters, joists and studding, involve more geometry, mathematical calculation, knowledge of the bearing

- - - - -

[2] Stanza five of "Builders" by Henry Wadsworth Longfellow.

power and the strains and the stresses of joints and timbers than the wisest individual could compute. My barn seems to be the fabric of today, but it is older than the Pyramids. It is made possible by virtue of experimentations made six thousand years ago on the banks of the Euphrates. The castings on the bearings of my hay-fork carrier are illuminated with a long list of patents running back through many years, and behind each patent lie wakeful nights, distressing disappointments and anxious hopes. My felt paper covering, for which I paid one dollar and ninety-five cents per hundred square feet, is enshrouded in mystery, buried in secrets, guarded by bristling patents. I fancy it is some by-product of that commercial centipede, the all-conquering and ever-to-be suspected Standard Oil Company.

Thus you see, he who would build a cow-barn today - for not more than eighteen cows - must make friends with all the arts, must count on all the sciences, must avail himself of the accumulated experience of the centuries, the common sense of the ages. There are rustless nails, ball-bearing wheels, devices to lift poison gases from the floor and bring fresh air from the ceiling, a dustless room for the milk separator, separator test-tubes - Babcock's triumph[3] - which tell awful tales about "robber" cows that look so comely, fat and strong, but who do not pay for their board, so thin is their milk. On the other hand, these tests often cover the modest, homely, obscure, runt-like little cow with compliments. Science has made the last of the herd first and the first of the herd last, in the estimation of the intelligent barn owner.

- - - - -

[3] Stephen Babcock (1843-1931), a Wisconsin agricultural chemist, devised an accurate and simple test for measuring the butter-fat content of milk in 1890.

BARN BUILDING 187

    This meeting of the sciences, this conspiracy of the laboratory, puts the cow in the lime-light, and the barn necessitates the reconstruction of the herd. Such a barn calls for cows that justify it. And so the barn-builder was busy that summer in studying pedigrees, problems of butter-fat, rations and ratios, the respective claims of Jersey, Guernsey and Holstein. As an immediate result, three adult cows were sold in order to find money enough to buy one calf with which to improve the herd.

    But the delightful trouble does not end here. Problems thicken, responsibilities deepen. A model barn, housing high-bred cows, even though it be covered with paper and the herd be made of eighteen heads, calls for masterly handling, a "herdsman" to grace the barn and to manage scientifically the bovine ladies housed therein.

    So the barn-builder must go in search of all this - the competent <u>man</u>, not a hired <u>hand</u>. The new barn called for no stable boy, but a dairy-man, one tutored of the schools, one who would love his charge and profit by the wisdom of the ages, one who could apply the latest inventions, profit by the experiments and use the formulas of the agricultural college and the dairy stations. All this must be found in the person of one who was still willing to work, and for farmer wages; and so the barn-builder laid hold of another modern contrivance - he advertised, and of course in the journal of highest standard - <u>Hoard's Dairyman</u>.

> WANTED: Man and wife to work small farm, equipped with dozen cows and the usual complement of horses, pigs, etc. Good house, with fair wages, privilege of keeping cow,

> two pigs, garden patch, wood, etc.
> Well equipped poultry yard to be
> run on shares with the wife. Must
> be tidy and careful workers in and
> out of doors. Position open about
> September first. Address Box 161,
> c/o <u>Hoard's Dairyman</u>, Fort Atkinson, Wis.

All this care and science, this caution and provision, for the sheltering, feeding, breeding and training of a cow! All this splendid combination of discoveries, inventions, mechanical patents, chemical tests, laboratory contrivances was in the interests of a quadruped, an animal of the barn-yard. The interest culminates in the cow chiefly because under this care she becomes a more marvellous milk-producing mechanism, a more fertile source of butter and cream, the indispensable factor in the great cheese industry of the world. Why not? Cheese and butter and cream are wholesome articles of diet, and the improvement of cow conditions is for the purpose of increasing her product, which is to feed the human world better.

But there is something more than an economic element, something more than dollars and cents, more than food and drink, in my barn problem. Here as elsewhere, beauty waits on utility; refinement and profit go hand in hand.[4]

What an exquisite product is the Jersey cow. She is the lily of the bovine world! The gentle but alert eye, the delicately sculptured head, the gracefully curved, tapering horns, which have almost wholly passed

- - - - -

[4] I have omitted the next paragraph about the island of Jersey, because it disrupted the flow of the sermon.

from a weapon of defense into a matchless ornament! And then the color, shading from delicate fawn to rich mahogany, and the slender tail with its ample bush! An artist may paint with pigment but no poet with words can possibly suggest the beauty of the Jersey. She seems to stand on the border-line where matter breaks into spirit, body takes on soul, the useful clothes itself with the beautiful.

"Treat your cow as though she were a lady", is the dictum which W.D. Hoard, the cow-loving governor of Wisconsin, has made famous. How could one do otherwise in the presence of a perfect Jersey cow? I always feel like taking off my hat to her and begging her pardon for my rudeness in staring at her.

The cow has improved the manners and to a degree transformed the morals of the western farm hand. The "hired man" of my boyhood was a profane, boisterous, banging fellow. He has given place to the quiet, courteous, respectful and respectable barn man. The owner of cows cannot afford to have any other type of man around. The insulted cow resents the indignity promptly by lessening the flow and degrading the quality of the wonderful return she makes to man for his care and guidance. Slowly but surely the cow is helping to transform society in the dairy regions of the West. Cheese factories and creameries are supplanting the country saloons which used to occupy the crossroads corners, and the traveler slakes his thirst with buttermilk or sweet fresh whey where he used to get his whiskey or beer.

Thus the cow becomes a minister of the beautiful as well as of the useful. In the construction of my barn the utilities alone were considered; the canons of severest plainness, cheapness and simplicity were enforced. But lo! to the surprise of everyone, the adequate windows, the provisions for air, light and feed, even the economical and suspect paper covering, with its battened joints and parallel lines, satisfy the eye; the farmer neighbor and city visitor to Tower Hill talk about the "beautiful" barn. It certainly shames its surroundings, the slattern horse-barn, the ragged pig-pen, the inadequate carriage shelter, the dishevelled yard with its clutter of tools and unwashed vehicles. As the barn approached completion, I noticed that the men began to pick things up, and there is an increased motive if not an imperative necessity for the snatching of more dimes and dollars from the current outflow of the preacher's pocket-book and putting the same away in the special barn-pocket, so that the barn-yard may not disgrace the barn.

The ministry of the barn will not only ameliorate the condition of the calves, but it will make the lives of the colts, the pigs and the chickens, the tasks of the farmer's wife and the surroundings of the new baby more comfortable, more humane, more righteous. If my paper barn transforms the Tower Hill barn-yard, the zone of its influence will surely widen. Neighbors will take note. Other barn builders have been watching the process and are already prepared to improve on my barn. (My successes they will copy; my mistakes they will avoid.) It is already advertising the "James patent swinging mangers", the "flint-surfaced felt roofing", the iron stalls and concrete floors, the patent milk-pails and the labor-saving contrivances looking towards neatness, economy and thrift connected therewith.

If the new barn is persistently lived up to, it will help uplift the county, contribute towards the

reformation of the State, and help bring in the kingdom
> Wherein no man can fail,
> Where whoso faileth and dieth
> Yet his deed shall still prevail.

But there is menace in the barn. I have not yet touched the innermost ethical elements in the new barn which stirred the mind of the Great Preacher of all the world. He called the barn-builder the "foolish one", but if I read the parable aright, the offense was not in the new barn or in the plentiful store of grain and goods, but in the complacency, the social indolence and spiritual apathy which said, "Soul, thou has much goods laid up for many years; take thine ease, eat, drink and be merry."

The sin of the New Testament barn-builder was not in the treasures that he had laid up, but in that he had laid them up for himself and was not "rich toward God". It was the satisfied ambition, the carnal indulgence, the materialized goal, the selfish life of the barn-builder which received the condemnation of the Master who rejoiced in sowing and sowers, who noted with pleasure the growing lily, the birds of the air and the beasts of the field.

Nature has long since passed beyond the quadruped in her supreme concern. The cow and all the wealth connected with her represent low rungs in the ladder of evolution, upon the higher rungs of which have long since been planted the feet of man. Today the battle line of creation is away up there, where human babies cry for pure air, where the children of men and women grow pale for want of nourishment, where souls grow faint, hearts grow sick, and minds grow vacant from over-work and under-feeding.

Well did the Master startle the barn-builder with the demand, "This night is thy soul required of thee. The things which thou hast prepared, whose shall they be?" Miserable is the triumph that layeth up treasures for one's self! Alas for the treasure-gathering, the barn-building, that leaves the man poorer in the things of God, penurious towards the soul, indifferent at the very point where goods become precious and treasure desirable, where self is lost in the fuller life of the community and things are transformed into ideas, possessions into powers, wealth into influence and plenty into character, social potency, civic righteousness.

It is all very well to preach the gospel of the cow. I think it is well to build larger barns, particularly better barns, but only when they make the soul "rich toward God", only when they enlarge rather than stultify the builder, widen his sympathies, and increase not alone his relish for food but his relish for good.

The question of evolution today, as John Fiske[5] said in his dying days, is the perfection of society, the development of the community, the construction of the state. And John Fiske did but tardily confirm, in terms of science, the purest, divinest declaration of the Nazarene prophet, the carpenter-preacher, when he declared that the Kingdom of God is at hand, that its foundations are within, that it is the kingdom of justice and purity, brotherhood and progress. Mere plenty, bursting barns, never saved a soul, never upheld and ennobled society or secured the permanence of the state. The poorest, most deceptive test ever invented

- - - - -

[5] John Fiske (1842-1901), an American writer who popularized the philosophy of Evolution. He was one of Jones' favorite authors.

by the politician is the test of "prosperity". The man who will go to the polls at the next election, guided only by the desire for a restoration of "good times" or a perpetuation of the prosperity that now exists, is Devil-guided and hell-inspired. Not that prosperity is to be regretted - nay, it is much to be desired; but when pursued as an end, when taken as a measure of civic values and public righteousness, it is a delusion and a snare. Prosperity may in the future, as it has so often done in the past, mark the damnation of the individual, the degradation of the family, the disintegration and ultimate death of the State. Corinth and Ephesus, Tyre and Sidon, Carthage and Memphis, Babylon and Nineveh, Alexandria, ancient Rome and modern Petrograd are indisputable cases in point, and it may be that Paris, London, New York, and Chicago will be added to the list before two millenia more have been passed. Aye, they are doomed by a law as inexorable as the law of gravitation to a place in the list unless they take timely heed and lay hold of the other law, as inexorable - the law of spiritual gravitation, the law that conserves ideas and ideals, the law that saves souls from the mortality of bodies and the decay of things.

 I have at last arrived at the real lesson of my paper barn. How do easy triumphs and our pride in them shame our deadly complacency, our awful indifference, the assumed helplessness and uselessness of soul-breeding, of society-housing and community renovation!

 My little barn among the bluffs of Wisconsin, awaiting its little bunch of a dozen cows, inviting the triumphs of the breeder, rises in accusing contrast to the wretched, rat-ridden rookeries, the solid blocks of fire-traps, in which Chicago men and women are living today, into which babies are being born by scores every twenty-four hours, places where no self-respecting breeder of Jerseys would harbor his calves, from which no health commission would accept the milk even of the best bred Jersey cow -- so infectious is the district, so unsanitary the surroundings, so corrupting to good milk and to good cows is the environment. And still, in such surroundings we are breeding men and women; aye, "breeding" is the word. How careful are we of the inheritance of a cow! How careless of the ancestry of a citizen! How wise are we getting concerning the laws of reproduction, the principles of generation, in the barn-yard! How reckless and defiant are we of the same laws at the marriage altar! Proudly, with pomp and parade, music, dancing and gifts, the capitalist of the boulevard gives his daughter in marriage to one tainted with a corruption, marked with a degeneracy, from the parallel of which he would religiously guard his brood mare. Today, among the most progressive sections of society, with the so-called "best citizens", the up-to-date men and women who form our so-called "good society", the laws of birth and breeding are more respected and better enforced in the stable than in the nursery.

We cannot ignore the distressing, heart-breaking revealments of labor conditions, chiefly of women and children in all our large cities - the horribly unsanitary atmosphere and inhuman strain in which women and children by the thousand make the cigars for "gentlemen" (if indeed such ever smoke "stogies"), make dainty the laundry of "my lady" of the boulevard and manufacture the crackers that reach the table of everybody from the boot-black to the millionaire.

Truly, we eat and drink to our damnation; we are clothed in unrighteousness, on the human side, to an extent that would ruin the dairy business and would supplant my paper barn with the fetid, mud-stained dung-heaps of the primitive pig-sty.

The gospel of the new barn cuts across social lines and arraigns with equal force and power the human husbandry on the "favored side", so-called, of society. O the social damnation, the human degradation, the spiritual and bodily debility, that so often go along with the greater barns bursting with the accumulated stores of wealth! I know not which is more to be deplored, the condition of the under-fed baby and the over-worked woman who dwell on the "other side of the river" or "behind the yards", or the over-fed baby and the wickedly over-dressed woman who is exhausted in using up her indolence and justifying her extravagance along our avenues, boulevards and lake shore drives.

Surely both are to be pitied; nay, the conditions of both should be remedied. My paper barn in Wisconsin sent me back to my work in Chicago with a newly dated commission, with my task freshly interpreted, which in brief is simply this: to join with others more effectively than ever before in applying the principles of good husbandry and progressive farming to soul-culture, to community-farming, to tilling the fields of heaven, making ourselves "rich toward God", which is being rich in justice, in beauty, in righteousness, generous toward the things of the spirit, diligent in the cultivation of soul.

It behooves the favored citizens of the country to hear and heed the voice of God speaking through the anguish of little ones, through the cry of the orphaned whose parents are still alive, of the widows with unburied husbands and the widowers with undivorced wives, the famished souls, the starving minds, the confused consciences about us, exclaiming in the stern tones of the Day of Judgment, "Foolish one, this night is thy soul required of thee. Thou hast been laying up treasures for thyself and art not rich toward God."

This chapter originally appeared in the **Wisconsin Magazine of History** 67:2, and is reprinted here with permission.

XIII

During the Chicago World's Fair of 1894 Jones gave up his summer holiday to work on the final preparations for The World's Parliament of Religion in that September. In compensation he took a holiday in March of 1895. From then on the "March escape" became part of his regular pattern. He frequently went South – partly for the weather and partly because he continued to be drawn to the places where he had fought as an artillery private in The Civil War.

Like his summer holidays, his March escape usually provided material for sermons on his return. He was as interested an observer of people and events as of nature, and the Murfreesboro Horse Fair comes to life under his pen. He goes to books for some "facts" about horses and their history, but the heart of this sermon is what he saw in the Tennessee city.

The lessons he means to draw are clear enough in general terms. He expresses his indignation at the inhumane conditions in the city by contrasting them with the care lavished on horses. The specifics, though, are not very clearly drawn. As often happened, he was more interested in the event itself and slighted the conclusions he wanted to draw from it.

"Breeding" was the fourth sermon in "The Gospel of the Farm" series for Hoard's Dairyman. It appeared in that newspaper on 15 April 1910, after it was preached at All Souls on 6 June 1909.

Jones had not yet selected the poem to be used as the preface to it in the book.

AT THE HORSE FAIR: BREEDING

In the spring of 1909 I found myself with a week's leisure at Murfreesboro, Tennessee, whither I had wandered during my usual March escape from Chicago. For in March that otherwise hospitable city is disposed to get me by the throat. I was drawn thither by the battle-stained surroundings and perhaps by the fact that, so far as I knew, nobody that I had ever known lived there. Consequently it seemed a place where I should be secure from lecture temptations and the dissipations of addressing school children and reading papers before women's clubs.

By a happy coincidence, I found that my week at Murfreesboro was also the week of the Annual Horse Fair - a fair so famous that I provoked the contempt or pity of my fellow-guests at the hotel table when I confessed my ignorance of this notable annual event, the triumphs and attractiveness of which were known to lovers of good horses everywhere. It had helped make the region round-about famous for breeding of beautiful horses, particularly of the saddle and carriage types.

This particular fair for 1909 was advertised as "the largest and finest exhibit of high bred and notably trained horses ever offered at this famous pavilion". The printed catalogue contained over four hundred numbers, graphically described. The auction sale lasted three days; buyers were there from all parts of the country. The hotel register showed a range of visitors reaching from Cleveland to Galveston, from Buffalo to Jacksonville, Florida, from New York to Denver. The corridors of the little hotel at which I stopped were cluttered with cots, and all the spare rooms in the little city were occupied by the overflow.

For two or three days preceding the great opening, the beautiful animals were arriving in palace cars or were led or driven into the city over the various "pikes", some warmly blanketed, others gaily caparisoned. As if conscious of the place of honour awaiting them, the elegant creatures came with mincing steps, prancing air, uplifted heads, arching necks and flashing eyes. The business of the little town was threatened, as well as enlivened, by these attractions of the street. The noble creatures filled with pride the hearts of their grooms and owners (and with envy the remainder of the human world, most of which was lined up along the streets). Those animals that pranced up and down the street looking so eager, impetuous and at times so fierce, were in reality submissive, gentle, obedient. Saddlers danced their artificial steps of single-foot, rack, canter, fox-trot and running walk, passing from the one to the other quietly and gracefully at the slightest signal of the rider. In those days, on the streets of Murfreesboro, the old Greek myth of the centaur seemed to have come true. Here was a composite animal with the head of a man and the body of a horse, one organism moved by one will, combining in perfect union the grace and agility of the equine with the alertness and intelligence of the human.

In and out among these gentle ladies and gentlemen of the stable, darted the trotters in their rubber-tire sulkies – strapped, banded, laced and padded – like college athletes, pushing with wild impatience, fretting and fuming for the trial, with all the grace of mind and body sacrificed to the one element of speed, to the one purpose of winning the game, of beating their rivals.

These painfully artificialized creatures – the trotters in harness – were relieved by the earlier victors of the race course – the running horses. The three-year-old, and often younger, fillies and geldings, with the minimum of trappings, were also out for exercise, their little black jockeys riding bare-backed and with single-rein bridles.

This fascinating and motley scene was accentuated and lifted into the dignity of a pageant by the high-stepping pairs and four-in-hands, with their clinking, silver-mounted harness and sumptuous "drags", carrying the swells which represented the "upper tens" – the less than "four hundred" – of Murfreesboro society and their guests. But for all the lace, the ladies' hats fearfully and horribly made, the silken parasols, the glistening linen and patent leather, the frail distorted bipeds had poor show in comparison with the elegant quadrupeds, over which they held the ribbons and waved the autocratic whip.

When it comes to beauty of line, symmetry of form and grace of movement, it must be admitted that civilization has done more for the horse than for men and women. Man's skill has greatly enhanced these qualities in the horse, while the human trappings often encumber, distort and weaken the human form divine. The processes of civilization sometimes cramp the body with artificialities, spoil the complexion with confections and pastry, neutralize, if they do not dim, the lustre of the eye and make awkward and grotesque the gait. However it may be with the mind and the instincts of the heart, commend me the supple Indian and the naked islander for litheness of limb, dignity of carriage, grace of motion and fleetness of foot.

But all this is but an overture that introduces the opera, a prelude that prepares the way for the real play which was enacted in the great horse pavilion beginning at nine o'clock each morning and continuing until nine or ten in the evening for three consecutive days. The performance was interrupted only by short intervals for the human feeding, which was expedited as much as possible by the enterprising church sisters of the town who, under a large tent erected close to the auction ground, catered to the jockeys and horse fanciers. With one gulp they satisfied the pangs of hunger, tested the cooking skills of Murfreesboro and helped pay off the mortgage on the Methodist church.

It was indeed a "Performance" which drew well. The steep rising galleries were always well-filled with spectators who sat for patient hours on the hard boards, giving to the performers absorbed, and sometimes excited, attention. Here sat ladies in fine feathers, old men with well-stocked memories of "affairs" in which they had won and lost, flattering themselves that they were still members of the supreme court that was to pass upon the merits of horse-flesh. Here were curious girls and boys, stopping on their way to and from school, traveling men who had hurried through business in order to look in on their way to trains, old soldiers, some of whom had worn the blue and others the gray, lawyers, doctors, bankers and at least one minister from Chicago, working his vacation for all it was worth. Most of these I have enumerated, like the parson from the North, were there with no commercial intent and were saved by sheer penury from the seductive temptations of the auctioneer.

O, what a show it was! Variety was the first conspicuous attraction, reaching from the Shetland pony - no bigger than a sheep, driven smartly into the ring in a little cart by "little Lord Fauntleroy" with short socks, naked knees and yachting cap - up through all colors and sizes, to the great speeder and stately coacher. One after another, in rapid succession, they dashed to the stand, stopped a moment -- as if conscious that they occupied the center of the stage -- while the auctioneer rattled off their chief points; an expert, in quieter, more gentlemanly tones - sometimes the veterinary, sometimes the owner himself - called attention to the subtler qualities, the more delicate points and the high breeding, which were in danger of being overlooked. Then, with a crack of the whip - the bark of which was much more fierce than its bite - the animal was put through his paces up and down the long saw-dust floor, while the bidding went on with such spirit that when the final, fatal "Gone!" was pronounced, the non-commercial auditors felt a keen sympathy with the defeated and a lively appreciation of triumph of the victor. The prices ranged all the way from the fifty dollars for little Lord Fauntleroy's Shetland up to the fifteen thousand dollars that bought the promising young race horse with a brilliant record. The average price would dazzle a plodding horse-breeder on a Wisconsin farm. It was a poor horse indeed that did not go beyond the two hundred and fifty-dollar mark, and five hundred-dollar horses were no surprise.

It was indeed a stupid attendant to whom this horse fair did not mean more than an auction sale.

AT THE HORSE FAIR: BREEDING 203

This was an historical drama reaching far back. It was a problem play, raising questions in pedagogy and making pertinent contributions to sociology. It gave to the student of public weal what the artists seek when they go to Paris, Florence or Rome - an "atmosphere" in which their studies can be carried on more propitiously. The love of the beautiful flourishes where the imagination is fed by gracious forms and pleasing colors.

Above everything else this horse fair, to the thoughtful, was a study in morals and religion. It was a parable of the higher life, a sample and symbol of spiritual achievements, a glowing chapter in the holy gospel of the farm.

Let us attend to some ethical values of the horse, by the help of this horse fair.

The history of civilization is the history of the domestication of animals. The dog, cat and cow alone antedate the domestication of the horse. The student of primitive races, in the past and the present, can find horseless peoples, but anthropology has been unable to go far enough back into the study of mankind to anticipate the dog and possibly the cat. But to go back of the horse is to land in the heart of savagery; it is to go back of the plow, the most potent of tools. Without the horse, barter could never have bloomed into commerce, and the prowess of the clan would never have risen to the dignity of the state. The story of civilization is essentially co-terminous with the story of the horse.

Says Professor Shaler in that great gospel-book of his, <u>Domesticated Animals</u>:

> ...man is not a strong animal nor is he so built that he can apply

the measure of strength that is in him to good advantage....With the first step upward, the advance depended on securing more energy than that with which he was endowed.... the progress of mankind beyond the savage state would never have been affected but for the bodily help which has been rendered him by a few domesticated animals....the races of men might well be divided into those which have and those which have not the use of the horse ....no other creature has been so inseparably associated with the great triumphs of our kind, whether won on the battle field or in the arts of peace....Lacking the help which the horse gives, it is almost certain that even now civilization could not be maintained.[1]

If we compare historic time, some six thousand years, with geologic time, we find that the period since life first appeared upon the earth is as five seconds to the day of twenty-four hours. Of course in this stretch of geologic time, the horse has a pedigree that reaches millenia back of the human. The horse, of all the vertebrates, has the longest and best established ancestral tree. His fossil ancestors have been traced far back from the one-toed, through

- - - - -

[2] Nathaniel Southgate Shaler, Domesticated Animals. (New York: Charles Scribners Son's, 1895, reprinted 1908), p 57.

the three-toed, to the five-toed tree climbers of the tertiary period. Professor Marsh, the great discoverer in the geology of the upper Missouri, found fossil remains of the three-toed and the two-toed horse, who were the unquestioned progenitors of our one-toed horse, remnants of the aborted toes being still left along the leg bones (often giving trouble to the horseman in the shape of "splints").

Notwithstanding these ancient antecedents of the horse of the Western Continent, it still seems probable that the modern descendants, now found in a wild state on the western ranges, are progeny of imported stock, traced back to Central or Northern Asia. There seems little doubt that the Indian received his pony from the white man. De Soto in the earlier half of the sixteenth century abandoned his horses, which are supposed to have given rise to the wild horses of Texas. The Spanish left the early progenitors of similar herds now found in different parts of South America. The second voyage of Columbus brought horses, but they perished. In 1519 Cortez landed sixteen horses in Mexico; in 1698 the French brought horses to Canada; in 1629 the Dutch brought their plodding breeds to New Amsterdam. The colonies of Virginia, Maryland and the Carolinas had their race-courses before the Revolutionary War. The blood of all these horses still flows in the veins of the modern American horse. Why should not the thoroughbreds at Murfreesboro hold their heads high and step proudly?[2]

The horse enters early into literature. The Bible tells of Joseph exchanging Egyptian corn for the

- - - - -

[2] The next sentence was an awkward repetition of the same point and has been omitted.

Syrian horses of his brethren. Horses, splendid horses, figure in the battle monuments in the valleys of the Euphrates and the Nile. Roberts, in his <u>History of the Horse</u>[3], gives a lengthy citation from Xenophon which describes the good horse and gives timely advice to the horse trader. His "points" are so well taken and so graphically described that the passage might well be printed as a leaflet by the horse departments of our agricultural colleges; it would be a document quite up-to-date.

King John of England in 1199 imported one hundred stallions from Flanders for the purpose of improving the farm horse. Edward II, two hundred years later, imported some Spanish horses for the sake of improving English horse-flesh. Henry VIII prohibited the exportation of the best horses and at the same time prohibited breeding from inferior stock.[4]

Although the Puritans were opposed to horse racing, perhaps because it gave too keen a zest to this mundane life, Oliver Cromwell, the great Puritan captain, had an eye for a good horse and loved to ride a fast one. His "White Turk", which he bought of a Mr. Place, was an Arabian importation, claimed at the time to be the "most beautiful horse ever introduced into England". The thoroughbred trotters of England still rejoice in pedigrees that reach back to Cromwell's "White Turk" and other famous horses in the stables of the Commonwealth.

France, Germany, all the countries of Europe, have their interesting horse stories; and always the

- - - - -

[3] Jones probably means Isaac Phillips Roberts, <u>The Horse</u> (New York: The MacMillan Co., 1905).

[4] A redundant quotation from Roberts has been omitted.

AT THE HORSE FAIR: BREEDING

story of the money, time and talent invested in horse breeding promptly oversteps those of commercial triumphs or economic achievements. The horse promptly gallops into the domain of romance. He stirs the affections and enthusiasms of men. The chivalrous man was the horse rider. Chivalry is allied to cavalry - the root word in both cases being <u>chevalerie</u>, meaning horsemanship -- knighthood.

Mr. Roberts, in his work on the horse, gives a list of twenty-one horse registry associations in the United States; stud books reach from the Shetland pony up through coach horses, to the mighty draft horses of the Norman, Shire, Clydesdale and Percheron stocks of imported origin, and our own native Cleveland Bay, Hamiltonian and Morgan stock. Our state institutions and the agricultural department at Washington are spending large sums of money and giving much scientific attention and intelligent affection to the breeding of horses.

Professor Alexander, of the horse breeding department in the Experiment Station of the University of Wisconsin, has for several years been putting forth elaborate bulletins, some of them one hundred and seventy-five pages in length, discussing various phases of horse breeding. He has secured the enactment of rigid registry laws, looking toward the perpetuation of the best, and the suppression of the poorest, blood in Wisconsin horses. When his words fail to make impressive his lessons, he summons the camera to his assistance and his pictures fascinate or alarm, as the subject may be fair or fell.

This high academic attention to horse breeding is justified on the severest utilitarian basis, and the veriest Gradgrind among the lawmakers justifies the expenditure looking towards the improvement of a vast industry and the protection of an indispensable element in the commercial world. The Agricultural Year Book for 1917 records the large returns from these small investments. Since 1890 the horse population of the United States has increased 50 per cent, and its money value has increased 60 per cent.

In 1917 there were twenty-one and one-tenth million horses in the United States, with an average value of $102.94 per head, aggregating nearly $2,175,000,000. During the preceding year of 1916, 15,556 horses were imported at a cost of over one and one-half million dollars, while 357,553 horses were exported at a value of seventy-three and one-half million dollars. And all this growth in the face of bicycle, trolley car and automobile rivalry. All the indications go to show that the horse is to remain, in the future as in the past, an indispensable element in civilization. The abused horse -- the "plug", which is the product of careless breeding, inefficient rearing and over-work - let us hope is to go. The neglected beast of burden, the abused slave, dragging almost impossible loads over equally impassable roads, is to go let us pray, speedily. Let man's brutal ambitions and inordinate greed exhaust themselves on the unfeeling forces of steam and electricity. Thank heaven, coal and gasoline, wood and steel have no nerves. But the horse of mettle and obedience, of beauty and spirit, of affection and loyalty is a creature of nerves and is to stay.

In the future, more than in the past, the horse is to have a place in the art, poetry, chivalry and spirituality of man. Obviously his first uses were martial, not industrial. The Norman horse was developed not for purposes of draught, but of chivalry. The horse that would carry the knight with a hundred or more pounds of armor must necessarily be a heavy one. In the institutes of Howel Dda ("Howell the Good"), the beneficent Welsh king of the ninth century, the hitching of a horse to a plow was prohibited. It was too ignoble a task for the lordly animal; that was the work of the humbler, less-ambitious ox. Clearly the hesitancy to eat horse flesh arises not from hygienic but from esthetic reasons. We eat the hog, notwithstanding his promiscuous diet and his wallowing habits; we refrain from eating the horse, notwithstanding the purity of his food and the cleanliness of his habit not only because he is too valuable to be eaten, but because he is too much beloved. To eat him is too much like eating a member of the family; it is approaching too near to cannibalism.

The horse has profoundly reacted on the spiritual nature of man. Theodore Parker spoke a great psychological as well as physiological truth when he said, - "The outside of a horse is good for the inside of a man." Goethe, in his famous pedagogical valley that was set apart for the training of youths, taught his boys courage and self-reliance by sending them into the pasture to break colts - a discipline that has far outreached the confines of the ideal valley hid in Alpine obscurity. Says Roberts, "A farmer boy is lonesome where there are no colts to be handled."

Beauty has always been an essential element in horse-breeding. It is to be regretted that in some sections of our country, the utilitarian instincts have asserted themselves to the degeneracy and disfigurement of the noble animal whose original and most characteristic traits are grace, agility, swiftness and endurance. The special prominence given to the breeding of the clumsy, ox-like, barrel-legged giants of the Shire and Clydesdale types is a curious illustration of how perversion of type can be hastened by breeding. The place of the deformed 2200-pound draught horse is in the fat stock show rather than in the horse show. His slow gait, clumsy movements and relatively short life place him alongside of the corn-fed, 1800-pound fat steer and the unwieldy 600-pound porker. The Berkshire pig and the Durham steer may be justified by the increased commercial value, but a Berkshire or Durham horse indicates science misdirected. It is a hopeful sign to find that the national government, the experiment stations in Colorado and private associations in Vermont, are busying themselves in the task of restoring - before it is too late - the beautiful, elegant, graceful, tenacious and all-round-efficient Morgan type, which economically, probably - surely artistically - represents the high water mark of American horse-breeding up to date. The auto-truck in the city and the good roads in the country will help restore the horse to his high estate. It is cheaper to macadam the road to the station than it is to pile sufficient flesh on the horse's bones to enable him to wallow along through the mud with half a load of farm truck. It was a delight to note the absence of the beefy, ponderous, imported horse at the Tennessee Horse Fair.

Were the horse to be supplanted in the industries of the world, he would still have a permanent place in the amusements, the refinements and the domestic life of the world. Shaler calls his horse "the finest product of man's care", and says, "He receives the best care of all domesticated animals unless it be the silk worm." No man can estimate the contributions of the horse to the gentleness of man and to the refinement of society.

AT THE HORSE FAIR: BREEDING

I have not yet spoken of the greatest, most delightful, most significant surprise of the Murfreesboro Horse Fair. The conventionalized type of the horseman in American literature - the old-fashioned horse trader so familiar to the gray-haired farmers, the tobacco-chewing, swearing, gambling, drinking, cheating bravado - was hardly in evidence at Murfreesboro. Rowdyism is eliminated from the barn of the successful horse breeder as surely as it is from the barn of the progressive dairyman. Quiet gentlemen, educated men, many of them college graduates, men prepared to discuss intelligently and graciously the problems of public wealth and civic welfare gathered around the hotel tables during this horse fair. Murfreesboro is a "Dry Town". During the week I mingled freely with these horse dealers and I heard little or no complaint on behalf of the bibulous interests, and my nose detected few hints of violated law. Horse breeding on the higher lines is anti-saloon business. The intelligent lover of the horse deplores the dignity of the capitalistic brewers, who would lend a touch of beauty and refinement to their nasty business by driving through the streets with their finely-bred and nobly-groomed animals hitched to the uninteresting and ill-smelling beer wagons. Gentleness, courtesy, patience, sympathy and high intelligence are the successsful conditions of horse breeding. All these were necessary to the bringing together of the magnificent animals at the Horse Fair; for horse flesh, like Opie's paints, must needs be "mixed with brains".

But enough of horses. What of men? How inevitably does the mind jump from the horse nursery to the human nursery! How careful are we of the ante- and post-natal conditions of the saddle horse! How careless are we of the antecedents and training of the boy who is to ride in the saddle! The science of eugenics is the science of man-breeding. How carefully does the horse breeder scrutinize the pedigree both of dam and sire! With great skill and fore-sight he labors to eliminate the less favored. With generous wisdom he provides for the perpetuation and nurture of the more favored. But how is it with our children? Read the awful facts which every social survey offers concerning the improperly clothed, the inadequately housed, the under-fed children of men, the voluminous products of reckless parentage and a careless state. The social investigators remind us of what we are too willing to forget: that winter in Chicago often finds as many as five thousand children attending the public school who are habitually hungry; ten thousand more who are insufficiently nourished, many of them having no beds to sleep in. The majority of these children are reported by experts as "living in damp, unclean, and overcrowded homes".

Colts are carefully provided for, their coming anticipated, their needs studied. Even in would-be well-ordered homes, children are social accidents, their advent deplored, their training often ignored and evaded -- more times subordinated to shallow, passing, commercial, social and other interests. There is in the United States today much more systematic thought given to the breeding and rearing of colts and calves than to that of boys and girls. The result is such as might be expected under such husbandry.

Beautiful are the humanities that gather around the horse. Eloquent and efficient are the prophets of the Humane Society when they plead for winter blankets and summer fly-nets for the horses, when they fight the

AT THE HORSE FAIR: BREEDING

cruelties of the over-check, the foolishness of the blinders, the barbarity of the docked tail. So efficient is their ministry that he who defies their pleas or disobeys their mandates is self-convicted of brutality. How stolidly skeptical and often-times cynical is the same constituency when the officers of the same Humane Society plead for the child who is robbed of his childhood by over-work, and whose well-being - physical and moral - is hopelessly defeated by the over-exhaustion of the mother before and after his birth.

Benign laws on the statute books of some of our states looking towards the proper breeding and development of horses are far superior to the laws concerning child- and woman-labor and the proper provisions for health and decency under which their labor is to be performed.

That was a touching funeral procession witnessed in Boston, headed by the file of unharnessed and unridden horses of the firemen. That week the cab and truck horses of Boston wore black rosettes in their bridles. They with their companions of the fire brigade mourned the loss of a friend, a champion who had stood between them and the cruel lash, one who had protected them from the over-load, one who, remembering their thirst in hot summer days, had caused thousands of drinking troughs to be filled with flowing water for their benefit. George T. Angell, the venerable President of the American Humane Society, was dead.

He was indeed a messenger of the Lord, an acknowledged apostle of the great friend of man "who went about doing good", one who deserved the divine approbation, "Inasmuch as ye have done it unto one of the least of these, ye have done it unto me. Enter thou into thy reward!"

The Arab in Robert Browning's spirited poem of "Muleykah" preferred to disclose the secret of the saddle to the thief who was stealing his "Pearl", and by so doing enable the thief to out-speed and escape forever his pursuers, rather than see the beloved child of his heart, the sharer of his tent, beaten in speed - even by the horse on which he himself was giving chase.

When shall we bring the chivalry of the home up to the standard of this chivalry of the stable? When will men guard the honor of wives and daughters as valorously as did the Arabian horseman that of his favorite mare? When will human tenements, wherein men and women bring forth and rear babes, be brought to the standard of the stable in point of good air, good water, good feeding and gentle treatment? When shall we have as good laws, as wisely executed, for the prevention and suppression of disease in human society as now are found on our statute books concerning the denizens of the barnyard?

Over and over again did the auctioneer dwell upon the spiritual qualities of the horses he offered for sale. "This, ladies and gentlemen, is a gentle animal: an educated creature. Note the intelligent eye. She is a lady's horse - affectionate, loyal. Little children love her!" And so on and on. And the bidding showed that even more than speed, size, color or grace, these spiritual qualities were prized. The well-trained and educated horse, when it descended from intelligent ancestry, went at a high figure.

Gentleness, obedience -- not slavishness -- good manners and good habits, are attained in boys and girls in exactly the same way as they are attained in colts. Roughness, profanity, vulgarity and - above all -

rudeness and brutality, must be excluded from the barns where the colts are to be transformed into gentle and kind horses, fit companions for ladies and children -- not slaves but co-workers, partners, with men and women. The same conditions are equally imperative in the home and school and the church, if boys and girls - wild, wayward and uncertain - are to be transformed into kind, trusted and faithful men and women.

One of the great religious books of the last century put forth by the American press, was Horace Bushnell's Christian Nurture. "Nurture" is the word; "training" is its equivalent. This is the highest word in the Christian vocabulary, and it finds its humblest exemplification and perhaps its most successful demonstration in the open life of the intelligent, humane horse breeder. "Christian Nurture" is the phrase that expresses the method necessary to produce good horses and good citizens. Not only our colleges, but our churches have much to learn from the men of the race-track.

The professors in our theological schools, as well as in our agricultural colleges, may well visit the horse fair whenever they can and ponder upon the revelations thereof. Let us rejoice in the achievements revealed there, for perhaps in due time the turn of humanity will come, and devout purposes will move the public spirit of progressive citizens with an enthusiasm to improve the human stock. Those purposes will be embodied in wise laws, enforced by an intelligent public spirit, that will produce progressive citizens and give us men and women who will grace - and not disgrace - the splendid lords and ladies of the paddock, matching noble mares and stallions with nobler men and women.

XIV

Beginning like the sermon on barns, with a description of the necessities of animal care, this sermon moves much more rapidly into the application of the idea to human beings. Little time is spent on pigs and the pigpen and a great deal on indignation at the neglect of children in the cities. Jones lines up solidly with the muck-raking authors of his time. He goes further, though, in his passionate, though somewhat unorganized, plea for intellectual and moral reform beyond the need for physical care of children.

The sermon is notable for a strong defense of continued immigration and its praise for immigrants. In 1914 or 1918 this was not a popular position. But Jones was accustomed to standing against public opinion.

Jones printed this sermon in <u>Unity</u> on 17 December 1914. The original manuscript is missing, but was very likely first preached shortly before then - early December 1914 - at All Souls. The manuscript as it now exists has been altered to fit its proposed publication in 1918 - after four years of war.

An observant searcher can still see the traces of the pigpen Jones refers to in the beginning of the sermon. The outline of its foundation is visible near the stone walls of the barn, at Tower Hill State Park in Wisconsin.

The poem for this chapter is Margaret Widdemer's "The Factories", an indictment of child labor. In his note he mis-attributes it to "Margaret Miller".

PIGS AND BABIES

> A good name is rather to be chosen than great riches
> And loving favor rather than silver and gold.
> The rich and the poor meet together:
> Jehovah is the maker of them all.
> A prudent man seeth the evil, and hideth himself;
> But the simple pass on, and suffer for it.
> The reward of humility and the fear of Jehovah
> Is riches, and honor, and life.
> Thorns and snares are in the way of the perverse;
> He that keepeth his soul shall be far from them.
> Train up a child in the way he should go.
> And even when he is old he will not depart from it.
>
> Proverbs 22:1-6

One of the minor disappointments of one of my summer vacations was that I had to return to the city before my Tower Hill pigpen was completed. The plain truth is that in order to qualify myself as a builder of a pigpen, I found it necessary to do a mass of reading and figuring, oral investigation, research by correspondence and not a little thinking by myself. By the time I was reasonably qualified to undertake the task, there was not time enough left for the assembling of the material and the work of the mechanics before I had to leave my pigpen-building for sermon-building.

To build a pigpen intelligently in the light of the latest science means a liberal education in agriculture. The literature of the pig is extensive; the science of the pig is absorbing. For nearly a half-century or more the Department of Agriculture in Washington has been engaged in the study of the pig and in the encouragement of pig-investigation and pig-exploitation. All the agricultural colleges of the country, and particularly in the Middle West, give much attention to pig-raising, and have issued many bulletins concerning the breeding, housing, rearing and feeding of pigs.

My pigpen when finished was to have two rows of windows on the south front that would throw the sun's rays into every corner of the pen. The sleeping corner in each compartment was to be floored with cork brick to save mother and little ones from the chill of the cement that formed the remainder of the floor. Scientific breeders of pigs recognize the need of privacy and quiet during maternity. It is also necessary to recognize the fact that the pig is peculiarly a social animal, with strongly developed social instincts. So the individual pen where maternity is to be respected is best separated from its neighbor by an iron grill-work, that the matrons may see one another and enjoy a degree of community life without interfering with one another's families or trespassing on family rights. This pigpen when finished was to have rear doors opening on an adequate paddock with shade trees for summer time and soft earth for the little pigs to wallow in and obtain due exercise. Of course this pigpen was to have convenient storage for food and proper arrangements for fresh water and the compounding of suitable diet.

The psychology of the pig is as important as, and to me more interesting than, its physiology. Professor Shaler of Harvard College, in what I consider his very religious book, <u>Domesticated Animals</u> (already often referred to), calls attention to the fact that the pig, of all domestic animals - perhaps of all quadrupeds - is most developed on its sympathetic side. When the cry of distress is heard anywhere in the hog pasture, the entire hog community rushes to the rescue, and under such a call even the domestic pig, from whose nature most of the savagery and courage has been bred, is fearfully aggressive. When a member of the pig community is in distress, you had better look to your line of retreat, as every farmer boy early learns.

Professor Shaler discovers a high degree of intelligence in the pig. He gives credence to, and analyzes with some detail, the achievements of one of the many "learned pigs" which have been exhibited. We are told that the pig trainer is careful in the selection of his pigs. He takes note of the brain capacity. He seeks those whose eyes are set far apart.

Civilization has done much for the pig. Put the modern Berkshire or, to me the more attractive and picturesque, Duroc-Jersey, over against their barbaric ancestor, the wild boar - rough, fierce, armed with tusks, swift of foot and terrible in battle, and you see how the commercial needs of men have modified the pig. He has become in the main a harmless, helpless animal. His progeny would soon die out if the sustaining and guiding hand of man were withdrawn. He is shy, timid; the merest child can drive him, and the bark of a puppy will scare him. Economically speaking, it was well thus to eliminate the virility of the wild boar out of the modern pig; you get more and better pork by the process.

All this lore and very much more must be acquired before a pigpen can be built intelligently - one which will embody the latest science and return the greatest profit.

There is ethical value in all this information. The academic study of the pig under government auspices and with legislative encouragement has been going on for half a century. Large sums of money have for years been expended in the encouragement of pig-raising, for the study of the diseases to which they are liable and their remedies, while the Child Welfare Department of our Government was not established until 1912.

To pursue this child study the Government called the Virgin Mother of Chicago, Julia Lathrop[1], to conduct research work and to direct the high business of raising children hygienically and training them along the lines of latest pedagogy. It is safe to say of this Child Welfare Work that it is still in its incipiency and is receiving grudgingly a scandalously small support compared with the amount invested in pig-study and pig-rearing. Fifty thousand dollars a year was all that Miss Lathrop dared to ask for in the beginning, and there was a time when it seemed as though that sum would be cut down. By 1916 the appropriation had reached only $164,000 and Miss Lathrop was asking that

- - - - -

[1] Julia Lathrop (1858-1932) was an associate of Jane Addams at Hull House. The two of them frequently worked with Jones in reform causes.

it be doubled for 1917. Even then it would compare but ill with the sums invested in pig-study.

The legislature of a would-be progressive state refused at a recent session to make an appropriation of five thousand dollars for the better supervision of her dependent children. The same legislature appropriated fifteen thousand dollars for the better care of hogs! The State of Mississippi had no money to support a factory inspector, but in the five years preceding it had spent over $300,000 for the replanting of its oyster beds. Louisiana at the time of this writing had no money for an inspector to protect the rights of the child, but it spent something over $25,000 in the protection of its game and fisheries.

In trying to bring the lore acquired in the study of pigpens to bear upon child-saving and child-training problems, I am justified of science, encouraged by history and, in so far as I succeed, blessed of religion.

We are beginning to realize the awful responsibility that rests upon the favored and the boastful in this direction. Jacob Riis[2] called attention to the fact that ninety percent of the children picked up on the streets of New York and distributed among its institutions die there. Figures show that 300,000 babies under one year of age die annually in the United States. Doctors estimate that one-half of them, at least, die from preventable diseases. Legislatures are just beginning to awaken to the fact that babies constitute a more important asset of the State than pigs, and viewed only from the economic standpoint are as

— — — — —

[2] Jacob Riis (1849-1914), Journalist, author, social reformer - especially concerned with city living conditions.

worthy of protection. The improvement of the pig within the last hundred years is a great achievement of science, while the degeneracy of the human in many sections of our crowded cities is alarming. Out of the twelve thousand applicants for enlistment in Manchester, England during the Boer War, eight thousand were rejected as being too defective for service, and out of the four thousand accepted only one thousand came up to full standard.

I believe all but six states in the Union have at the present writing some kind of child-protecting laws, but that they are inadequate in scope and not effectively enforced is the open scandal of our country. The Federal Child Labor Law, passed only after much long and bitter struggle, and now administered under direction of the Children's Bureau, is a distinct advance, but its standards are none too high and its provisions too easily evaded.

One of the best books to come to my table is entitled Children in Bondage, written by our commanding poet, Edwin Markham, assisted by Judge Ben Lindsay of Denver and George Creel.[3] Eleven out of these eighteen chapters were written by Mr. Markham. The table of contents is both statement, argument, appeal and conclusion; each chapter is a challenge and a rebuke. Listen to these calls to conscience: "The Sacrifice of Golden Boys and Girls", "The Crimson in Our Cotton", "Little Slaves of the Lamp" (the glass industry), "The Sweatshop Inferno", "The Cost of Coal, not in Dollars but in Human Lives", "The Grind Behind the Holidays".

- - - - -

[3] Edwin Markham, Benjamin Lindsay and George Creel, Children in Bondage. (New York: Hearst's International Library, Co., 1914). It was reprinted by the New York Times in 1968.

Read these challenges and then complacently think of your Santa Claus lists. Read them before you are hypnotized with the reckless, wicked, un-Christian season we call Christmas. Read of these "Spinners in the Dark" (the silk business), the "Curse of the Canneries", "The Child in the Perils of the Street", "Why Do Children Toil?", "The Great American Cancer", "Curing Symptomatic Evils", "Uprooting Causes".

It is well that we should grow indignant over this awful useless war raging in Europe. It is well indeed that our moral nature should cry, "Hold!" to that barbarism which desecrates art, breaks up communities, crushes homes, tears human flesh into shreds. But let not these horrors blind us to the equal or greater, but less obvious, horrors nearer home. "Half of the babies that die annually, die from preventable causes" - I repeat the verdict of physicians. This means that a hundred and fifty thousand babies born a year ago would be alive today, responding to the music in parent hearts, had it not been for the greed and selfishness, the grasp and competition of our American commercialism. If we accept three million as the total number of deaths on the European battlefields in the first four years of the war, the above figures show us that <u>preventable</u> deaths of infants less than one year old in the United States alone for that same period have equalled one-fifth as many as the war total. Let him that is without sin cast the first stone; let him with clean hands make the arraignment and summon the guilty into court.

In relating the mortality of children to the poverty of parents, we are no longer dealing with sentimental ethics, nor are we trusting to <u>a priori</u> logic. We are not talking about what ought to be or what in the nature of things must be, but we are talking of how things have been and how things are now. We have as definite data to go by in estimating a child's prospects of life as the insurance companies have in calculating the expectation of a grown man, a thing no underwriter ventures to estimate until he has before him a careful life-history of his subject. Who were his parents? How long did they live? When and where was he born? What is his health history to date? And what is the present accurate result of an expert physician's examination of his physical condition?

With facts as obstinate, and many of them more easily obtained and conclusive in their application, the life prospect of any baby born into the world today is a computable quantity. Every day adds more conclusive evidence of the intimate relation between high child mortality and parental poverty and squalor. The carefully collected figures are no sooner published than they are outgrown. So we are dipping out of a flowing stream when we quote from any statistical table. The latest figures available at present writing will answer my purpose. I need only remind my readers that the next year's figures will be different, more conclusive, and, let us hope, a little less ominous. Slowly but very surely the life of both babies and pigs is brought under the protecting hand of science and beneath the care of more and more intelligent nurses.

The experts of the Children's Bureau have recently published the results of a survey of infant mortality made in Manchester, New Hampshire. I can select but one or two facts from the valuable array presented. The infant death rate for the United States is estimated to be 124 per thousand births, which means that in round numbers one of every eight children born alive dies before it has completed its first year. Among the Manchester families studied, this death rate <u>doubled</u> in families where the father's income was less than $450 per year - one baby of every four born into these families died, and this was the income of more than 13 per cent of the families.

In families where the father's income was from $450 to $850 (and these constituted 60 per cent of the families studied), the death rate was one to every six babies born, or one-fourth higher than the average for the United States. In the 13 per cent of families whose wages were over $1050 per year, on the other hand, the death-rate fell to just half that of the average rate for the country. Of these babies only one in sixteen died during the first year, while the 12 per cent of families whose wages were between $850 and $1050 per year lost one baby out of every eight born - the rate being the same as in the nation at large.

The first ethical point in connection with my pigpen building is that as a nation, as expressed in federal and state laws, we are more careful of the physical well-being of the pig than we are of the baby. Ten thousand children or more in this city of Chicago, sleep o' nights and wake every morning under physical conditions that would not be tolerated by the successful pig breeder. And what is sadder, the up-to-date farmer is better informed as to the proper balanced rations of a growing pig, and he gives more attention to the compounding of these rations than this city of Chicago gives to the rations on which its children are expected to grow. I am not now thinking of the outrageous parents - the wicked, the idle, the foolish fathers and mothers, but rather of the successful farmers and successful businessmen in the United States, multitudes of whom on Sundays are sitting in Christian pews and praying the Lord for forgiveness of their sins, never stopping to catalogue these same sins as they appear in the eyes of the informed student - nay, as they are reflected in the worn faces of ill-fed and ill-housed children. If the children could only be treated with respect such as the favoured pig receives - that is, if they were only housed, fed and protected in such a way as to bring them to their maximum vitality, what a cloud of gloom would be lifted from the life of today. The child's needs run a long way on the same line as the pig's needs.

This brings me to another gruesome arraignment. The economist reminds us that the pig is the only domestic animal raised for food purposes alone. Therein lies the source of man's great interest in him. Economically speaking a pig is an asset, a baby a liability. You make money in raising a pig; it costs money to raise a baby. But if you raise a baby on pig-standards only, though he be fat and healthy, you have raised only a little animal.

And this point of departure where the baby's well-being takes leave of the pig's well-being is the most important point in our study. Certainly the well-being of a baby is not to be tested by avoirdupois. A well-fed child is not necessarily well cared for. I know not which to pity most, the child of the washerwoman, who must begin life's grim battles at twelve and face the terrible strain of long hours, or the children of some of the women whose clothes the washerwoman renovates, whose intellectual development, spiritual growth and social habits are delegated largely to hired assistants. For surely a child thus raised, and with parents so practical they scoff at "dreamers", may profit by all the scientific prudencies thrown around the pig-sty and still be left to revel in the ethics of the trough, compelled to lead an anemic life of the spirit, wanting in ideals worth living for, deficient in the initiative spirit which fills the soul with energy. Such children, over-blest with things and cursed with spiritual poverty, remain in the country as rust on iron, dry rot in the rafters on the house - carrying weakness, dismay and death far beyond the community in which they live.

General George Brinkerhoff[4], a noble friend of the unfortunate, Ohio's great humanitarian of the last generation, made himself famous by substituting for the old three R's, the three H's: head, hand and heart. These point to the greater needs of the child. They represent the most cruel neglect of our children.

"Social Service" is the slogan of our educators today. The elective studies in sociology are crowded with the better class of young men and women in our college courses. But by the confession of the students themselves, and by the attention given to the "investigation" and the "surveys" in this direction, too much of the social service in the interest of children and mothers is still on pigpen levels.

Recently I was talking to a graduate of a prominent college who means to give his life to social service, but he confessed that "social service", as he meant to pursue it, was primarily the question of housing, feeding, ventilating. He was prepared with an arraignment of the churches because of their failure to

- - - - -

[4] Roeliff Brinkerhoff (1828-1911) was a leading figure in prison reform after the Civil War.

render "social service" in these directions. Far be it from me to offer any apology for existing churches. I admit the thrust of his impeachment. Organized religion has been too indifferent to the physical conditions of life. It often fails to heed the demands of science. Food and environment do enter into the problem profoundly, but there are other social services than those connected with bread-and-butter benevolence. Hungry stomachs and shivering backs are often results of needs farther back and farther down, which cannot be supplied out of the flour barrel, the coal-bin or the loom. In the higher evolution of "social service" there comes a more adequate sense of the intangible sufferings of human nature, and our primal sympathies go out to the spirits that are underfed; when they are nourished, the housing and diet problems will be better cared for.

When this United States with its broad acres and fertile soil, with its expanse of fields and blooming orchards leaves a percentage of its citizens poverty-stricken to menace their neighbors and become a burden to the state, it gives proof of its spiritual profligacy. It denotes a stupidity and stolidity of conscience somewhere.

There are those in college and commercial circles who are sounding notes of alarm concerning the immigrant "horde" always threatening our country. Perhaps after all in this fresh tide of virility, this new stream of spiritual as well as physical potency, lies the hope of our country. We may look forward to future degeneracy, decay from internal weakness, and death as the end of this as of other nations. Perhaps this reinforcement which comes through the immigrant ports of the United States may save it.

PIGS AND BABIES

Two most striking and interesting books touching this phase of the subject have recently been published. One is From Alien to Citizen[5], by Professor Steiner of Grinnell, Iowa. It is the story of a wandering lad reaching our shores from that distrusted and little understood section known as "Eastern Europe". He was the child of conservative parents. He belonged to the distrusted, always underestimated and abused, Jewish race. We learn in this book how he wandered through our country, a veritable tramp from necessity - not from choice.[6] He was made familiar with the terrible hardships that belong to a man without money and without the language that would serve as a means of adequate communication with his fellow beings. This man had to learn the inside agony of the iron mills, the coal mines and the far-off harvest fields of the Northwest. He had been lured hither by the ideal America, "the land of the free and the home of the brave". But after his rapid disillusionment, he soon passed from the distrusted alien to the invaluable and indispensable citizen. He became the leader of men, the inspirer of youth. Because there was kindled in the heart of the little lad by the Jewish father and mother the unquenchable flame of the ideal, he has come to be a power in the United States. He is welcome in all the pulpits in the land; he is a leader in thought, a prophet of reform.

Scarcely less exciting, and quite as instructive,

- - - - -

[5] Edward A. Steiner, From Alien to Citizen: The Story of My Life in America (New York: Fleming H. Revell Co., 1914).

[6] One persistent topic in the newspapers of the late 19th and early 20th century was the danger of "tramps".

is that other book entitled A Far Journey[7], by Abraham Rihbany. This is the story of a lad born on the hill slopes of Syria, under the shadow of Lebanon, into a home of the simple, primitive life which obtained in that land in the time of the Nazarene carpenter. He drifted hither on the waves of a holy heart-hunger and landed in New York with nine cents in his pocket. The battle for bread was so fierce that at times he, like Elijah of old, would fain pray that his life might be taken away. Today that man occupies the pulpit of James Freeman Clarke in Boston, a pulpit than which there is none more honourable in the United States. He is in the most splendid apostolic succession that the American ministry can offer, and he is still a young man.

Now where is the economist who can estimate the value of these two great assets in American life: Professor Steiner of Grinnell College, Iowa, and Pastor Rihbany of the Church of the Disciples in Boston? There is ample justification for the opinion that these men are no glaring exceptions, no sporadic or spasmodic manifestations of power. They themselves are conscious of being types of a large class borne hither by the great inflowing stream that has been vitalizing this country from its inception. If you want to complete the list, call the long roll of the great nation-builders of the United States who were borne here on the crest of a dream, who wandered hither in search of the ideal. In 1848 and the years immediately following, the Middle West country was dotted with prophets and poets of whom Carl Schurz[8] may be taken as spokes-

― ― ― ― ―

[7] Abraham Mitre Rihbany, A Far Journey (New York: Houghton, Mifflin and Co., 1914).

[8] Statesman and Newspaper editor (1829-1906).

man. They came to interpret for us, who had preceded them by only a short time, the gospel of democracy, and they were ready to serve that gospel by their lives.

A southern "Daughter of the Confederacy" said to me some years ago in discussing the painful situation from 1861 to 1865, "No wonder that you won and that your people did not feel the awful weight of the struggle, because you had foreigners enough to fight your battles for you. You won through hired soldiers. A friend of mine in Lee's army at Gettysburg told me that he had found whole regiments from the North, members of which could not talk a word of English." The Southern sister was half right, but she overlooked the far more important truth. It is true that many of the soldiers who fought for the Union were foreign-born and foreign-bred; many of them speaking broken English rose to positions of responsibility, but it was no filthy lucre that brought them to the battle front, but rather an intelligent dream of democracy, an ideal of liberty, an appreciation of citizenship more valuable to them than any soft bed, white bread or ventilated palace.

I plead for the babies. I beg for them everything that the favored pig receives at the hand of the intelligent pig-raiser. And then I plead for the something more - a tremendous plus. If we are satisfied when the baby receives the fullness of pig-privileges, and are content to rest when it is cradled in pig-plenty, then hog-trough morality will control the business and direct the industries of the United States.

We spend much time and waste much breath in trying to fix the responsibility of the awful war now waging in Europe, but we are short-sighted and miss the mark unless we go back, back and back to the babies that were nursed at the breasts of queens, until we go back to the nurseries where were cradled the sons of kings, the children who were fed with false dreams of power and the malicious philosophies that justify crowns. Such scions of aristocracy - such sons of kings - grow up like the offspring of wild boars with developed tusks and an agility in their use.

Miss Taylor, the author of The Man Behind the Bars[9], was, for over a quarter of a century, the Angel of the Joliet prison. She not only brought comfort, life and light into numberless prison cells, but laid subterranean wires that reached into the homes of convicts, sustained the spirit of waiting wives, tutored the hearts of depressed children. In this book she tells the story of "Alfred Allen". Through her I came to know the real name of this Welsh boy who came out of Joliet under her guidance. He was sheltered for some time under the roof of the old All Souls Church. The remainder of his short and pathetic life was spent largely within my knowledge, part of the time under my direction. In the early '70's, bereaved of father and mother, this little Welsh waif became one of the "gamins" of the Chicago streets. He was starved, frozen, chilled, battered and beaten as such children were in those days. (Happily that type of "gamin" is scarcely to be found in Chicago today.) Finally he was trained, in what were under the circumstances perfectly normal ways, to be an expert assistant to a burglar-employer. He was small, wiry and alert. He could be placed in out-of-the-way places, could be passed

- - - - -

[9] Winnifred Louise Taylor, The Man Behind the Bars (New York: Charles Scribners Sons, 1914).

through small openings, and in many ways he proved useful to the one who to him was a "good friend". Miss Taylor found this boy a grown man in prison. A cellmate, hardened in crime but cultivated in mind, had stirred in him a love of reading. He became deeply interested in works of political economy. This Irish criminal turned his best side toward his Welsh fellow prisoner, and the boy reached after culture on high lines. In the course of his reading he fell upon the work of an Englishman who admired America. In that book he read that "in America every man feels called upon to do some service for his country and to feel a voter's responsibility". This struck the heart of the convict. He thought, "I have never done anything for my country and I am an American." From that time forth a new life began to grow in that starved soul. With broken body but with a kindled mind he came out of prison with a holy purpose to do something for his country. The story as you find it in the book is too long to be told. I know it in longer meter than is given there, but the end of it all is that this assistant robber beat out the fragment of a life still left him in a pathetic and heroic quest for usefulness. He did seek an education, he did master a craft and did find the joy of human love, knew both the pride and the heart-break of a father who received and lost a baby love.

The point I want to make is that it is better to be a convict in Joliet in communion with high teachers and great philosophers than to be cradled in luxury with intellectual companionships that are trifling, debilitating, silly and selfish.

I plead for that higher nourishment of babes uncalled for by the pig-sty at its best. I beg for air for the soul, bread for the heart. The call is for development of conscience in the child. O Americans, lift your little ones into an atmosphere of courage and hope, however meager the bodily nourishment may be. They only are the "favoured children of Providence" who are guided upward, strengthened in thought, chastened in spirit; on these the nations must depend.

Scientific pigpens for pigs, palaces for babies if you can afford them - and there is enough wealth of this kind to go around if the game is fairly played; but the little pig parts company with the little child on the psychical thresholds of life. You cannot save the baby with only physical benefactions prefigured by the most modern of pigpens. The first step in the redemption of the slum, I believe, is the burning down of the uninhabitable dwellings. Acres of such intolerable, unredeemable shacks are waiting the application of the torch by order of the city council. But the work is only begun when the shacks are burned and modern tenements take their place. You cannot save a family with more coal or better bread, though these are mighty factors in the salvation we seek. Work effectively on the other line and eventually they will buy their own coal.

Elizabeth Barrett Browning was right in her plea for the ragged children of London. She cried: "Put a thought beneath their rags to ennoble the heart's struggle."[10]

In the absence of ideas and ideals give your dollars to those who have both, to spend them for you; but if you have ideas and ideals that have been a comfort to you, then in the name of high Heaven invest

- - - - -

[10] From "Song for the Ragged Schools of London".

your dollars and your lives in the nobler charity, the greater benefactions of mind, the holy forces of love and tenderness.

XV

"The Gospel of the Manger" was an addition to the manuscript. A preliminary list of proposed chapters had in its place a different sermon on the same theme, "Sub-Human Contributions to the Humanities".

The explicit focus on the birth of Jesus -- even in a Christmas sermon -- is unusual for Jones. He puts it into an evolutionary and sociological context that gives it quite a different emphasis from that of most Christmas sermons, yet he does not lose the centre of the Christmas proclamation.

Peace becomes the theme which he develops -- although in the beginning, the material seems far away from both peace and Christmas. Like some of the other sermons in the collection, this one has been revised to be more appropriate to the time of The Great War. Jones' optimistic faith in evolution and human progress sounds naïve in our time, but his passion for peace, disarmament and human unity has not lost its power or its relevance.

The sermon was first preached, before the War, on 17 December 1911 at All Souls. Both <u>Unity</u> and <u>Hoard's Dairyman</u> printed it in their Christmas issues the same year. (Its pacifism is so intense that <u>Hoard's</u> could never have printed it by 1917.)

Jones intended this sermon to be prefaced by "Brotherhood", an early poem by Edwin Markham. Jones and Markham were close friends. Markham even wrote a poem on Jones: "To J. Ll. J. - The Dream".

THE GOSPEL OF THE MANGER

A recent book by Royal Dixon has the startling title of The Human Side of Plants.[1] It is not a book written by a poet or a sentimentalist. No playwright marshals the plants in masks as Rostand did the animals in "Chanticler". It is written by a botanist and with botanists in mind. It is the work of a scientist, anxious to state scientific realities. It deals in the main with the well-established and well-acknowledged facts taught by botanists.

This book tells us of plants that walk, eat, catch insects, fish, defend themselves, keep a standing army and navy, employ aerial squadrons, keep servants and livestock -- aye, plants that plunder and murder and build airships. Here we are told of plants that soar, that carry life insurance, kidnap and entertain. There are plants that hide their blossoms and their fruit, that court and join in solemn marriage. In the final chapter we are not much surprised to find the audacious title, "The Mentality and Spirituality of Plants". The mentality and spirituality of plants! Think of it! Mr. Dixon tells us that plants have a psychic sense in addition to the five senses with which we are endowed. Plants see and feel and hear, smell

─ ─ ─ ─ ─

[1] The beginning must be a later addition to the sermon, since Dixon's book was not published by Frederick A. Stokes Company until 1914. The book is much more an entertaining exercise in popular science than "by a botanist with botanists in mind".

and taste, and they have that other psychic sense which enables them to grow over the obstructions which they cannot see or feel or smell and find the wall behind the bank, upon which they are to climb.

Everywhere in the plant world we see the beginning of that struggle for existence which reaches towards the co-operation of human communities. The story of wheat antedates the pyramids. The story of barley and rye and Indian corn is inextricably associated with the story of human civilization. Every new plant erected by the skill of man, developed as a human resource or companion, is another addition to the rational life, a reinforcement to the gospel of love. Kaffir corn, alfalfa, rape, spineless cacti and the new berries and fruits developed by Burbank[2] are headings for recent chapters in the story of human progress. They indicate more than can be put into words of how the human life-line, if adequately measured, must be traced back and back and down into the animal kingdom and into the vast realm of plant life.

When we cross the very uncertain boundary between plant and animal life, how much fuller and more gracious and profound is that bible of God whose pages have been written in Nature's book! Studying the animal world, we find that which enriches our sympathies, restores our faith and lifts us higher and still higher onto the highlands of brotherhood. In this profoundly impressive story even the battle fields of Europe are but incidental episodes of the march.

Long before we find men on this earth, we find human attributes blooming in brute realms. Not

— — — — —

[2] Luther Burbank (1849-1926), a developer of new plants whose activity captured much public attention.

only is there a human side to plants, but there is a human side to all life on this earth. The more we study our little brothers and sisters in fur and feathers, the more do we learn of the higher and better economy of the human state. The old text said: "Go to the ant, thou sluggard!" The old aristocrats of earth did that and learned lessons of industry and thrift. The new man, Tolstoy for example, went to the ant and found a sociological gospel of mutual helpfulness, of public spirit, of community forbearance.

Next in the evolution of the race to the power of kindling and controlling fire is the domestication of animals. Without their co-operation the poor, unweaponed and unclothed human creature could never have risen to the supremacy which he now occupies. The student of primitive man has not been able to find any monumental or historic trace of a race so primitive that it is unaccompanied by the dog.

The contribution of the dog to the spiritual life of the race is greater than his contribution to its physical prosperity, great as that is. Professor Shaler[3] tells us that the greatest triumph man has ever achieved over any organism, including his own body, is that represented by civilized - I use the word advisedly - the "civilized" dog. His ferocious ancestor -- the wolf, the hyena or some allied species living by prey -- has been transformed into a thousand forms, with aptitude and skill developed by human wit. Through the alchemy of spirit and the chemistry of brains, the natural foe of the lamb has come to be the lamb's best guardian, the most heroic and skillful of shepherds.

- - - - -

[3] Another reference to Nathaniel Shaler's <u>Domestication of Animals</u>.

Add a little more of this spiritual solvent and the frightful beast becomes the companion of women, the playmate of children; a little more human sagacity, and the sneaking thief of the forest becomes the reliable watch dog, who stands guard over your property; a little more brains introduced into the canine laboratory and you have the hound whose keen scent and marvelous agility make the latest achievement of the rifle insignificant and oftentimes of no avail. By the same alchemy of wit, we have the dog of the old descent reduced to a fluffy plaything which milady carries in her muff with room still left for her gloves.

One of the masterpieces in American oratory is Senator Vest's tribute to a dog, delivered in the line of his practice as a lawyer before a jury. He said:

> Gentlemen of the jury, a man's dog stands by him in prosperity and in poverty, in health and in sickness. He will sleep on the cold ground when the wintry winds blow and the snow drives fiercely, if only he may be near his master's side. He will kiss the hand that has no food to offer, he will lick the wounds and sores that come in encounter with the roughness of the world. He guards the sleep of his pauper master as if he were a prince. When all other friends desert, he remains. When riches take wings and reputation falls to pieces, he is as constant in his love as the sun in its journey through the heavens. If fortune drives the master forth

THE GOSPEL OF THE MANGER 241

an outcast in the world, friendless and homeless, the faithful dog asks no higher privilege than that of accompanying him, to guard against danger, to fight against his enemies, and when the last scene of all comes and death takes the master in its embrace and his body is laid away in the cold ground, no matter if all other friends pursue their way, there by his graveside will the noble dog be found, his head between his paws, his eyes sad but open in alert watchfulness, faithful and true even in death.

How the pages of English literature would be impoverished if we took out of them the stories of the bird, the dog and the horse. The tenderness of Robert Burns would shrink in an expurgated edition that would leave out the poems to "Mousie" and the "Ould Mare Maggie" and his ewe lamb "Mailie".

Where would the march of empire be without the beasts of burden which accompanied the human -- the camel, the ox, the horse, the ass -- and still more the later bovine benedictions of the cow, the foster mother of millions of children, the humanitarian agency in millions of homes?

Later perhaps in order of time, the reindeer and, when climactic conditions demand, the dog have reinforced the human power, supplemented the strength of man's back, enlarged the carrying capacity of his arms and added to the fleetness and endurance of his feet to a degree immeasurably greater than anything done by the more recent triumphs of steam and electricity. Compared with the transporting service of these more primitive express trains and freight-bearing caravans, the transcontinental railroad trains and the transoceanic ships are recent luxuries known to but comparatively few of the children of men.

Doubtless the ox not the cow was man's first conquest. The earliest bovine was the beast of burden -- the yoke-fellow of man. Mark the yoke, how much it means to human progress -- the ox-yoke hewn out of the maple log, with its hickory bows. This is an extension of divine providence that reaches clear down into our day. Rich am I in memories that reach back to the ox-yoke. It was with oxen that we cleared the forests and plowed the earlier fields of Wisconsin. It was oxen that broke the prairie sod of Illinois. Oxen drew the prairie schooners across the arid deserts of the West and lodged the adventurous pilgrims in the gold fields of California.

The era of the ox as a beast of burden, as a draft animal, in our land is largely past, but the era of the cow, which began later, is still in its infancy. There is sociological warrant and economic justification for the old Hindu piety that, in an early Veda, sang the hymn of the cow:

> I charge you, O my sons, to follow a herd of cows, smelling the dust raised by their feet day by day and at night lie down and guard them. O thou mighty Indra, make our pastures wide, give us wealth in cows, for he that hath cows will delight in cows, for substance is the delight of man and he that hath no

THE GOSPEL OF THE MANGER 243

substance hath no delight.[4]

Professor Shaler constantly emphasizes the truth that in the domestication of animals human sympathies were developed and the boundaries of love extended. He says that domestication represents "one of the modes of action of that sympathetic motive which, more than any other, has been the basis of the highest development of mankind".[5] He tells us that the element of sympathy, love for another's life, is the inspiration that has brought the lower realms of life, animal and vegetable, into the service and companionship of man. He shows us that while the primitive inhabitants of this continent had but the dog and three or four plants under control, the present inhabitant has domesticated to his will and his purposes perhaps a hundred different species of animals and a thousand different plants, fully one half of which, he says, are cultivated for the gratification of the aesthetic tastes and interests. They are bred and cultivated for pleasure, for the joy of companionship, for the beauty of garden, lawn and fireside. Take the pets out of the family and the flowers out of the garden, and man again becomes the hard, fierce, cruel companion of the tiger and the serpent.

Barnum's Happy Family[6] was the joke of the menagerie, but the farmer's happy family -- where the fowls of the air, the beasts of the field, the lamb and the dog, the cat and the bird, live in amity -- is in every

- - - - -

[4] These lines are not from any hymn of the Rigveda. Whatever their origin may be, Jones would have found them in a secondary source.

[5] Shaler, <u>Domestication of Animals</u>, p 221.

[6] A circus exhibit of several incompatible animals in the same enclosure.

well-ordered barnyard an accomplished fact; it is not a prophecy, but a realized "kingdom of God on earth".

Sturdy sailors shed salty tears as Buffalo Bill Cody bade good-bye to his comrade and champion, his gallant horse of the wild west. As he lay on the deck of a great steamer wrapped in the American Flag, before he was consigned to his watery grave, his master said:

> Charley, but for your willing speed and tireless courage, I would many years ago have lain low as you are now, and my Indian foe would have claimed you for his slave. Yet you never failed me, Charley, old fellow. I have had many friends, but of very few of them would I say that. Men tell me you have no soul, but if there be a heaven and scouts can enter there, I'll wait at the gate for you, old friend.

I love these stories from the widening realms of human life which show how the "triumph of the Cross" is rooted not in "civilized" nor "Christian", nor yet in "human" life but in <u>life</u> -- that which reaches farther down than our study can go and higher up than our experience has reached.

In preaching the "Gospel of the Manger", the emphasis is generally laid on the <u>gospel</u> found in the <u>lowly</u> manger. The <u>cattle</u> in that Bethlehem stable are too much neglected. "In the fulness of time" is the Bible phrase. The times were ripe for his arrival, for the cattle were there to welcome the arrival of the "Prince of Love".

These four-footed additions to the <u>genus homo</u> -- the two-footed animal -- accompanied man on his upward

THE GOSPEL OF THE MANGER

climb through vast stretches of time before the dawn of the manger era. The herdsman antedates the farmer by many, many generations. The earlier master of the flocks must needs follow his herd from one valley to another, from one altitude to another. Not until man ceased to be nomadic and built for himself a fixed habitation, not until he learned to master the seasons, to conserve the over-supply of summer for the under-supply of winter, not until he learned to "make hay while the sun shines", to turn the sod and plant the seed, did the era of the manger come.

A babe laid in a manger must needs represent an advanced stage of human development. The manger is relatively a modern achievement. Primitive man led a precarious life, skulking in caves, hiding in hollow logs, seeking protection for his young in the limbs of trees as he waged his unequal battle with the relentless forces of nature -- cold and heat, storms, rains, winds -- and the still more relentless wild beasts that thirsted for his blood. The fruits and roots of the forest were his meager support until out of his dire necessity, his pitiful helplessness, he won by his wit the cooperation of his humbler relatives of the animal kingdom.

When the Christ-child was laid in a manger, he was cradled in the lap of civilization; he entered into a vast and noble inheritance of the past, and he rested on the high prophetic vantage-ground from which he could look forward to a measureless destiny for man, in which there would arise the kingdom of God, the reign of peace, the era of brotherhood on earth.

It is true that the words of the Hebrew law-givers, sages and reformers were back of him, but farther back than all these were the uncounted triumphs over field and forest and the inhabitants thereof. The beasts of the field and the birds of the air were ready to be his loyal attendants and royal escort. When he came these were there ready to welcome him. They made room for him in the manger.

Legend, poetry, painting have rejoiced in this manger story. Artists throughout the Christian centuries have loved to paint Mary the mother and her babe in the neighborhood of the cows. The barn and the manger have been the favorite theme of both preacher and poet. The symbolism of the manger is perhaps an overworked commonplace of the Christian pulpit. It has been made to typify the poverty, the unwanted hardships, the primitive simplicity of the cradle-conditions of the Christ-child. But legend, poetry and art, at their highest, fall below the inspiration of the plain, hard reality.

Theologians make much of the Biblical phrase "in the fulness of time", in regard to the advent of the Master. They love to show how the elder prophets of Israel predicted the forthcoming event, and they argue that when the clock of the old civilization had run down and pagan power was at its extreme ebb, there came into the world this renewing vitality, this energizing personality, this redeeming of the race. There are texts at hand to justify, within limits, this reasoning.

But science throws the rays of its searchlight far, far back of Hebrew text and historical records and discovers a Messianic preparation for the man-child that renders the chronology of the Biblical theologian, as Emerson suggests, "but the tick of a kitchen clock".

When the Christ-child was laid in the manger and holy motherhood was companioned by the gentle-eyed

THE GOSPEL OF THE MANGER

cows, he came into a fulness of time for which the struggling souls of men had battled through untold millenia.

Zoroaster, the prophet of Persia, thus counted the early rounds in the ladder of civilization:

> What is the first place on earth most acceptable to Ahura-Mazda, the holy one?
> <u>It is where man has built himself a place for wife and child</u>.
> What is the second place most acceptable to Ahura-Mazda, the holy one?
> <u>It is where man has turned the sod and planted seed</u>.
> What is the third place most acceptable to Ahura-Mazda, the holy one?
> <u>It is the field that man has fertilized by the dung of cattle</u>.[7]

The child laid in a manger started from the high vantage-ground of progress. The manger implies settled homes, cultivated crops, fertilized fields, the domestication of animals. Who, then, would learn the gospel of the manger must learn of science concerning the dawn of the human in sub-human realms, the slow climb of man from the troglodyte - the cave-dweller - through the nomadic herdsman to the settled farmer.

What a charming Christmas story is this. Forget for a time the winged angels; let the cloud-choirs of the sky cease their singing. Banished be Santa Claus with his tinsel and bells, while with bowed heads and unsandalled feet we stand in the great cathedral of the

-----

[7] There is a passage similar to this in the <u>Vendidad</u> (Fargard III, "The Earth"). A note by the <u>editor in Sacred Books of the East</u> says it was a favorite theme that occurs in several variations in many different texts.

past, the dim but solemn aisles of history, and realize as best we may the bringing of a manger into the effulgence of Christmas joy. What tiresome marches, what bloody struggles, what sweaty toil lie back of our Christmas carols.

The child cradled in a manger is a foundling of democracy; he is qualified to become a prophet of human brotherhood, an exponent of the love of God on earth.

Aristocrats in their conceit may be born to downy couches, cradled in marble and ebony, draped in silks and satins, but thereby they may be excluded from the sunshine of universal love, from the inspiration of inclusive sympathies. From the loving brotherhood in which there is neither Jew, Greek or barbarian, black or white, rich or poor, high or low -- a brotherhood which embraces all in the adequate love of the Father of All, whose dearest son was cradled in a manger. Out of this fundamental brotherhood he rose to be the friend of sinners, the confessed brother of the sparrow and the "Prince of Peace".

It is inspiring to remember that he whose message has broken down the arrogant claims of conquerors, the superstitious pride of descent and class, the prejudices of creeds and races found his cradle in a manger. The cattle welcomed him. What more fitting place for one who said of the sinner: "Neither do I condemn thee; go, and sin no more," who commended the humility of the contrite publican, whose broken prayer, "Father be merciful to me, a sinner," was heard above the arrogant piety of the high-headed, blood-proud, purse-proud, creed-confident Pharisee who said: "Father, I thank Thee that I am not as other men are."

In the manger, if nowhere else, the Christ-child is still at home. The gospel of the manger is no mush

THE GOSPEL OF THE MANGER

of concession, no gush of sentimentality, to which we turn our thoughts once a year and then forget it while we remain deaf to the cry of the toiler and blind to the claims of the hungry. The gospel of the manger is as hard as steel, as inevitable as gravitation, as permanent as the laws of mathematics.

When kings, czars and kaisers misread their mission, misdirect the energies of men, pervert the human state and render of no avail the decisions of justice, love and service proclaimed on Sinai and Olivet - exemplified by the master souls of Socrates, Buddha, and Jesus - then the religion of the bird's nest, the persuasive plea of the dog and of that perpetually humiliated man-made product, the mule, restore our faith. Then the gospel of the manger reassures us that after all "the earth is the Lord's and the fullness thereof" and that the meek are to inherit it.

This larger brotherhood of life is ever groping, climbing -- and at times soaring -- towards the heights of "peace on earth, good will to men". It lifts us above petty jealousies and mocks the heroics of nations, the conceits and prejudices of races. All these narrow enthusiasms seem so small, mean and transient.

When we stand by the Christ-child, cradled with the cattle, how petty are the dividing lines between Teuton and Briton, Frank and Slav! As we study the profounder reaches of the law of brotherhood, we come to the unities "above the battle". If we have a place in our hearts for the Russian hound, what about the Russian man who trains him? If we have admiration for the dachsund, have we no place for the German who loves him? He who is a pro-Jersey cowman must necessarily be a pro-Briton, knowing who raises the Jersey cow. If we make room for the beautiful Ayrshire, we must make room for the Scotsman who developed her.

When the human marauder who lived by conquest was transformed into the soil-tiller, tribal bonds gave way. The next step in the process will come when national enthusiasms are merged into international comity. Then peace on earth will follow, and the gospel of the manger will come into full power. Someone has said that the dog is already "more than dog", and surely the dog stories that delight the philosopher as well as the child justify the statement. When the gospel of the manger comes full-orbed, the lion will lie down with the lamb or else the lion will have been eliminated. It is the mission of man to give to the Lord his own by the elimination of the brute, the representative of selfishness, dominated by greed and force, whether the greed be of quadruped or biped, whether his weapons be horns, fangs or sabers. The forces that make for schism and hatred and unholy rivalries are doomed by the gospel of the manger which is the gospel of love, expressed in the gentleness that is conquering the world.

The "Christmas spirit" -- so called -- is cosmic before it is Christian. Any successful attempt to bring the angel songs down to earth must make common cause with the force that has been, and is, eliminating horns, claws and fangs, supplanting them with the marvelous hand, the deft fingers, and the dome of thought -- bringing up angels out of clover fields and farm yards.

Notwithstanding the gruesome quarrels among the nations, I still celebrate Christmas with a right good heart, because I put my back up against the Universe. I remember that I belong to the Pleiades, that I am allied to that Providence which draped this naked earth with the beautiful green grass and noble trees. I am allied to the rose; I am neighbor to the robin. I am akin to the elephant in P.T. Barnum's menagerie of whom this story is told: An ugly splinter, deeply rooted in her ponderous foot, was extracted by a dexterous surgeon, who with great danger to himself probed the wound and prepared the way for a speedy healing. A year and a half passed and the elephant was again in that town. When the surgeon visited his former patient, she raised the healed foot and caressed him with her trunk.

I love such stories because they reinforce my Bible and rebuke my dogmatism. I find in them an escape from the Calvinism that still would write the message of God in lurid terms of hell-fire. They help me escape from that interpretation which would crown with power some devil of mischief or malign Satan. These studies teach me that there is a groping toward beauty, a leaning toward duty, a climbing toward the light, and everywhere discoverable in the mighty precessions of life -- growing more and more mighty and more gracious in every upward reach. Within the whole circumference of the universe there is no spot upon which the foot of an unmitigated devil can rest. In all the immensity of space, there is no abiding place for a Satan untouched with a thirst for righteousness. In the long run there is no permanent place for the bayonet-armed man any more than for the bayoneting animal. Both are doomed. The time will come -- it is nearer now than we realize -- when the brute elements will be eliminated from the human as life-destroying and progress-thwarting. If I fail to find a gospel in the creeds and forms of Christendom, if Bible texts confuse, I can still move the previous question and seek the gospel of love in the bird's nest and in the manger with the cows.

Wellington's defeat of Napoleon at Waterloo fixed the map of Europe for a century. He was called the Iron Duke, but I like better the story of the Wellington who comforted a sobbing boy because he had to go off to school and leave his pet toad unattended. "I will take care of your toad," said the great general, and he took him home and became a human providence to that much underestimated co-worker with men, his assistant gardener. He even wrote the lad of how the toad was getting along. In the balances of the Almighty, the heart of the man who could make common cause with a boy in the interest of a toad may have been a more valuable contribution to the coming Kingdom of God than the skill that conquered at Waterloo. Back of the triumphant general lay the military achievements of history, the ambitions and triumphs of the Alexanders, Caesars, Hannibals, all fused into the will of an "Iron Duke", but the tenderness of mothers unborn, the spirit of gentleness and pity, the hearts of the saviours of the world are found in the story of the toad. Waterloo belongs in the past; the toad story to the future.

In this dire predicament which now overhangs the nations we call Christian, there is no justification for gloomy discouragement. The pessimist still has no place on which to stand. Even on the reeking battle fields of Europe, human nature is still dominant. If it has harked back instead of pushing forward, it cannot go far back. Let the sword-bearers do their devilish work to the utmost, yet the peasant life of Germany, France, England, Russia, Austria, Belgium will remain. It will continue to be sweet, tender, loyal, so long as there are little lambs to be nurtured, little calves to be fed, little colts to be trained -- so long as there are little chickens to be loved by

THE GOSPEL OF THE MANGER 253

little boys and girls, aye, so long as there is a flower to be watered by care-burdened homekeepers. While man continues to plant trees, set out parks, preserve places of beauty, so long will the procession of life -- not of man alone but of all life -- move toward the heights of gentleness, tenderness and forgiveness. Many peaks along the way may be cross-crowned, but the goal is the land of love.

The solution of all our war troubles is to be found in the gospel of the manger. The Texas steer with its branching weapons is giving way to "the cow with the crumpled horn", and she is making way for the cow that has no horns. Farmers are breeding the horns off their cattle as fast as they can, and if perchance the process is too slow to meet the humanities of the barnyard, the humane farmer saws off the horns, knowing that the momentary agony is overbalanced by the permanent peace that will prevail ever after in the barnyard.

"Why did you choose this breed for dairy purposes?" I asked of a farmer as his handsome herd of Red Polls quietly passed through the barnyard gate in intimate contact with each other. "I believe, sir," was the reply, "it is because they are so gentle. They are so kind to one another and to everybody that it is a pleasure to handle them." There is a whole system of political economy in that answer. Nay, here is the gospel of the manger in barnyard philosophy and cow demonstration. Here is a suggestion for the international code-makers.

The Red Polls are a hornless brand. They have left the gospel of force behind them. They have already forgotten the attributes that belong to horned animals. They are developing a new psychology, a higher political economy for the barnyard, and their success is for the council of chambers of nations. The times are as ripe for dehorned nations as for dehorned cows. The unarmed man is justified of nature and of history. His bloodless quests are practised by the marching hosts of life, reaching from the humble earthworm -- without whose services this globe would still be a barren place -- up and on to the conquests of reason, to the universal brotherhood.

Let us gather up the fragments of this lesson. The manger came in the fullness of time. The child cradled therein had back of him an heroic and measureless ancestry. He was born into an economic bounty, the wealth of which we are just beginning to realize, the economy of which is still in its infancy. He was born into tenderness, doomed to gentleness and love. He was born into a brotherhood wider than the widest human reach. He was a comrade of the kine, a companion of the birds, at home in the fields.

The child in the manger made possible a new era of economic justice; it recognized that the only gospel is the gospel of democracy. The word "international", which now is pronounced so hesitatingly, will soon become the chosen word of preacher, journalist and orator. It was first a suspected word, brought into prominence by the working men of Europe. It was beaten out on the anvil of the blacksmiths when the Brotherhood of Labour was established. The order rose above the prejudice of race or the ambitions of nations. Then, lo! the scientist, the artist, the statesman and at last the preacher began to claim the word. Soon we will all be internationalists. But no internationalism can be achieved except that which is founded on the manger gospel of love. Man sallies forth on the high adventure of conquering all the forces of this earth for the domain of reason and the service of life. Thus the gospel of the manger opens out into the greater brotherhood and the larger freedom of the ages. It is the gospel of love.

XVI

In 1916 Jones began a series of sermons on The Book of Genesis. He used, as he always had, the most recent Biblical scholarship - continental "higher criticism" - to shape his interpretation, and he set the Biblical texts within the frame of evolutionary thought. He preached the third of that series - on the creation of woman - on 19 November. Changing its cumbersome original title for the book, it became "The Milk of Human Kindness".

Without the original title, there is nothing in the sermon itself to indicate its source in the book of Genesis. Despite apparent discontinuities in subject matter - evolution, motherhood, the dairy industry, social conscience, women's liberation - the unity becomes visible at the end. It is a sermon on the growth and influence of "feminine" characteristics in human culture.

Jones was as much a spokesperson for the emancipation of women as he was for peace. In this sermon he combines the two. His treatment of "the uprising of women" has a strikingly modern ring to it, despite the fact that his specific examples are much out of date.

The introductory poem for this sermon was to have

been one by Charlotte Perkins Stetson Gilman, an active feminist of the time. The note Jones made indicates that the poem is to be taken "from Bynner's New World". Witter Bynner did publish a book in 1915 called <u>The New World</u>. It contains only one long poem, written by himself; there is no poem by Mrs. Gilman in it.

The sermon was printed in <u>Unity</u> on 4 January 1917.

THE MILK OF HUMAN KINDNESS

Herbert Spencer[1] dwelt upon certain "critical points" in the evolution of life on its way to man. John Fiske called them the "high bridges" over which life passed on its upward climb. Such a critical point was passed when life left the water and ventured to try the land, and animals became air-breathing. Another critical point was passed when the animal left the ground and took to the air - when the reptile became a bird. A more sublime bridge was crossed still earlier than these, when the uni-sexual life, which was propagated by division, became bi-sexual, and life was perpetuated by male and female. Perhaps the most profound of all triumphs in the evolution of life came when the egg-laying mother gave place to one who gave birth to her young alive, and the infant - first nourished within the body - was then fed by the same body through a period of helplessness into self-reliance. This triumph marked what John Fiske calls "the dawning of the spiritual life", the first appearance of altruism. Progress was accelerated and made inevitable by

- - - - -

[1] Herbert Spencer (1820-1903), a British philosopher who attempted a unified view of all knowledge through evolution.

the prolongation of infancy, enabling the individual to organize new experiences and form new habits of thought and action. Then followed an unlimited demand for love; when egoism gave way to altruism another high bridge was crossed on the upward road.

Preachers talk much about "the milk of human kindness"; they revel in rhetoric, indulge in poetry concerning it, but he who would understand the full purport of this phrase must needs consult the biologist before he can appreciate the poet. Primarily – fundamentally – the "milk of human kindness" is mother's milk. This is a biological necessity before it is a psychical comfort. Literally through mother's milk has come, as Fiske has shown, the development of the home and the ever-enlarging circle of that home, until now the brooding care of the fireside reaches out through the commanding industries of the world and wraps the globe in a provident mantle all the more divine because woven by human hands.

Harriet B. Bradbury, in a recent book entitled, Civilization and Womanhood[2], says that marriage is the result of man's early recognition of his relation to his own children -- a most significant remark, for biology teaches that there were great eras of life in which the male parent knew not his own and the mother was the sole parent burdened with the responsibility of the offspring. Indeed, often this responsibility became so urgent that she must needs protect the child from its own father.

But this conscious fatherhood – this monogamic necessity of the higher life – is no later-day product of what we call civilization. It is not even an

– – – – –

[2] Published in Boston by Richard G. Badger in 1916.

experiment on the part of the human, for monogamy – a deliberate union between one male and one female through life for the maintenance of a family – reaches down into sub-human realms. The birds sang songs of love, and father birds guarded the brooding mother and helped provide for helpless offspring on this earth long before man had erected himself on two limbs. Before his appearance there was the vigilant prowess of the male defending his offspring and his mate. Those who would make light of this necessity of the higher life – those who would evade the bond "until death do us part" – are merely kicking against the pricks of destiny, proving disloyal to the deep-laid necessities of progress rooted in pre-human life. They are harking back to brute selfishness and inefficiencies.

It is now quite clear that what Tylor calls "the arts of life" – spinning, weaving, skin dressing and tanning, pottery, basket-making, mat and carpet-making and hut-building – came by the hand of woman. All of them were born out of the divine necessities of the child. It was a woman's hand that domesticated the barnyard animals, the milk-producing, wool-growing, egg-laying reinforcements of the larder and the wardrobe. The students of primitive man have never been able to go back of the domesticated dog, which was probably the triumph of the hunting male, unless, indeed it was the triumph of the child, which made of the primitive dog what he still is – a household pet, before he was the companion of the chase or the guardian at the gate. But surely the cat is woman's conquest; at one time it was woman's invaluable ally in her battle with the vermin that menaced her supplies. The root cellar, and if you like, the granary – which antedates the barn, were builded by and for women.

Perhaps the greatest triumph in the history of humanity was woman's conquest of man, changing the hunter into the planter, supplanting his instinct to provide by killing with the more sure provision from the breeding and rearing of herds and flocks and the raising of crops. Thus did she compel the father to share first the primal burdens of parentage and then the ever-increasing and widening joys of the home.

To fight dirt and flies, to keep out the rain and vermin are difficult tasks assigned by common consent to woman, but the extended interpretation of motherhood, the increasing vigilance imposed upon her by science, the rapidly unfolding life of the race, have brought the more severe battles in which there can be no division of labor between the sexes. It requires the combined energies of father and mother to carry on the more complicated warfare against the subtle enemies of life - the deadly microbes, the poison gases and the seductive narcotics.

Economically speaking, the cow is the greatest food-producing machine perfected by man. The cow transforms the roughage of forest and field, of mountain-side and swamp into the most palatable of food, adapted to the needs of babes, invalids and strong men. Grass, timothy, clover, alfalfa, potato-parings, pumpkins, turnips, cabbages, bran, barley, oats, rye, cotton-seed, even the refuse of the maltster - the material which the brewer could not wholly spoil - are put into one end of this machine, and presto, in an unspeakable short space of time, milk, with all which this implies - milk, sweet, luscious, delectable, milk, a fitting nectar for the gods of the old mythology - milk, with all it contains, cream, butter, cheese,

THE MILK OF HUMAN KINDNESS

custards, pies and puddings - is drawn from the other end. One quart of good cow's milk is said to have the nourishment of eight eggs or two pounds of salt codfish. Milk is the only food that contains all the elements necessary for the human body. One cow in her full development furnishes the milk necessary in the modern day for fourteen adults, though as a matter of fact, it is claimed that in the United States there is a milk cow for every four and a half persons.

The products of the cow machine are almost equaled by the marvelous story of its by-products as developed by modern skill and invention. An auctioneer, famous as the vender of dairy cows, has epitomized these by-products in a passage familiar to cowmen. He tells us that there is nothing, from nose to tail, that is not utilized by man.

> Her horns give us combs, her tail makes soup, her blood is used to make sugar white, her bone fertilizes our soil; card-board is made out of her stomach and, by further elaboration, the finest quality of false teeth comes from the same source; and added to all this, her flesh and that of her progeny feed the nation with its most staple meat.

Where the cow is most honoured, there the wealth of the field is most successfully conserved. The devastated fields of the profligate farmer are renewed, and the denuded plantations, rendered sterile by the cultivation of cotton and tobacco, are promptly brought back to fertility and to civilization by the help of the cow.

If we would understand the full import of the phrase, "milk of human kindness", let us study the dairy interests of our day and become conversant with the triumphs of motherhood as it has been extended beyond the resources of human bodies into that milk-industry that now constitutes, it is claimed, one-sixteenth of the food supply of the world. He who would appreciate the great gift of Providence through motherhood must begin by trying to appreciate the statistics of the milk industries of the world.

Ten billion gallons of milk were reported as the product of American farms in 1916, making a lake, as one writer estimates, large enough to float the navies of the world. Let this suggest the motherhood that is expressing itself in the economic joys and prosperities of our day.

There are over a million and a half dairy cows in Wisconsin and in Iowa, half as many in Michigan; Illinois has over one million. Chicago uses daily over one million-and-a-half quarts of milk gathered from a radius of sixty to one hundred miles. These are inadequate, and doubtless imperfect, figures which out-reach in their thrilling significance the most pleasing measures of the poet.

A pioneer orchard-maker and breeder of blooded cattle in Wisconsin has written the autobiography of a cow. It is a humble companion to the classic Black Beauty. To this book also I make grateful acknowledgement.[3] "Queen Vashti", was a thoroughbred Guernsey cow; the story of her descendants reaches from Oregon to Massachusetts. They carried with them wherever they

- - - - -

[3] A.J. Phillips, Queen Vashti (La Crosse Wis.: The La Crosse Engraving Co., 1906).

went not only beauty and gentleness, but the astounding profits of the milk pail. Prosperity followed them. It is not for me to give the dollar-and-cents triumphs of this one family that produced cow after cow for the "Advance Register". Let this one item suffice to show the possible achievements of the barnyard.

"Queen Deete", daughter of "Queen Vashti", gave in twelve months, 14,501 pounds of milk, which yielded 781 pounds of butter. At forty cents per pound this will bring three hundred and twelve dollars and forty cents.[4] This lady of the manger began her career on a bluffy farm in Wisconsin and ended it on a rocky farm in Massachusetts - and she carried cash and contentment wherever she went. Can we render this achievement in terms of prophecy, translate these dollars and cents into prospective homes, extend the care and love of these few breeders into the care and love of communities - into the companionship that comes by man's conquest over nature? Can we eliminate the pride in things, the conceits of culture and the cruelties of wealth - at last reaching the heights which give a scientific basis for the hope that man is to triumph over the kingdoms of nature, not by the power of might but by the power of love?

Strange to say - though not so strange as beautiful - milk, the indispensable condition of life of the higher animals, offers the best culture ground for the germs which threaten that life. We now know that the bacteria of typhoid, tonsilitis, scarlet fever, tuberculosis and other enemies of human life are more rapidly multiplied and more readily transmitted

- - - - -

[4] The real value of this figure can be seen by comparing it with figures for family income used by Jones in Chapter XIV, p 225.

into the body of the child through milk than through any other media.

Thus the milk problem becomes the health problem of our day, and the dairy business becomes necessarily a life-saving or a life-destroying business as the case may be. The prosperity it spells is not counted in dollars and cents, though it is a profitable business, but it gives that prosperity which represents the only true wealth of the nations which Ruskin had in mind when he wrote:

> It may be discovered that the true veins of wealth are purple - and not in Rock but in Flesh - perhaps even that the final outcome and consummation of all wealth is in the producing of as many as possible full-breathed, bright-eyed, and happy-hearted human creatures.

The modern milk problem, properly interpreted, is an extension of motherhood -- a maternal provision for the health of babies. The present movement for pure milk reaches back at least thirty-six years when Denmark, still the leading nation in dairying interests on so many lines, grappled with what is now the quest of every well-ordered city on the globe.

An intelligent butter-dealer, noting the despondency of an employee over the menaced life of the little babe at home, was told that the primary difficulty was the question of milk suitable in quality and quantity. The doctors had pronounced the milk unsatisfactory, and his milk dealer was unwilling to supply him even with the poor milk in sufficient quantities. Dr. Busck heard a call in this necessity, and he instituted the now famous "Milk Furnishing Society" of Copenhagen. A small company was organized, to operate under a commission consisting of three university professors, a philanthropist, an eminent diplomat, a physician and a lawyer. It is noteworthy that there was not even one business man - and still the company meant business. The motto of the company was "Pure milk from sound cows." This involved a combination of science and humanitarian instincts blended with commercial sagacity. The company began with the meager capital of several hundred thousand dollars.

Its effort after cleanliness is shown by the fact that a few years after its initiation, it was sending six thousand pieces to be laundered weekly - these being the sanitary costumes of its four hundred and thirty employees, of whom two hundred and thirty were boys, one hundred and twenty, men and eighty, women.

It fits into my contention to remember that these women were selected because their sense of taste was more keen than that of men. Their work was to test the milk by its taste. They were not allowed to labor more than one hour at a time, for it was discovered that the delicacy of the sense of taste was blunted by longer use. Burbank, the plant wizard, said fifteen years ago that he preferred women assistants in the delicate operations of his laboratory for the same reason; their sense of taste was more sensitive than that of men.

The milk rejected by these tasters was relegated to such by-products as would kill the dangerous microbes, and was disposed of at a lower rate - while the producer stood condemned in the estimation of his fellows. In the business of the company only bottles sealed by authorized experts and duly labeled "Infants' Milk" is permitted to be given to babes.

This extension of Providence through the domestication of animals, the care of the herd, the elaboration of milk into its by-products of butter and cheese lends a glory to motherhood, gives a meaning to the phrase "milk of human kindness" that no poet or orator, unilluminated by these facts of science could ever reach.

Motherhood, in the fulness of time, breaks through the darkness of ignorance in spite of the brutality of savage life, the coarseness of life-takers - hunters and warriors of the masculine gender. Motherhood brings in the era of clover, alfalfa and the silo. It was the dire necessity of motherhood that, combined with scientific sense and insight, helped Professor Babcock of the University of Wisconsin to reach the great milk-treating process which has made co-operative dairying possible throughout the world and his name famous wherever there is an intelligent love for the cow.

The story of Professor Babcock is too much neglected in the teaching of the children in our public schools, who need to understand that to such minds as his the desire to serve the people is a supreme incentive, and that in giving to the people this priceless invention made during his employment by the State of Wisconsin, Mr. Babcock has received a reward far superior to the immense royalties that would have been his had he patented his device in the usual commercial manner.

"The milk of human kindness!" This phrase leads us into the higher humanities, the ultimate sobrieties. The immediate anxiety of the laboring man in the Copenhagen butter-house arose from the fact that his milk dealer, who was at the same time the dispenser of

THE MILK OF HUMAN KINDNESS 267

beer, had refused to sell him milk because he abstained from beer; hence he was an unprofitable customer. The milk industry is slowly but surely crowding out the beer industry. During my horseback-riding days the fact was as obvious as it was significant that the old roadside taverns, the country saloons, were being rapidly supplanted by creameries and cheese factories. My good horse Roos knew full well that her rider would dismount at a creamery and refresh himself with the buttermilk ever available. She could also find her way back to the pump which was always waiting to provide for her comfort.

The Pasteur Institute of Paris issued a bulletin urging the value of milk as a stimulant and recommending that it should take the place of alcoholic drinks in war trenches, as well as in hospitals. It reports that more courage and inspiration comes from clean, pure milk than from the most delectable wines or fiery absinthe. It is obvious that the growth of the milk industry runs parallel with the higher life of the community. More milk refinement on the farm, health in the city. It banishes profanity and cruelty from the barnyard and is to drive the saloon out of business.

"The milk of human kindness!" I have not tried to keep the spiritual and physical meanings of this phrase apart; they are inseparable. The realizing of the one promotes the other. Seventy percent of the revenue of the state of Illinois, legitimately expended, is spent on the mothering industries of the state - the care of the dependent, the defective, the sick, and the education of the child. These are maternal cares, lifted above sex-lines into parental anxieties. Mother-instincts have taken possession of both male and female parents. The joint work involved in the nest-building, the brooding and feeding loves has been extended beyond the limits of narrow firesides and is becoming a human providence concerned in the well-being of infancy everywhere.

The mother who is partial, and selfishly devoted only to her own family, is a case of arrested development. It is womanhood tarrying on sub-human levels. Some of the most menacing bigotries, iniquitous selfishness and cruel foes to progress are found in the selfish mother who in her upholstered home dotes on her own delicate darlings to the neglect and injury of some other mother's darlings on the same street. It is an unmotherly love that permits or compels little children to shiver in inadequate clothing and to grow pale for the want of proper nutrition, while one's own little ones are wrapped in softest down and fed with dainties from the profits made by the toil of the fathers and mothers of the underfed and shivering children.

A mother's love ought to be so profound and so divine that it would make her anxious for the well-being of all children whose welfare is inseparably connected with the well-being of her own. I recognize no demands of motherhood for those of one's own fireside that are not also the demands of universal motherhood. It is a slavish and dehumanized mother who has not room in her heart for every child of woman, of whom the Master said, "Of such is the kingdom of Heaven."

We had a typical case of a certain type of motherhood one summer at Tower Hill. Five young lambs disappeared from my little flock of sheep. Three neighboring lads, skilled in wood lore, undertook to solve the problem as to what became of the lambs. They promptly detected in the pasture-lot wolf tracks - in that country from which the wolves are supposed to have been driven long ago. With great dexterity they traced the invading mother from my happy sheepfold, out of which she had torn five little lambs from their helpless mothers, to her lair two or three miles away from the sheepfold where four of her own beloved wolflings were waiting for her maternal caresses. This was brute motherhood - beautifully exemplified, triumphantly realized by the forethought and marvelous skill of the wolf mother, marooned, it was supposed, on the wrong side of the river by the premature breaking up of the ice-bridge in the spring. To that mother no home was too vigilantly guarded or too tenderly protected for little wolf darlings, and no other home was too sacred to supply the needs of her own sweet little ones. But this is wolf-motherhood; not until motherhood is interpreted in broader terms than those of one's own fireside, of alleged "ties of kin" and claims of caste or tribe or nation, will wolfish motherhood rise into human motherhood.

Woman was given as a "help meet to man". Her function from the first has been to emphasize the cooperative cares of man and woman necessary to the perpetuation of the race. Women came in response to the biological demand for prolonging the period of infancy, so that the greater number of new impressions might be incorporated into habit, organized into intelligence, formulated into ever-widening comprehension.

"The uprising of woman" is comparatively a new phrase in state-craft. Ellen Key in her <u>War, Peace and the Future</u>[5], enforces the truth that sex lines are

- - - - -

[5] Translated from Swedish by Hildegarde Norberg. New York and London: G.P. Putnam's Sons, 1916.

comparatively superficial scratches on the surface of the human globe. Archaeology and biology teach us that there were great depths of life before bi-sexual lines appeared, and a study of the spiritual nature of man shows that there are high reaches of communal humanity above all sex lines and passions. Just beyond the interests of our own children lie the interests of all children. The serenity of our homes is safeguarded only by the well-being and love-ties of the race.

"How are we going to prevent war?" is the question propounded in Ellen Key's book. The answer comes promptly and forcefully, "By making humanity really human." She deplores the spirit of the German mother who gleefully told of her little girl who refused to accept a hat when incidentally the milliner spoke of it as being made of "English" straw. Her patriotism rejected the commercial term. "Mother," says our author, "is the word most frequently heard on the lips of dying soldiers, mangled by human ingenuity." She calls upon mothers to hasten to bring up their sons to be saviours of humanity "if they are to avoid the horrible results of war". She tells us "war is born out of spiritual neglect". We are anxious to inoculate our children against disease. "Why not," says the Swedish prophetess, "inoculate them against hatred?" "Woman," she says, "has been hypnotized by the nationalistic idea of power and glory", and she turns to America as "the land of youthful courage and initiative" to lead in the correction of this lamentable limitation of the human by brutal instincts.

Miss Key reminds us that sixty-five years before her writing her fellow country-woman, Fredericka Bremer, visiting the United States told the American women that "war was like a bleeding wound ravaging people and countries". She called upon the women of America to "combine in counteracting the effects of war and securing an era of peace", and this, her latter-day sister, looking the horrible facts of today squarely in the face, says:

> Many women are already now, during the days and nights of the war, asking: Was it for this that I in agony bore my sons, watched and labored over their tender years, and filled their souls with the best of my heart and mind? Many women ask further: Is it really true that the life and future happiness of my country necessitated a policy that led to all these sacrifices? And a few ask no longer; they have already set their nay against man's yea. These few are increasing. What I now with my faint voice say will some day swell with the chorus of millions of women's voices: We will - and we shall - quench the hell of war and create a paradise of peace.[6]

In enforcing this pronouncement, Miss Key recalls the old mediaeval story of a woman appearing in the market place with a can of water in hand and a flaming torch in the other, declaring that it was her purpose to put out the fires of hell with the water and set fire to Paradise with the torch, that men and women might serve the right -- regardless of their own

- - - - -

[6] Key, p 118.

selfish interests, the hope of future reward or the dread of future punishment.

Literature is full of the apotheosis of woman. Dante's Beatrice, Goethe's Margaret, Shakespeare's Ophelia and Browning's Pompelia, all represent womanhood lifted into regal power and purity. But these women of literature pale in the presence of the greater women of history: Michaelangelo in his old age rekindled his creative fires with his love for Vittoria Colonna; Petrarch found a new inspiration in Laura; Tasso had his Leonore; St. Francis was matched with the benignant Santa Clara, the little virgin who created the world-encircling organization of "The Little Sisters of the Poor".

The mythologies of all religions make much of virgin-mothers, who alone were deemed fit to give birth to saints and saviours. (This is an unnecessary indignity to fatherhood.) But the virgin-mothers of theology are pale and weak in the presence of the glorious line of childless mothers who have fed the world with the "milk of human kindness" drawn from their spiritual breasts. Call the roll of the great virgin-mothers of America. Take note of those who have thrown maternal arms around neglected children, who in the combined potencies of love and wisdom have penetrated through the selfishness of motherhood and the coarseness of fatherhood and made parental the co-operative life of the community, made divine the providence of the state: Susan B. Anthony, Elizabeth Cady Stanton, Frances Willard, Lucretia Mott, Louisa Alcott, Lucy Larcom, Clara Barton, Jane Addams, Mary Bartelme, and Julia Lathrop - all these from our own land, to say nothing of the sisterhood across the sea with Joan of Arc and Florence Nightingale at the head of the line.

THE MILK OF HUMAN KINDNESS

The old text-books told of society rising from a patriarchate, the venerable elder on horseback, the valiant grandfather who could summon the greatest number of his progeny to defend his right in case of invasion as to justify aggressive assaults on neighboring clans. But the new books tell us that society began, not with the father-warrior, but with the mother-guardian of the hearth. There was a matriarchate before a patriarchate was possible. One of my books has a frontispiece entitled "The Unit of Society". It is no man with a sword, no hunter with his booty, but a primitive woman, defenceless, meagerly clothed, holding a babe at her breast. There did society begin. The first sacred office was that of protector of the fire on the hearth.

The mother's breast was the fountain of love that nourished human society, and only by the advancement of this mother love - which has long ceased to be exclusively woman-love and has become human-love - is society promoted. Just as manly men have ceased to be masculine, so have womanly women ceased to be feminine in the higher affairs of home and state. The old division holds only on the militant levels where muscle counts more than brain, and the regime of brawn - the dominations of the conqueror - for the time overshadows gentleness, obscures patience, and wages a losing battle with the sympathies and loves of the human heart.

These forces are now arrayed in the final Armageddon, not of Teuton against Anglo-Saxon, but of physical force against the power of mind. On the one side are the weapons of wit, the armaments of love; on the other side are the cold steel of hate and armor-plated sectional pride and national hatreds. This division does not run parallel to sex or race lines. For this battle there is being developed on the side of love a manly line of women and a womanly line of men. What were once peculiarly women's problems - housekeeping and baby-tending tasks - have long since passed into the joint care of father and mother.

No longer does man hold a monopoly on the strenuous activities, as Europe now sadly realizes. There plows are steadied by the hands of girls; fields are seeded by woman's skill; harvests are gathered, handled and housed through the wit and muscle of mothers and grandmothers. On the other hand the trouble and toil of the loom, the burden of the kitchen, the care of the larder are shared by man. The most successful chefs of today wear trousers and are not disgraced by their profession. The largest herd of Jerseys exhibited at a recent Minnesota State Fair conspicuously displayed the names of woman owner and a woman superintendent. Work - all kinds of work - has gotten away from sex lines, and I regard with grave apprehension the vigorous attempt on the part of some blessed women to revive and perpetuate the old sex lines in the higher industries of humanity. The world has waited too long on man-managed politics; may Heaven save this country from woman-managed politics! May we have instead politics managed by men _and_ women in intelligent and equal co-operation! May the light of universal brotherhood and sisterhood break through the sex consciousness and interfere with the "feminine clubs" and female social activities. By the same token I would banish masculine clubs and male conceits. When woman in her impetuosity and ardor tries to play the game of life alone -- to push the interests of independence and civilization by herself -- she will find herself hoist on her own petard. She will have lost much time and many graces.

THE MILK OF HUMAN KINDNESS

The great and last call of religion, as I understand it, is the fusion of the male and female - of man and woman - in the common enterprises of humanity.

In the realms of art, science and political emancipation, the dictum of the Nazarene applies; in the heaven of future democracy, they "neither marry nor are given in marriage, for they are equal with the angels". Men and women are yet to be fused in the higher life of common duties, human loves and human tasks.

I am ashamed to find myself associated with any distinctive band of men from which women are excluded. I grieve over the tendency to absorb the best energies, the noblest thoughts and the maximum of time of the most gifted women in the perpetuation of sex-consciousness, sex-partialities and sex-consciousness, sex-partialities and sex-elegancies. Just as sure as we are evolving out of masculine domination, we are menaced by a feminine domination. Unless women can catch the high note that comes from their feminine triumphs and are lifted out, above and beyond sex lines to join hands with men in the common struggle to escape family exclusiveness, sectarian dogmas and national conceits they will miss their highest opportunity and defeat their noblest aims. Men and women should grow ashamed of narrow segregations and geographical patriotisms, in the fullness of the joys belonging to man and to woman - in the achievements of the <u>genus homo</u>.

Through unnumbered aeons has life climbed up from the solitary cell, risen from the ooze of pre-Adamic seas, crawled onto the land - and the end is not yet; the ascent physical - a thrilling story - is to be supplemented and continued by the greater ascent spiritual. Life is to escape out of the selfishness that protects one's own progeny into the mutual care for all helpless offsprings.

A parenthood that has crowned with sanctity motherhood is at last to make tender, vigilant and loving fatherhood; maternal and paternal loves are to be spelled in parental fidelities. "The milk of human kindness" is now the joint product of men and women working together, the substance and symbol of happy lives nobly lived.

XVII

Rarely does Jones reveal his intimate life in his sermons. He frequently uses his experiences, but keeps himself in the role of observer. This sermon and an 1891 sermon, "The Creedless Church" are the only two known to me in which Jones let his audience into the formative events of his personality.

"A Grave in the Woods" is the earliest sermon in the collection. It was first preached at All Souls on 3 March 1895. That sermon, moreover, was a revised version of a sermon, entitled "Short Range Skepticism vs. Long Range Faith", written for his Janesville, Wisconsin congregation on 8 December 1878.

The two themes of this sermon make it a fitting conclusion to the volume. The hardships and determination of the pioneers are made real in the life of one unknown man. The unshakable optimism for the future that Jones holds - even in the face of The Great War - is buttressed by the long range effects of the lives of men like his uncle. Jones may not have believed, in orthodox terms, that Jesus died for him, but he knew that Uncle Jenkin had -- for him and for all.

The grave that Jones refers to is still there, in a cemetery near Ixonia, Wisconsin.

This sermon has never been published before, but Jones did send it to his nephew, Chester, a few weeks before he died. Chester eventually worked it into Chapter Four of his family history, <u>Youngest Son</u>, published privately in 1938.

Another poem by Edwin Markham, "The Conscript of the Dream", was selected as the preface. Jones' note here may mean that he had the poem in manuscript, prior to its publication.

THE GRAVE IN THE WOODS

<u>Pe lladdai efe fi, etto mi a obeithiaf ynddo ef</u>.

The above text is taken from a small blackened limestone slab that still stands, somewhat awry, over a grave that was dug many many years ago on the top of a little hill in the deep Wisconsin woods. At the foot of the hill in the clearing stood the rude but ever radiant log-house which formed my early childhood home. To this grave under the trees on quiet Sunday afternoons the gentle mother was wont to lead her little ones away from the fatigues of the household and the routine of daily tasks, and there she taught them to lisp this text in the softer consonants and the minor melodies of a tongue unintelligible to most of my readers, but which even yet holds for me the sweeter harmonies of piety, the deeper rhythms of trust and hope.

Beside this rude slab the story of the family's first great grief was told. It was the earliest grief to touch the heart strings of the children. It was the story of a humble, faithful, helpful life which shaped for the little lad his first ideal hero. It was the story of the man for whom I was named and whose traditions are still a part of the moral capital and spiritual wealth of the family circle to which I belong.

It was a simple story of an early immigrant, the tale of an obscure life touched with helpfulness to all those who came within its reach. But obscurity did not prevent it from being the story of a strong earnest man, tutored by labor, sanctified by strong and rational religious convictions deepening into a brave purpose, which ripened among the sterile but ever lovely hills of Wales.

This man had wealth of manliness with which he might have richly endowed a woman's life, but that privilege was denied him. Perhaps some secret pang, some unrecorded disappointment, closed his heart forever against the conjugal joys for which he was so well fitted. There might have been a time when, like Philip in Tennyson's story, he groaned

> And slipped aside, and like a wounded life
> Crept down into the hills of the wood;
> There, while the rest were loud in merry-
> making,
> Had his dark hour unseen, and rose and passed
> Bearing a life-long hunger in his heart.[1]

But this passed, and there grew with the years great heart-room for the babes whom he saw gathering round an elder brother's knee. To these little ones he gave the uncalculating paternal affection which was an uncle's privilege. He loved his brother's boys and girls as if they were his own. He settled into the brother's fireside, became a genial helper around the family hearthstone, a loving elder brother to the

- - - - -

[1] From "Enoch Arden".

slender mother, a foster-father to the growing children, often more welcome – because more indulgent – than the real father.

The pretty stone cottage in Wales with its slated roof, festooned with ivy and honeysuckle, and its garden patch hedged with box became overcrowded. The cramped life of old world conditions, hampering customs and outgrown traditions, threatened the growth of the little circle. To the open-minded, radically-disposed guardians of the home fires the mental as well as the physical freedom of the growing children was menaced by the lack of room. These loving hearts, reinforced by open minds, found but few paths leading to scant privileges opening up before the blithe and heedless brood.

From across the mighty waters came tidings of unclaimed acres, untold possibilities where the mental and spiritual atmosphere was as free as the air that swept over vast mountain ranges and across measureless prairies and deep forests. They read with avidity of the possibilities over there where a poor man might own his home and cultivate his own acres, where he might provide against the winter of old age and, more attractive than all that, where all these privileges were haloed with free thought – a rising gospel of human brotherhood and educational opportunity. In this little Welsh cottage there was a prayer-altar and time for high thoughts and the discussions of great principles. These home-keepers dreamed that the gospel of the open mind and the unrimmed fellowship which made a shrine of the hearth in the little cottage might find richer soil and more room to grow if transplanted to the beckoning fields of America.

The most imperative of all these beckonings was the thought that in the new land in America the poor

THE GRAVE IN THE WOODS 281

man's children might rejoice in schools and perchance wear the regal crown of learning, while all the family could know the joys and powers of independence. While the partner-brothers were still making hats in winter and tilling the ten-acre croft in summer, America had become the dreamland of their fancy -- the unvisited home of the heart -- until the divine attraction finally drew the soul as the moon draws the sea in its mighty tidal flow, and America became the irresistible destiny of this little family group. By a spiritual compulsion it was torn from the cosy complacency, the social contentment and the religious fraternity in which those thrifty home-makers had nested.

He who would understand the old Bible tale of Abraham's westward move and of Israel's yearning for Canaan will do well to study this hunger for America in the heart of the old-world fathers and mothers, whose large plans for their children have compelled millions of them to expatriate themselves for their children's sake.

To the eyes of the elder cottagers the low, naked hills in their very barrenness were beautiful. The hedges were so green, the dear church with its fellowship so helpful, the loving kindred with whom they had prayed, worked and sung, so dear; parents and grandparents, kindred and comrades many, whose ashes rested in the venerable churchyard, held them in the bonds of deathless love.

America had no charm to balance these, no attractions to tempt the mature away from this home. <u>But the children!</u> Ah, the prattling, playing, happy children! For their sake the breathing spaces of America, where the waiting tasks of a republic - the training grounds of democracy - held for them room to grow and scope to act.

So the wifeless and childless member of that circle said to the partner-brother, "You stay and guard your own. I will go first and find out the way, discover the place for the new home in the new world. I in the wilderness will prepare for you the way and make ready for the wife and children you will bring when I send the word."

Thus the unmarried man pioneered for the family. He sought, as it seemed to him, the frontier of the world. There were two years of lonely grappling with the rugged mysteries of a new country - a new language, a strange life - the story of which can never be told nor realized even by the inner circle - the children for whose sake all this sacrifice was made. This much is known: the father-uncle learned to swing the American ax -- that wonderful instrument fraught with such potentialities, such profound efficiencies. He learned deftly to "carry up the corner" in a log house-raising, and, potent accomplishment, he learned to use the English language. A few more dollars were earned with which to pave the way into the still-farther West. And then the word went back over the sea, "Come!"

They came - father, mother and seven children. The uncle waited for them near the Eastern shore of the new world. After trials and tribulations known only to the immigrant who antedated railroads, post-offices, printing offices and road ways, the little group found their way into the heart of a "wilder West" than now exists anywhere. Wisconsin in 1845 was deeper in the solitudes than is today any section of Idaho, Montana, New Mexico or Washington.

Deep in that wilderness two fathers for one family were none too many. To feed ten hungry mouths even with coarsest fare was a large task. The courage that faced an unknown continent shrank before what seemed the desert dreariness of the open prairies in their apparent unfertility and bleak inhospitality. With curious shrinking, yielding to a blind inherited instinct, they picked a home, in the depths of a vast forest of oak, elm, basswood and their lesser kindred.

As soon as a sufficient number of the brave old trees were felled to let in the sun and make room enough, the pioneer home was reared. For the first six months it was roofed with basswood bark, for not only had the trees to be felled but the skill had to be acquired to rive the oak and shave the "shakes" into shingles before the permanent roof could be placed.

Once more spoke the uncle-brother: "It is not for me to enjoy the children. You grapple with these trees, carve a field out of this forest, plant your garden, comfort your wife, help care for the children and I will go out and work for wages to supply food until the ground begins to yield of its wealth."

He went to his work, blazing the trees as he went, to mark the trail to be re-traced. It was only six miles distant but it was six miles of deep forest shades which made intense the loneliness at both ends of the path. His work was in a saw-mill to which other pioneers with Yankee skill had hitched the little stream by means of a crude dam. It was on the very spot where now Chicago's wealth, fashion, pride and boasted culture are wont to resort when midsummer heats come. The old mill pond has become a lake. The stumps have given way to flower beds. The settlement in the clearing has given place to palatial homes with their park-like lawns.

Each week the uncle brought his little pile of coin and slipped it into the mother's purse, never forgetting the bits of sweetmeats for the babies and whatever was available to hearten the life of the little family in the woods. More valuable than any tangible witnesses of his love hidden away in his pockets was the story of the swiftly approaching opportunities, tidings of the widening prospect, the rapid resistless advance of the settler tides. Each week he had new tales of the things that were being done and, still more interesting, of the things that were being felt, reached after and finally grasped. In his frontier village he felt the throbbing life of a new metropolis forty miles away - the growing Milwaukee. Into the ears of the older boys and girls he poured hopeful tales of how civilization with its schools and churches was pushing its way through the woods and would soon be there.

Brave, prophetic days were those when a woodman's hands laid strong hold on a century, when his ax hewed at once materials for house and barn and for the walls of the state. Great days were those when the simple, honest eye of the pioneer could see beyond the bogs and marshes, the stone and forest trees to the goodly school houses, colleges, attractive churches, stately court houses and teeming cities of the future.

Swiftly did the weeks pass by. But one Saturday evening the expected figure did not emerge from the gloomy forest above the house; the familiar step was not heard upon the threshold, and no clear voice lifted the gloom. On Sunday morning the simple devotions of that fireside were touched more with anxiety than thankfulness. On Monday a messenger came - the brother was very sick at the mill. The father hastened to the bedside, a humble cot in the loft of the sawmill. In a few days he returned with heavy step, bearing the little bundle of clothes with the high-top lumberman's boots tied on the outside. This told the story which the strong man could not phrase. Ere another Sunday came, the fever-blighted body was brought into the new home touched now with an abiding desolation.

The time of silence was very near when the brother reached the sick man's couch. There were but few words to speak, but they were words of cheer and hope. "Bury me under the trees in sight of the house," he said, "and when better days come, inscribe on my tombstone the words, "Though he slay me, yet will I trust in him."

Beneath the great oaks a grave was dug by the brother's hands, for there was no near neighbor to perform the friendly act; no representative of an official priesthood or of formal religion was near to speak the word of hope and resignation. The rude coffin was lowered, the grave closed and the voice of the brother - who was ever a priest in his own household - sang the favorite hymn in the old mother-tongue and read the great texts with scarcely a falter. Loud and clear the voice echoed through the vaulted aisles of that forest temple as he spoke the prayer of triumph which rose through the tall tree tops. Memories of it remained to their dying day in the hearts of the few who heard his words. Once back in the forest cabin, the others bent beneath their great grief, but the strong brother broke, and nature righted herself in a period of deep unconsciousness.

Now the reader will understand why I did not locate the text at the head of this narrative in the sacred writing of the Hebrews. I take it not from the Hebrew classic, the book of Job, but from the more sacred inscription on the tombstone that marks the resting place of the ashes of a humble pioneer who helped make possible a home in the wilderness. I was the baby in that home, the recipient of his caresses. Into those brave traditions was I born. And his name is a part of the rich endowment which was bequeathed to me and which I have proudly carried through the lengthening years.

What do I care about the proper rendering of the fifteenth verse of the thirteenth chapter of Job? That is a question for Hebrew scholars to decide. In its present form this is to me a text taken from the holy scripture of human experience. It is a sacred text spoken in the vernacular, not of Israel but of Wales, into which I was born. Job is the ideal hero shaped in the brain of some great unknown author. But my text belongs to a man who through life was clothed in the habiliments of the common laborer, to whom the ministers of religion in his day would scarcely grant the name "Christian", of whom church members stood in fear. Upon that gentle, generous soul were hurled the opprobrious epithets of "heretic", "unbeliever", "Socinian", "Unitarian". In a very real and proud way he would have confessed with Paul: "After the way which they call heresy, so worship I the God of my fathers."[2] He knew the inspirations that belong to the free thinking mind.

After long waiting and with much hesitancy, with the audacity that belongs to gray hairs, I have ventured at last to give publicity to this tender bit of personal wealth.[3] I have lifted just a corner of the

— — — —

[2] Acts 24:14.

[3] This is a bit misleading, since the text of this chapter goes back to a sermon from 1878.

THE GRAVE IN THE WOODS

curtain behind which is a gallery of pictures too sacred for aught but confidential and sympathetic inspection. I tell this little story hoping it may throw a ray of light over many of the dark places in human experience and dissipate the anguish which streaks the radiance of the world and darkens the sunshine of the human lives.

What is the reasonableness of a trusting faith in the presence of such grief? What justifies hope in such times of sorrow? What is it that breeds courage out of despair?

Measured by what seems to be the stern and exacting standards of human experience, who can but pronounce the life I have hinted at as a very sad one? There seems to be so little to justify the trust called for in this text from the cryptic language of Wales scratched upon that crumbling limestone slab. Here was a heart-hungry life, unendowed with a wife's love or with posterity - though he richly deserved both. Into this life fate poured great yearnings, noble longings, far-reaching interests, which with cruel relentlessness were denied gratification. The few privileges, though they were of a high and precious kind, seemed to have mocked him on the parental soil. He tore himself from the homeland surroundings. He robbed himself of the amenities belonging to it. Some will-o'-the-wisp in the shape of a finer ideal lured him into a wild, crude, cold country. Here not only was his heart chilled by foreign surroundings, his fellowship cribbed by a foreign tongue, but his body was stung by exposure and hardships and he was ruthlessly cut down in the prime of life. Malign poisons - typhoid infections - cut him off at the threshold of a patriotic ambition to become a useful American citizen. He was girding himself for the task of shaping the institutions that in due time would bring blessings not so much for himself as for the children of his brother's loins - of his own heart, of whom I am one.

Studied at short range, who can pronounce these thirty-eight years other than years of thwarted ambitions and blasted hopes. Starting from this premise, how easy it is to carry the logic in all its severity to the grim conclusion that the so-called "order of things", in this case at least, lands in disorder. Is not the pessimist's cry, "What's the use of trying?" justified? The skeptic says, "Does it pay to strive?" The interpreter of the apparent facts of life may well answer with shaking hands when he notes how in this world the honest are defrauded, the innocent made to suffer with the guilty. They seem to get on best who care least for principle. Peace and prosperity are disturbed and sometimes demolished by one's devotion to the right.

This good uncle's grave may well be taken as a symbol of many, if not of all, lives. This grave in the woods is multiplied indefinitely in the memory of the countless home-seekers who came from all quarters of Europe to find in the forests, or on the prairies of the waiting West, not the homes they dreamed of but graves prematurely opened. Can we call that providence which ends in so much improvidence?

This story but reminds us of innumerable stories still more pathetic -- of innocent babes torn from loving arms, of unsympathetic lines surveyed through growing homes, of ships cracked like hickorynuts by the storm, of churches and school houses demolished, homes scattered, barns leveled by the tornado, of pestilence in slippered feet walking in the darkness of the night smiting the innocent, of floods leaving behind them starved bodies and discouraged spirits, of belated rains flooding sunburnt crops and early frosts rendering fruitless laborious tilling.

Following these lines of apparently legitimate reasoning, one is tempted to quote texts in justification of despondency, of faithlessness not of faith. How the oracles of despair rush to the memory. "To be great is to be misunderstood" says Emerson. "To be good is to be miserable" exclaims Renan. "Nature is gory in her cruelty, hard and relentless, inflicting wanton torture upon her children", echoes with more audacity, John Stuart Mill. Confronted by these hard, uncompromising facts, honest souls in all ages have been at times compelled to exclaim out of their agony: "There is no God!" Nay, more, they have prayed: "Heaven save us from immortality at such a price!"

The short-range study of life runs into distrust at every turn. It brings a skepticism concerning every hope. It teaches us to quote the satirical words of Hudibras, the caustic sentences of Byron, the venomous stings of Voltaire, the satire of Ingersoll. The social, moral and religious world studied at short range seems to bring confusion worse confounded, and the fitting scripture comes to us from the visionless author of Ecclesiastes, who out of the bitterness of his soul exclaimed:

> "Vanity of vanities, saith the preacher; all is vanity."

There are more pessimists, I fear, than we realize. Honest minds are wont to ease the strain and dispel the gloom of life by evasion. They exclaim, "Give it up! The riddle cannot be solved. There is no meaning discoverable in the pattern of life's tapestry, woven through blinding tears. Make the best of it but do not take life too seriously. Faith and trust are the children of fancy and not of fact, offsprings of sentimentality, not of reason. The wise, not the fool, saith in his heart, 'There is no God'!" These are the unspoken sentiments of unnumbered souls.

Even the melodious Tennyson chants with the grim rhythm of a Druid bard of the inhospitalities of Nature:

.....but what am I?
An infant crying in the night;
An infant crying for the light,
And with no language but a cry.

Are God and Nature then at strife,
That Nature lends such evil dreams?
So careful of the type she seems,
So careless of the single life,

I falter where I firmly trod,
And falling with my weight of cares
Upon the great world's altar stairs
The slope through darkness up to God,

I stretch lame hands of faith, and grope,
And gather dust and chaff, and call
To what I feel is Lord of all,
And faintly trust the larger hope.

"So careful of the type?" but no.
From scarped cliff and quarried stone
She cries, "A thousand types are gone;
I care for nothing, all shall go."

THE GRAVE IN THE WOODS

> Man trusted God was love indeed
> And love creation's final law –
> Tho' Nature, red in tooth and claw
> With ravine, shriek'd against his creed.
>
> He loved, he suffered countless ills,
> He battled for the True, the Just,
> Is blown about the desert dust
> Or sealed within the iron hills.[4]

Must then the text which the broken man asked to have inscribed on the obscure stone slab that was to mark his grave in the woods be discounted? Did the high words of Job betray him? Did he go out of life a defeated man?

No! Man is a far-seeing animal and, to the far sighted, cosmos not chaos is the law of the universe. The far horizon is ever touched into beauty. Method and not chance, reality and not sham are the assurances of history as well as of reason. In the judgement of him who takes note of the movement of generations, who lays hold of the faith that still makes faithful, the revelations of centuries – the swing of destiny from atom to planet – is ordered, and short-range pessimism ever gives way to long-range optimism. Browning glimpsed this when he said:

> This world's no blot for us,
> No blank; it means intensely and it means
>   good.
> God! Thou art love! I build my faith on
>   that.
> So doth thy right hand guide me thro' thy
>   world.[5]

— — — — — —

[4] From "In Memoriam", excerpts from sections liv, lv, and lvi.

[5] From "Fra Lippo Lippi".

To the near-sighted the soil of the field is mud when wet, dust when dry, and we grow petulant under the annoyance that comes from either condition. But to the far-sighted mud and dust alike are something that through the alchemy of nature, manipulated by the art of human nature, are convertible into bread and honey, milk and raiment.

The common life about us to the near-sighted is dross. To such, says Mrs. Browning, our age is

> A pewter age, – mixed metal, silver-washed;
> An age of scum, spooned off the river past,
> An age of patches for old gaberdines,
> An age of mere transition, meaning nought
> Except that what succeeds must shame it quite
> If God please. That's wrong thinking, to my
>   mind,
> And wrong thoughts make poor poems.
>   Every age
> Through being beheld too close, is ill-
>   discerned
> By those who have not lived past it.[6]

To many house-worms who are never out at night except when bent on small purposes and following the lead of low desires the heavens above are but rain-fields spattered with meaningless lights, but to the tent-living shepherd-priest of the East the starry hosts came forth in martial array and their broken hearts are healed by the uncounted procession. The devout star-gazers worshipped the belts of Orion and listened for the music of the Pleiades.

The stars may send a shiver through the belated traveler on a wintry night, but the astronomer in his

- - - - -

[6] From Book 5 of "Aurora Leigh".

solitary observatory through his far-reaching glass discovers the majestic movement of distant worlds. He sees the planets pursuing their "unhasting and unresting" rounds. He sees Mars nod to Mercury, and Venus, with the deliberation of infinite courtesy, to Saturn. So sure is the mathematician of their unfailing precision, that he points to the place where a planet ought to be. The man at the telescope takes note of the suggested time and searches the hitherto vacant spaces and, true to the requirements of the multiplication table, he finds Neptune awaiting him.

Every longer vision discovers a missing harmony. Even what seems to be the unkindly invasions of the rights of the human soul are belted with law which by the longer measuring line squares the account. The winds are no longer fickle; man is learning to count upon them. He weighs and measures them and anticipates their journeyings. To the wise there are no more accidents. All the uncalculable forces are calculable farther on or higher up. The informed railroad engineer knows that there is a limit to the endurance of the axle of his locomotive. His calculation of it averts calamity. Every piece of iron put into the modern bridge is registered; its power of endurance is marked and the date and limit of its safety is noted. As a result, we sleep in undisturbed security in flying transcontinental trains.

The same law holds good in regard to the social and moral forces of the world, did we know how to estimate them -- and our social engineers are becoming more expert each year. Some day moral calamities and social tragedies will be evaded by the more adequate calculations. Certain virtues will inevitably build the state, certain vices as inevitably destroy it. The far-seeing prophet is assured that the wheel of law is ever climbing upward. He sees forces of chemistry pushing themselves into botanical forms, vegetable forms reaching into animal powers; the reptile strains toward the bird, the quadruped reaches toward the man and the darkened souls of men grope toward the light - ripening ever and anon into the white souls of history.

>A fire-mist and a planet,
>   A crystal and a cell,
>A jelly-fish and a saurian,
>   And caves where the cave-men dwell;
>Then a sense of law and beauty
>   And a face turned from the clod --
>Some call it Evolution
>   And others call it God.[7]

Looking back over the long story of the human, we see how he has been now coaxed, now pushed, onward and upward. Who, tutored by this longer story, can say: "I do not believe"? The maid's coarseness is written upon her face, spite of powder and ribbons. The woman's selfishness and pride are etched in wrinkles, while a life of service wreathes the aged face in tender lines and genial smiles. Note how the debauchee is lighting the lamp that enables other people to see his disgraces engraved upon his face, accentuated by his unsteady step.

The pestilence stalks through alley to boulevard because of the rotting garbage in the back-yards. The epidemic sends its horrors throughout the land, bringing sinners to their knees. The thrill of agony is driven through the heart of humanity until sectional

- - - - -

[7] "Each in His Own Tongue" (stanza 1) by William Herbert Carruth (1859-1924).

differences, personal selfishnesses are forgotten and streams of love and helpfulness flow into the devastated city.[8] Even to war-broken communities, love finally ministers, and in time the white-winged dove of peace sows flowers on battle graves.

The longer view discovers a possible hero in every man, persuades us

....that in all ages
Every human heart is human,
That in even savage bosoms
There are longings, yearnings, strivings
For the good they comprehend not,
That the feeble hands and helpless,
Groping blindly in the darkness,
Touch God's right hand in the darkness,
And are lifted up and strengthened.[9]

The longer vision inspires belief in a divine element that works through all human experience. If our triumphs are insignificant, our shames are not; if our virtues seem to mean little, our vices have a profound significance that is demonstrable. The contempt which ignorance brings upon us is a sign of the value of knowledge.

It is our short-sighted habit to acknowledge the beauty and perfection of nature while we bemoan the depravity of man. Who would not rather be a depraved man than a spotless lamb, for all its high symbolism! Better taste the hemlock with Socrates or feel the nails with Jesus than share the complacency of an owl.

I believe in God because he slays me with a

─ ─ ─ ─ ─

[8] I think he refers to the national response to the Chicago fire of 1871.

[9] From Longfellow's "Song of Hiawatha" (Introduction).

tremendous charge of moral responsibility; I will trust in him though I break under a surplus of reason or of hope.

> Let the great forces, wise of old,
> Have their whole way with thee,
> Crumble thy heart from its hold,
> Drown thy life in the sea.
> And aeons hence, some day,
> The love thou gavest a child,
> The dream in a midnight wild,
> The word thou wouldst not say -
> Or in a whisper no one dared to hear,
> Shall gladden the earth and bring the golden year.[10]

I acknowledge the corruption that mars the foreground while I still confess the eternal God that I glimpse on the radiant horizon. While I acknowledge the selfishness, confess the worthlessness, I still must recognize God in my very recoil from the life I despise - in my dissatisfaction with present attainments. I confess the distrust born out of my bitter experience, while I rejoice in the longer vision that lifts me above the conceptions of a broken universe and an unworthy God.

I take my stand beside the grave in the woods that nearly three-quarters of a century ago put out the light of a household. I weep with the father, and my heart bleeds for the mother in their desolation. There is a void in my heart for the uncle I cannot remember, whose bravery has been a life-long inspiration and responsibility. But the longer vision of it all and the light reflected by the tardy years enable me to read

- - - - -

[10] I have not been able to locate the source of this poem.

into the Welsh text the chant of the optimist:
> Whither shall I go from thy spirit?
> Or whither shall I flee from thy presence?
> If I ascend up into heaven, thou art there;
> If I make my bed in Sheol, behold, thou art there.
> If I take the wings of the morning,
> And dwell in the uttermost parts of the sea;
> Even there shall thy hand lead me,
> And thy right hand shall hold me.[11]

The law of life has been vindicated in that death. Kindness has come out of pain. That which remained guarded the household with added vigilance and all homes were made somewhat stronger and safer for that woe.

With the light of seven decades thrown back upon his somber tombstone, the inscription is splendidly vindicated:

<u>Though he slay me, yet will I trust in him.</u>

The disappointments of the near vision have been more than compensated by the over-realization of his fondest hopes. Many homes rich in unforseen privileges and unexpected opportunities have come into the elongated life of that childless man. Two generations have learned to call blessed him whom they never knew. Well might he trust in the God who slew him.

The tender Welsh uncle died leaving the brother and sister bereft and their children orphaned, a helpless little cluster in the lonely woods. But the sun shot through the tall tree tops and the pioneer's ax finally cleared the trees and put the grave on the hill-top in the daylight. Weeks of clearing extended

- - - - -

[11] Psalm 139:7-10.

into months; the years tallied the milestones on the road of progress, bringing to his loved ones much more than he foresaw. Better housing, more freedom from the threatened want, books, schools, chapels, colleges, universities -- the pride of multiplied homes all came in the fullness of time, as realizations of the dream that bore the emigrant group across the stormy sea in a tumbling little sailing vessel.

That bachelor uncle lived long enough to give a start to the "settlement" which in due time became the pride of the state and a strength to the nation. Why should he not with his dying breath exclaim:

<u>Yea, though he slay me, yet will I trust in him.</u>

Though men's vision is short, God's love is long. Earth's defeats are heaven's beginnings. Every apple tree has long roots; every rose draws its blushing fragrance from mysteries hidden underground. We may not trace these roots; we cannot prove them, but everywhere we must recognize their existence.

Over three-score and ten years ago the poor "mill hand" - as his employer knew him - lay dying in a sawmill. Doubtless a small group of foreigners gathered round the humble cot in mute helplessness. A brother came and bent over him and caught from his parched lips his chosen epitaph, and the babe who bore his name is now trying to interpret the text that softened the hard death-couch and lightened the gloom of the funeral hour. Not the words now written by the namesake, but the mystic weavings of history justify the selection.

The story of this grave in the woods is only one more symbol of the great law manifest to the wise everywhere.

A stone cutter's son became interested in the young men of Athens. He was suspected and in the

THE GRAVE IN THE WOODS

interest of the state he was slain. Now the greatest crown of Athens lies in the fact that Socrates lived and was martyred there.

A truth seeker, aweary, lay down by the roadside to rest. A shepherd boy passing by thrust a sprig into the ground to shade the sleeper from the burning sun. The twig took root and grew and a slip from that twig became the great Bodhi tree which the generations have gone on pilgrimage to see. The wayfarer slept twenty-five hundred years ago but he has made Asia mild.[12]

A Galilean peasant, after gathering a few fishermen about him, died ingloriously; but Europe and America would now fain call themselves <u>Christian</u> in his name.

A camel driver caught a vision and began to speak words of sanity, to teach brotherhood and reverence to his clansmen. And Muhammad reconstructed the life of millions, reshaped the religious geography of the world.

A short range estimate of any one of these lives would land us in a dreary pessimism, while the long range study of them establishes an invincible optimism. The long vision restores to us our faith and persuades us that this world is instinct with meaning; this life is charged with power, and love not hate, life not death is the law of the universe.

When I turn from this one grave in the woods to study all graves, I confess the doubt which the near vision at all gravesides brings at times to all souls — the gloomy insinuation that the grave is the end of all. But by the same token, I must confess that through the longer vision the soul regains its courage,

─ ─ ─ ─ ─

[12] This is one story associated with the Buddha.

and among the tombs we dare confess the trust in him who slayeth and the belief that the soul which once animated the broken form must abide somewhere, somehow, as a continuous asset, an economic resource in a divine universe. The longer vision hints at the larger economy that brooks no waste. It gives glimpses of an architect who ever out of the crumbling walls of time builds the nobler structure of eternity. The tenement may be mutilated by bullet, ravaged by disease, but the tenant must survive. Homes are blighted by crime, damaged by success, thwarted by the recklessness of love, but still there is that which will reconstruct, restore and redeem.

The renovating power of shame, the redeeming help of sorrow, the infinite grace of God has pierced the gloom that once hung over the solitary grave in the woods, and it has become a center of light.

The longer range gives faith, enables us in the twilight to apprehend the truth which sustained the spirit of the dying uncle, who left a bequest so vast that it required the master-hand of Israel to state it adequately:

Though he slay me, yet will I trust in him.

STUDIES IN AMERICAN RELIGION

1. Suzanne Geissler, **Jonathan Edwards to Aaron Burr, Jr.: From the Great Awakening to Democratic Politics**
2. Ervin Smith, **The Ethics of Martin Luther King, Jr.**
3. Nancy Manspeaker, **Jonathan Edwards: Bibliographical Synopses**
4. Erling Jorstad, **Evangelicals in the White House: The Cultural Maturation of Born Again Christianity**
5. Anson Shupe and William A. Stacey, **Born Again Politics and the Moral Majority: What Social Surveys Really Show**
6. Edward Tabor Linenthal, **Changing Images of the Warrior Hero in America: A History of Popular Symbolism**
7. Philip Jordan, **The Evangelical Alliance for the United States of America, 1847-1900: Ecumenism, Identity and the Religion of the Republic**
8. Jon Alexander, **American Personal Religious Accounts, 1600-1980: Toward an Inner History of America's Faiths**
9. Richard Libowitz, **Mordecai M. Kaplan and the Development of Reconstructionism**
10. David Rausch, **Arno C. Gaebelein, 1861-1945: Irenic Fundamentalist and Scholar**
11. Ralph Luker, **A Southern Tradition in Theology and Social Criticism 1830-1930: The Religious Liberalism and Social Conservatism of James Warley Miles, William Porcher Dubose and Edgar Gardner Murphy**
12. Barry Jay Seltser, **The Principles and Practice of Political Compromise: A Case Study of the United States Senate**
13. Kathleen Margaret Dugan, **The Vision Quest of the Plains Indians: Its Spiritual Significance**
14. Peter C. Erb, **Johann Conrad Beissel and the Ephrata Community: Mystical and Historical Texts**
15. William L. Portier, **Isaac Hecker and the First Vatican Council Including Hecker's "Notes in Italy, 1869-1870"**
16. Paula M. Cooey, **Jonathan Edwards on Nature and Destiny: A Systematic Analysis**

17. Helen Westra, **The Minister's Task and Calling in the Sermons of Jonathan Edwards**
18. D. G. Paz, **The Priesthoods and Apostasies of Pierce Connelly: A Study of Victorian Conversion and Anticatholicism**
19. **The Agricultural Social Gospel in America:** *The Gospel of the Farm* **by Jenkin Lloyd Jones,** Edited with an Introduction by Thomas E. Graham